The Eye of the Beholder

Nathan Edelman

THE EYE OF
THE BEHOLDER

Essays in French Literature

edited by Jules Brody

THE JOHNS HOPKINS UNIVERSITY PRESS

BALTIMORE AND LONDON

The Johns Hopkins University Press, Baltimore, Maryland 21218
The Johns Hopkins University Press Ltd., London

Library of Congress Catalog Card Number 74-6813
ISBN 0-8018-1621-1

Library of Congress Cataloging in Publication data will
be found on the last printed page of this book.

Contents

Preface

IN OUR PROFESSION, we commonly speak of our "research" and "writing." During his many years as a department chairman, first at Johns Hopkins, then at Columbia, Nathan Edelman often spoke to me, wistfully and with fatigue, of needing time to "study." This expression rings strange in English; even more so in French, Nathan's first language. How many of us say or think that we are "studying" when we read Molière or Villon or Montaigne? Students "study"; professors "do research" and "write," don't they? It finally occurred to me, however, that Nathan's odd use of the word "study" translates, exactly, the Hebrew and Yiddish expressions that are commonly used to describe the activity of the *Talmid chacham*, the student of traditional Jewish learning. And in another generation, and in another country, Nathan probably would have been that kind of *talmid* or "student"—the rabbi, the Talmudic scholar, the teacher, constantly at grips with the sub-message in a text, struggling to explicate the implicit, to give form and visibility to what he used to call with a nervous, impatient gesture of thumb and forefinger, "the inner meaning" of a text, to liberate the spirit embedded within the letter. Nathan's research consisted in searching or, to use another of his favorite words, "probing" documents for their secret. And his writing consisted in rewriting. Most of us do research and write; Nathan searched and rewrote. His writing, like his reading, was a search; not an act of exposition, but a sustained process of inquisition.

Among Nathan's papers I found a fragment of the introduction to a projected major work on Renaissance and classical aesthetics. In its substance, this introduction deals with the historical and aesthetic

vii

sensibility—the "anatomy of the mind," as Nathan called it—that underlies French classical doctrine. But as much as with their content, I was taken with the title that these pages bear: *The Eye of the Beholder*. In this carefully chosen cliché I saw in a flash the image of an entire career, the emblem of the student, the writer, and the man. I could visualize that studious eye beholding its subject, contemplating, piercing it, narrowing down its field of inquiry, working in on it like a corkscrew, cutting through the known to the unknown, and arriving finally at that one resistant fact or detail—a striking metaphor, a recurrent word cluster, an ostensibly insignificant stylistic habit—that one irreducible element, beyond biography or history, that had to be explained if the poem or the passage or the play were to have meaning, structure, or unity. This was the eye that beheld and penetrated the mixed metaphor in Descartes, the language of motion in Boileau's *Art poétique*, the imagery of light and darkness in *Phèdre*.

In the same folder with his most recent draft of *The Eye of the Beholder*, Nathan had been saving six earlier versions—each one approximate, partial, tending in a special direction, and all of them chopped up, marked in red and blue and green, far more ruthlessly than he would ever have done even with the most mediocre term paper or dissertation. And as I compared these multiple drafts, I could see the "eye of the beholder" turned inward on itself. I could track the probings of that relentless gaze, I could visualize the eye of that restless, exacting mind as it beheld its own words, weighed their implications and associations, as it searched for sharper, more precise, more powerful expression—as it struggled to give voice to the unsaid, to capture the ineffable.

A colleague of ours at Columbia once asked Nathan how such a careful and deliberate man in everything else could drive a car as fast as he did. This was Nathan's answer: "Driving to me is like classicism, power under control." And this is what studying and writing were for him as well: a way of beholding, getting hold of, holding onto the intellectual and spiritual energies of language.

Many of us are no more than the sum of our publications; still others are even inferior to what we write. Nathan left an important and impressive bibliography, and yet, as a human and professional presence, he towered far above his publications, in the same way that deep experience always outstrips and transcends the mind's capacity to describe it.

More than a teacher or a scholar, Nathan Edelman was an intellectual, always a rare bird in a profession like ours that is constant prey to positivists, technicians, virtuosi, and faddists. An aesthete who could exult in the music of a Racinian alexandrine, a sensitive moralist who could ponder the dark wisdom of a Spinoza, a joyous optimist who could chuckle at the tolerant, gentle ironies of a Montaigne, a rationalist who could delight in the logic of a Plato, Nathan lived a profession that most of us merely work at. He lived the life of the mind and taught his most edifying lessons by the example of his life, the power of his spirit, and the beauty of his soul.

I would like to end this tribute—which surely would have irked Nathan—with a quotation which surely would have pleased him: "j'ai plus de soin," wrote Descartes to Mersenne in 1630, "et crois qu'il est plus important que j'apprenne ce qui m'est nécessaire pour la conduite de ma vie, que non pas que je m'amuse à publier le peu que j'ai appris."

Jules Brody

Pour un ami

Pourquoi ne pas le dire tout haut? Ces quelques souvenirs si personnels, je les rédige le coeur lourd. C'est qu'il nous manque beaucoup, Nathan Edelman.

Et puis, j'ai toujours pensé qu'on ne devrait pas parler de ses amis; on risque d'en parler mal. On ne sait jamais où la candeur devrait l'emporter sur la discrétion. Un mot de trop, un accent mal placé et tout est gâché; l'amitié pardonne tout sauf le manque de tact. La fidélité est ici dans le secret. Et le silence.

Et pourtant. Se taire n'est pas une solution—pas quand il s'agit de nos amis disparus. Ne pas les évoquer serait ne pas combattre la mort.

Alors on en parle. En désespoir de cause.

Je me souviens de notre première rencontre. Il y a une dizaine d'années, dans un restaurant typique de Manhattan. C'est incongru, voire ridicule, je l'admets, mais malgré le bruit infernal, nous trouvons le moyen de citer Rabelais—en raison du menu peut-être. Puis nous discutons Montaigne, bien entendu. Ses quêtes, ses angoisses. Son goût pour le paradoxe. Son style. Sa technique, sa manie de semer le doute autour de lui. Je crois avoir lu quelque part qu'il était d'origine juive, ce qui expliquerait certains mystères planant sur certaines périodes de son existence. Tiens, comme pour Villon? Pourquoi pas. *Frères humains qui après nous vivez* . . . . Nous parlons, nous parlons.

Ils sont trois à table. Lui—yeux clairs, pénétrants; voix traînante, légèrement enrouée—me frappe par l'étendue de ses connaissances; elle—gaie, chaleureuse, débordant de fougue—par son enthousiasme pour les études et la culture juives; et leur fille—jeune collégienne timide, curieuse—par sa manière d'écouter sans ouvrir la bouche.

Lors de notre prochaine rencontre, un an après, à Baltimore où je suis venu faire une conférence, ils ne sont plus que deux. Abattus. Eteints. Les parents ne disent rien, moi non plus. Il n'y rien à dire: je suis au courant. Je ne connaîtrai leur fille qu'à travers leurs silences; je n'entendrai la voix de Jeannie que dans ses poèmes. Je les ai lus beaucoup plus tard et je sais pourquoi ils m'ont ému; ils sont ses regards blessés.

Les Edelman reviennent s'installer à New York et dès lors nos liens s'affermissent. Nous nous voyons fréquemment, régulièrement. Je participe à leurs projets comme ils participent aux miens. Nathan traduit ma pièce de théâtre, Lily en fait autant avec deux de mes ouvrages en prose. En politique, nos positions sont proches; en littérature, identiques. Je leur présente mes amis; je fais la connaissance des leurs. Invités à un événement que ma future femme et moi désirons célébrer à Jérusalem, dans la vieille ville, ils y viennent sans un instant d'hésitation. Nos deux familles sont désormais si proches que les joies de l'une seront celles de l'autre. Et les peines aussi.

Evoquer Nathan ici, c'est reconnaître son absence. Et pourtant.

Je le revois: jamais pressé, jamais de mauvaise humeur, il vous accueille et trouve aussitôt le ton juste pour vous mettre à l'aise. Vous l'observez: la pipe qu'il rallume sans cesse, la lueur espiègle dans les yeux, il est dans chacun de ses gestes, dans chacune de ses paroles. Il arbore le même air intéressé et amusé en jouant aux échecs—où il gagne souvent et souvent à contre-coeur—ou en commentant l'actualité—où son pessimisme prend des accents prophétiques—ou en disséquant le dernier roman d'un auteur dont l'oeuvre lui tient à coeur—et il n'y en a pas beaucoup.

Aimant saisir la pensée et dans son cheminement et dans ses soubresauts, il l'analyse avec un mélange de respect et de soupçon. Son intelligence est aiguë mais sans ruse, son jugement sûr mais non rigide. Il aspire à convaincre et non à plaire. A comprendre autant qu'à se faire comprendre. Ses propos sont brefs, percutants, jamais ambigus, jamais équivoques, dépourvus d'effets faciles. Patient, tolérant, il ne s'emporte—sans toutefois le montrer—que devant l'intolérance et l'imposture. Il ne s'indigne que lorsque la conversation touche à la guerre—n'importe laquelle—et alors il ne se gêne nullement de manifester ses sentiments. Parfois nous regardons les nouvelles à la télévision: un visage d'enfant affamé le met dans tous ses états. Vietnam, Bangladesh, Biafra: nous regardons les images, nous écoutons les titres . . . que faire, ciel, que faire? Hurler? Détourner la tête? Ce sentiment d'impuissance et de culpabilité rend fou. . . . "Il faut tenter de vivre," dit Nathan citant Valéry.

Humaniste, il ne peut s'empêcher de croire, de miser sur l'homme, de prendre au sérieux même ce qui ne le mérite pas. Son sens de l'humour est dénué d'animosité; son rire n'est jamais offensant.

Il aime donner et se donner—et, de lui, on aime recevoir. Conseils, lettres de recommandation, opinions sur votre travail: avec lui, vous ne vous sentez jamais endetté. Seulement enrichi. Ce qui explique, en partie, pourquoi ses étudiants l'admirent et ses pairs le respectent: c'est un être entier.

Mais là je dois avouer que je parle un peu sans savoir. J'ai connu Nathan Edelman sans vraiment le connaître. Je veux dire: sans être informé de ces mille et un détails et épisodes qui transforment une biographie en vie et cette vie en destin.

C'est que Nathan, pourtant si ouvert dans ses rapports avec autrui, se voulait renfermé quant à ce qui touchait sa·vie privée, sa vie d'*avant* sa rencontre avec vous. Excès de pudeur ou timidité mal maîtrisée? Il se livrait peu et fort rarement. Durant toutes ces années, je ne l'ai presque pas entendu parler de ses parents, de son enfance, de ses expériences estudiantines. Ses premières déceptions, ses premiers triomphes? Je n'en sais rien. Des découvertes intérieures qui portent l'homme ou des pièges qui l'attirent, il ne disait rien. Parfois nous lui tendions la perche; il l'écartait. Pourtant il ne s'agissait point de dérobade, ni de refus. C'était autre chose. S'il persistait à vouloir rester dans le présent, c'est parce qu'il y voyait un aboutissement. C'est dans le présent que l'homme est saisissable et nulle part ailleurs. Et il lui appartient de vaincre la vie, et même de la changer, en donnant au présent la densité et la richesse mystérieuse du passé.

Penseur, enseignant, essayiste, il savait mettre cette idée-là en pratique.

Rien ne lui procurait bonheur plus intense que de donner vie aux textes anciens, à leurs personnages et à leurs créateurs. Lire avec lui un poème de Ronsard, une page de Montaigne, c'était une aventure: du coup vous viviez sur deux plans, à deux niveaux, vous deveniez pont et miroir où se rencontraient en se disputant deux époques, deux univers, deux systèmes; grâce à vous, les morts parlaient aux vivants; grâce à vous, les vivants, conscients de leurs facultés créatrices, s'élevaient au-dessus de la durée. Que disais-je? Grâce à vous? Non: grâce à lui.

Aussi est-ce avec déchirement que j'en parle au passé. Il existe des absences que les mots ne comblent point. Ses élèves le savent car ils lui doivent beaucoup; ses disciples le savent aussi, car ils lui doivent bien davantage. Quant à ses amis, ils lui doivent une certaine conception de l'amitié et de l'homme qu'il a su incarner.

En nous séparant de lui, nous avons envie de dire tout bas: merci, merci Nathan, merci d'avoir vécu.

Élie Wiesel

The Eye of the Beholder

Editor's Note

THE SEVERAL ESSAYS that appear here for the first time I found among Nathan Edelman's papers at various stages of completion. Two of them—"The Unity of Villon's *Testament*" and "The Central Image in *Phèdre*"—were long-range projects that he had tentatively worked out as public lectures, with a view to recasting them later along more formal lines. In some places, his essential meaning and intention could only be guessed at. Where inference or reconstruction proved necessary, I tried to emend in a way that I felt would be consistent with Edelman's known habits of thought and style, even if not with the meticulousness which influenced this great scholar and critic to withhold from public view for too long some of his most brilliant insights. In preparing for publication manuscripts which, by Nathan Edelman's exquisite standards, were not yet in publishable form, I was guided by this conviction: many of his rough-hewn stones prove in the end more valuable than a basketful of someone else's polished gems.

Jules Brody

The Vogue of François Villon in France from 1828 to 1873

VILLON, in our time, has again become the celebrated poet that he was in days of old. The snows of yesteryear fall once more; the beauties of old, swept away by the winds of destiny, have been rediscovered. But this did not come about overnight. In fact, it has taken almost four centuries for Villon's recent prestige to overcome the silence that had engulfed him. And yet, without investigating the actual historical facts, we have tended to picture a Villon already crowned by the school of 1830. What is surprising is that we owe this impression —false as it turns out—to Sainte-Beuve, who contributed most to spreading the idea that Villon was "très apprécié des romantiques."[1]

Coming from so great a critic, this assertion quite naturally invites a search for the abundant and enthusiastic praise that he seems to have in mind, although he himself mentions no more than two or three examples. In the course of this search, one finds reason for doubt. The works of Villon, moreover, when read attentively, reveal a confusing mélange likely to prove disturbing to a certain kind of romantic idealism—so much so that Sainte-Beuve's remark must appear as hasty and thoughtlessly conceived. But his error, as will be seen, does not stem from negligence alone.

Originally published as "La Vogue de François Villon en France de 1828 à 1873," *Revue d'histoire littéraire de la France* 43 (1936): 211-23, 321-39. Translated by Jules Brody and Kathleen Duda.
[1]*Causeries du lundi*, 14: 280.

1

In 1854, "le bibliophile Jacob" (Paul Lacroix) put out a new edition of Villon's poetry, and here is what we find at the beginning of his preface (p. 5):

> La dernière édition des œuvres de F. Villon, publiée en 1832 par M. l'abbé Prompsault, est bien loin de mériter le discrédit dans lequel on l'a vue tomber peu de temps après son apparition. Ce discrédit fut le résultat d'une querelle littéraire qui s'était engagée alors entre l'éditeur de Villon et M. Crapelet, éditeur de la collection des *Monuments de l'ancienne langue française*.
>
> Cette querelle donna lieu a une polémique très ardente, où l'avantage parut rester à M. Crapelet, qui signalait deux mille fautes dans la publication de son antagoniste.

For a scholar trying to restore a neglected text, it is rather unfortunate to begin with an error! It was the Abbé Prompsault and not Crapelet who raked over the alleged two thousand mistakes on the part of his adversary. A short notice in the *Journal des Savants* of 1835 provides ample proof: "*Discours sur les publications littéraires du Moyen Age*, suivi d'errata comprenant près de deux mille corrections ou rectifications, par M. J.-H.-R. Prompsault, Paris, librairie d'Ebrard, 1835, 555 pages. C'est particulièrement dans les publications de M. Crapelet que M. Prompsault veut trouver un grand nombre d'inexactitudes."[2]

Crapelet's response was not long in coming, but the advantage probably did not stay with him, for the Abbé managed to renew his attack; it was he, according to the *Journal*, who had the last word, in September 1835, in a thirty-six page *Lettre à M. Crapelet*.[3]

Jacob's error is thus indisputable. But this did not stop Campaux from reproducing it without further research in the doctoral thesis that he defended at the Sorbonne in 1859; without suspecting that Lacroix had confused the roles of the two editors in this quarrel, he called Crapelet unjust for having attacked the work of Prompsault![4]

It was to this thesis that Sainte-Beuve, on September 26 of the same year, devoted the *causerie* cited earlier. He, too, repeats the words of the *bibliophile* and the *docteur*, adding an explanation of his own: it was Crapelet, "éditeur lui-même de vieux poètes, et jaloux comme le potier l'est du potier," who "relevait dans la publication de l'abbé Prompsault jusqu'à deux mille fautes."[5]

---

[2]*Journal des Savants*, June 1835, p. 377.

[3]*Ibid.*, September 1835, p. 572.

[4]A. Campaux, *F. Villon, sa vie et ses œuvres* (Paris, 1859), p. 384.

[5]*Causeries du lundi*, 14: 280.

Two thousand errors: "à peu près le chiffre que Méziriac prétendait retrouver dans le *Plutarque* d'Amyot," observes Sainte-Beuve; "mais Amyot avait de quoi survivre, et le Villon de l'abbé Prompsault en mourut—l'édition, non le poète." The poet was "très apprécié des romantiques."[6] Here, then, are two errors: one concerning the two thousand mistakes and the other concerning the popularity of Villon among the Romantics. We will want to deal here with the second one in particular; but the two errors are closely related, and in a way that must be clearly understood.

According to Jacob-Lacroix, it is "la dernière édition" (that of Prompsault), and not the poetry of Villon, which fell into undeserved disrepute. If the poet had the ability to attract public attention—as Jacob seems to suppose, since he attributes the defeat of the Abbé to a quarrel that was extraneous to the poet's own merits—why, then, did the edition fail? According to Lacroix' preface to his edition of Villon, this happened solely because of Prompsault's supposed scholarly failings—imaginary failings that were based, as we have seen, on a misunderstanding. Moreover, Jacob did not know that Prompsault's edition, printed by Béthune in 1832, had been republished in 1835 by "Ebrard, libraire-éditeur, et Delaunay." That is no sign of disfavor. Besides, "la querelle des 2000 fautes" did not take place until three years after the 1832 edition, and could not have influenced the immediate result of the publication.

But—one could argue—it was the 1835 reprint that failed, as might be inferred from Lacroix' rather vague reference. Nothing supports this supposition, which is invalidated by an examination of the passages from Villon cited after 1832 (before the first critical study of the poet) and by a comparison of the editions from which commentators took their quotations.

All these passages except three appear in works later than Prompsault's edition and earlier than Jacob's. Thus the only choice open to critics between 1832 and 1854 was to reproduce either Prompsault's text or some other pre-nineteenth-century edition. I will indicate only the obvious conclusions, without going into the details of the differences in transcription.

At first glance, the evidence is far from favorable to Prompsault in all cases. The lines from Villon quoted by P. Clément in 1853 do not correspond to the 1832 edition.[7] At times he seems to prefer sources that Jacob will follow a year later; at other times he presents texts which neither the Abbé nor Jacob accepted. Demogeot is not

---

[6]*Ibid.*

[7]*Jacques Cœur et Charles VII* (Paris, 1853), 2: 95–99.

much more faithful to Prompsault.[8] He seems to follow him in certain respects, but he also deviates from him at will—most often with the ostensible purpose of modernizing him, which is not necessarily evidence of disdain for the Abbé's text. F. Génin, who uses some lines from Villon to prove certain philological points, also departs from Prompsault.[9] But in another work, published after 1854, he scorns Jacob as much as his predecessor did, and looks back to older texts for passages where the spelling fits in somewhat better with his theories.[10] Nisard, who quotes from Villon in 1844,[11] and Sainte-Beuve, whose *Tableau historique et critique de la poésie française au XVIe siècle* was reprinted in 1842, took no more account of Prompsault's edition than did Clément and Demogeot. Michelet, citing the *Ballade des dames du temps jadis* in 1844, also believed that he should modernize the spelling, without regard for the Abbé's text.[12] One might note in passing that in the posthumous 1879 edition of Michelet's book no one thought to correct the Villon quotation according to Jacob's edition.

All these negative facts, however, do not prove that Prompsault's edition was completely forgotten. Géruzez, who published his *Histoire de la littérature française* in 1852, relied directly on this edition; it is surprising that he used the 1835 reprint, the only edition that could have fallen into disfavor. Moreover, the quotations from Villon were retained up through the eighteenth edition of the work in 1885.

Even more interesting is the comparison of the 1830 and 1858 editions of Villemain's *Cours de littérature française*. In the first of the two, Villemain reproduces readings that Prompsault will follow two years later; the correlation, however, is not perfect; surprisingly, it is much closer in the *Cours* of 1858. Someone took the trouble to review and correct the Villon texts quoted there and, rather than copy them from Jacob's edition, which had appeared in the interval, touched them up using Prompsault's spelling and punctuation.

Here is a rather curious example. In the *Cours* of 1830, we find this line from the *Ballade des dames du temps jadis*: "La royne blanche comme ung lys." In Prompsault we read: "La Royne blanche comme ung lys." In Jacob there is an inversion of the capital letter: "La royne

---

[8]*Histoire de la littérature française* (Paris, 1851), p. 252.

[9]*Des variations du langage français depuis le XIIe siècle* (Paris, 1845), pp. 101, 557.

[10]*Récréations philologiques* (Paris, 1856), pp. 230–32.

[11]*Histoire de la littérature française* (Paris, 1844), pp. 209–18.

[12]*Histoire de France*, 6: 44.

Blanche comme ung lys." Villemain, in 1858, uses the line and chooses Prompsault's reading.[13]

There is yet another piece of evidence. In 1832, the respected critic Daunou praises Prompsault in a way that Thuasne is right to call "incolore." Still, he scrupulously points out all of the virtues that he was able to find both in Villon's genius and in Prompsault's edition—which he does not criticize at all, although his praise remains on the faint side. Daunou's enthusiasm, however moderate, does no discredit to the editor: "Il se peut que les deux testaments et quelques autres vers du même auteur attirent désormais plus d'attention ou qu'ils obtiennent plus d'éloges; et M. Prompsault y aura contribué."[14]

Thus, it is certain at least that the 1832 edition had not been brushed aside; between 1832 and 1835 there are no other references to Prompsault's scholarship. As for the reprint of 1835, I have already cited reasons for believing that the quarrel between Crapelet and Prompsault did not destroy Prompsault; nor did it prevent at least two important authors from referring to it.

Jacob, vaguely recalling a quarrel between Prompsault and Crapelet, confused their roles and probably concluded that the Abbé's work had been buried under heavy opprobrium. Or else, in order to justify and facilitate the publication of his new edition, Jacob wanted to give the impression that in 1832 it was not Villon's work itself but the edition that had been judged defective.

But this is of minor importance. The essential point is to see the birth of a tradition, continued even by Thuasne, of a Villon "exalté par l'école romantique."[15] Campaux, in passing on Jacob's error, which he cites, adds a new element: "L'édition de Prompsault parut . . . . Le bruit qui se fit autour de cette édition, qu'accueillirent les plus injustes attaques, fut tout au bénéfice de Villon."[16] He sees proof of this in the articles by Daunou and Gautier which appeared in 1832 and 1834. We already know that the alleged "injustes attaques" did not take place until 1835. This error thus mars the testimony of Campaux, Villon's fervent apologist, who would have liked to prove not only that the poet himself had attracted the attention of the lettrés, but also that the "querelle des 2000 fautes" had actually contributed to keeping this attention alive!

---

[13]There remain two or three differences between the lines of Villemain and those of the Abbé; an interpolated comma by Villemain, a capital *V* for the *Vierge Souveraine*. But, for the rest, there seems to be a distinct preference for the 1832 edition.

[14]*Journal des Savants*, September 1832, pp. 556–57.

[15]Villon, *Œuvres*, ed. Louis Thuasne (Paris. 1923), I: 98.

[16]*F. Villon, sa vie et ses œuvres*, p. 300.

With the edition dishonored and the poet acclaimed, only one further element was needed to complete the tradition: that the poet had been acclaimed by the Romantics. It was Sainte-Beuve, of course, who took the decisive step, and it is not difficult to see why.

Throughout his essay, Sainte-Beuve criticizes Campaux' excessive admiration for Villon, and takes issue with his exaggerated romanticism. In denigrating Campaux' romanticist taste for Villon, it is quite possible that he generalized the connection between his taste and his romanticism through a polemical instinct which he did not always put aside when writing about contemporary authors.[17]

Lacroix, Campaux, and Sainte-Beuve, following the "vogue romantique" for Villon, fell thus into one error after another. But aside from their faulty testimony, might there not be other, more stable grounds for this notion of an *enfant de Paris* who was extremely popular among the Romantics? An examination of all the romantic judgments on Villon will compel a negative reply. For if one looks for a general reaction to the poet, one soon becomes aware that before 1873 (i.e., before the discoveries of Longnon) this reaction was more or less diffuse, and oscillated more than is commonly believed between the positive and the negative. Besides, it will be clear that the Romantics were not the only ones to be interested in Villon and that other writers, including the neoclassicists, and even a Parnassian, contributed significantly to the diversity of judgments on Villon.

II

In 1844, Charles Labitte devoted an article in the *Revue des Deux Mondes* to the *Grotesques* of Gautier. We find nothing there on Villon, however, although he occupies the first rank in this series of "figures grimaçantes" and "gloires éclopées." Labitte is concerned solely with responding to what Gautier had written on the forgotten writers of the seventeenth century.

This disdain for Villon stems in large part, no doubt, from Labitte's personal taste, and we would be mistaken to see in it a symptom of the times. But one is also struck by the pleading tone of some of Villon's defenders—and defenders is certainly a more fitting term than admirers. Henri Murger, the least polemical of them, provides this interesting bit of information in the *Préface* to his *Scènes de la vie*

---

[17]Campaux, nevertheless, has some new and penetrating views which Siciliano, among others, has pointed out (*François Villon et les thèmes poétiques du Moyen Age* [Paris, 1934]).

de bohème (1851): "Au reste, parmi tous ceux dont l'œuvre peu connue n'a été fréquentée que des gens pour qui la littérature française ne commence pas seulement le jour où Malherbe vint, F. Villon a eu l'honneur d'être un des plus dévalisés, même par les gros bonnets du Parnasse moderne."

The *"gros bonnets"* of the nineteenth century have been thoroughly studied, and yet no one seems to have found among them any trace of Villon's direct influence. But Murger goes on to explain: "telle ballade" and "telles stances amoureuses" of Villon are found, to be sure, "métamorphosées en galanteries de beau lieu flairant le musc et l'ambre." By these standards, the most fanciful influences would be easy to demonstrate! It is true that disciples will often move away from their masters, but to write this kind of *galanterie* and still consider oneself among Villon's heirs is, of necessity, to have misunderstood him rather badly.

It is not clear, however, why Murger's testimony should be disregarded concerning the "œuvre peu connue" of the poet whom he loved. Murger's opinion of Villon is completely favorable, and he would not gratuitously tarnish his reputation. Quite the contrary, it may be that he was reluctant fully to admit, and wanted to conceal, a neglect of Villon.

In the case of Campaux, there was an obvious need to answer the detractors. With all the impassioned zeal that he brings to rehabilitating Villon—for he feels he owes him this service—he attacks "ceux qui s'autorisent de deux ou trois passages" in order to invalidate Villon's religious faith. Elsewhere, again with reference to Villon's personal attitudes, he adds: "aussi a-t-on contesté sa sincérité sur ce chapitre."[18] There were detractors, then, but who is "on"? Campaux does not tell us, although he never tires of quoting at length those who share certain of his favorable judgments. Can it be that this critic, so taken with Villon, invented straw men for the mere pleasure of knocking them down? In such a case, he surely would have chosen objections that were less serious and less difficult to refute. One need only read his book in its entirety, moreover, to understand that his ardor could only have been elicited by polemical necessity. Campaux says "on," as will be seen, for a very simple reason: he has no interest in letting it be known that those very critics to whom he refers—quoting them incorrectly— included some who were hostile to Villon.

Now, what should we make of the *dizain* that concludes Banville's *Trente-six ballades joyeuses*:

---

[18]*F. Villon, sa vie et ses œuvres*, p. 314.

Pauvre Villon, dont la mémoire fut
Navrée, hélas! comme Iphigénie,
Tant de menteurs s'étant mis à l'affût;
Dans ta légende stupide, moi je nie
Tout, grand aïeul, hors ton libre génie.
O vagabond dormant sous le ciel bleu,
Qui vins un jour nous apporter le feu
Dans ta prunelle encore épouvantée,
Ce vol hardi, tu ne l'as fait qu'à Dieu:
Tu fus larron, mais comme Prométhée!

What "légende stupide" is he talking about here? The one (already refuted by Prompsault) that made Villon into the hero of the *Repues franches*? To judge from the last two lines, Banville seems, rather, to want to poeticize Villon's criminal tendencies by excusing them in the name of genius. Could he be talking, then, about another legend, a legend that would have condemned the poet for the vices of the man? And could this *dizain* of 1873 be a retrospective reply to some rather recent detractors? Murger, Campaux and Banville without supplying details, merely point to the poor reception that Villon had received. The critics against whom they were reacting, however, were much more specific.[19]

As early as 1828, before Prompsault's edition, four rather distinguished critics made pronouncements on Villon's work: Sainte-Beuve in his *Tableau historique et critique de la poésie française au XVIe siècle*; Villemain, in his lectures on French literature (delivered in 1828–29 and published in 1830); Saint-Marc Girardin in his *Tableau*, and Philarète Chasles in his *Discours sur la marche et les progrès . . . de la littérature française depuis le commencement jusqu'en 1610.*

What is the overall impression that these works could have produced? Going along with Campaux, one would be tempted to believe that even before Prompsault's edition, Villon was "très apprécié." He does not insist much on Villemain, who praises Villon only to subordinate him to Charles d'Orléans, "le seul vrai poète" of the fifteenth century. But what do the others tell us? "Je ne me serais pas arrêté sur Villon (says Saint-Marc Girardin), si par son ton de mélancolie gracieuse ou insouciante il ne me semblait avoir un caractère à part dans notre littérature, et si, par son tour d'esprit,

---

[19]Campaux has left us a list of writers who were interested in Villon up to 1859; I have added to it names that he neglected or could not have known. Considering Campaux' enthusiasm for Villon, he probably neglected none of the favorable interpretations before 1859. As for the adverse critics, whom he appropriately forgets, I have found many whose number and importance are revealing.

il ne représentait le génie libre-penseur de notre vieille France, tel qu'il est dans les fabliaux et les romans des trouvères."

Whatever the intrinsic merit of this judgment, Campaux is not wrong in emphasizing the favorable note. He was not entitled, however, to choose arbitrarily the passage that suited his purpose, for there are others where Saint-Marc Girardin turns out to be rather unsympathetic: "Villon, . . . fripon moitié par besoin et moitié par espièglerie, fut pauvre et malheureux; mais sa vie et ses malheurs n'ont rien de grand ni de poétique. . . . A voir sa vie et le sujet de ses vers, rien ne répond si peu à l'idée qu'on serait tenté de se faire du père de la poésie française. Holà! archers, où conduisez-vous notre Homère? Au Châtelet ou à Montfaucon? Voilà son Parnasse!" (p. 49).

The unacceptable idea of Villon as the father of French poetry derives, as we know, from two lines in Boileau:

> Villon sut le premier, dans ces siècles grossiers,
> Débrouiller l'art confus de nos vieux romanciers.

Coming from Boileau, this is an unexpected assertion that will have to be explained later. For the moment, let us just note the enormous importance that this couplet attributes to the author of the *Testaments*. We can be sure that it would not have occurred to many critics to denigrate Villon, nor would others have been so stingy with their praise, had it not been for Boileau's favorable comment. Witness Saint-Marc Girardin, in the present instance, who cannot bring himself to recognize Villon as the French Homer.

Campaux also emphasizes Philarète Chasles' judgment: the morals of "l'enfant de Paris," "son style, ses vices, son génie, tout chez lui est essentiellement populaire. . . . Les mots gaillards, répétés par le bas peuple, les sermons comiques de prédicateurs étaient ses seules inspirations; sa raillerie amère et sa poignante gaîté lui appartenaient en propre; nulle influence étrangère ne les avait modifiées"; "il mérite son antique réputation."[20]

We might wonder this time what the ellipses were meant to suppress. Nothing good for Villon, whom Chasles reproaches for his

mœurs grossières et licencieuses. Entre lui et le duc d'Orléans, qui l'avait précédé de plusieurs années, tout est contraste; la naissance, les mœurs, le caractère, le tour d'esprit. Si le noble captif a trouvé dans ses sentiments chevaleresques et dans son infortune la source de ces simples élégies qui doivent une grace idéale à l'amour de Dieu, de la

---

[20]Quoted by Campaux, *F. Villon, sa vie et ses œuvres*, p. 300.

patrie et des dames—Villon, né au sein de l'obscurité la plus profonde, élevé au milieu de la tourbe des écoliers libertins, semble représenter, dans sa nudité la plus effrontée, le génie populaire de la satire allié à l'impudence de la débauche. . . . La franchise ou l'orgueil de ces aveux étranges où il vante sa diligence

A voler devant et derrière,

porte témoignage et contre lui et contre l'immoralité de son siècle, qui accueillait en riant ces confessions d'un escroc. . . . Il n'avait pour héritage qu'indigence et roture.[21]

Campaux is equally inaccurate concerning Sainte-Beuve. In 1828 he was much more indulgent towards Villon than he was to be thirty years later, when he condemned him, the better to ridicule the Romantics. It would even be fair to say that his commentary on Villon, full of verve and good humor, is the most sympathetic, or the least unfavorable, of the four. Nevertheless, Villon comes out pretty well demolished by his compliments, for Sainte-Beuve is not content to say that he was a "novateur et chef d'école," "l'aïeul d'une nombreuse famille littéraire, dont on reconnaît encore, après des siècles, la postérité à une certaine physionomie gauloise et française"[22]— Campaux enjoys quoting this part—but elsewhere he enumerates the vagabond's vices and faults and concludes: "En voilà pourtant plus qu'il n'en faut, ce semble, pour dégoûter les honnêtes gens; mais avec un peu d'indulgence et de patience, . . . en remuant son fumier, on y trouve plus d'une perle enfouie."[23]

Add to this a comment by Villemain: "Enfant de Paris, comme on disait alors, ses idées, ses sentiments, ses images vous montrent ce qu'était la corruption d'une grande ville. C'était un . . . homme qui avait fort mal étudié [we would question this today], dont la vie fut misérable, déshonorée, et dont l'imagination fut abaissée souvent à ce qu'il y a de plus vil."[24]

I have cited these four critics at some length in order to draw attention to an extremely important point: it was the poet Villon, and not the Abbé Prompsault, who had to overcome a public opinion that the critics had prejudiced against him before the edition of 1832.

---

[21]Philarète Chasles, "Discours sur la marche . . . de la littérature française . . . jusqu'en 1610," in Jean-François La Harpe, *Cours de littérature* (Paris, 1840), 3: 607–8. Chasles incorrectly attributes to Villon the *Repue franche*, where we find the line: "A tromper devant et derrière."

[22]Quoted by Campaux, *F. Villon, sa vie et ses œuvres*, p. 299.

[23]Sainte-Beuve, *Tableau historique et critique de la poésie française au XVIe siècle* (Paris, 1828), p. 12.

[24]*Cours de littérature française* (Paris, 1830), p. 242.

Certainly, there was no lack of appreciation of the poet's popular origins, his subjectivity and melancholy, the poetic beauty of certain lines on death, the universally admired *Ballade des dames du temps jadis*. On the other hand, along with sporadic expressions of admiration there remains the distaste that Villon inspired in his critics.

One wonders why. Apart from Saint-Marc Girardin, who was to become hostile to the new tendencies, we might imagine that the criminal in Villon would appeal to the Romantics, for whom the outlaw enjoyed a vogue with which we are familiar. But there are outlaws and outlaws. The Romantics since Schiller had always greatly idealized theirs, making them into a type whom Villon, the "vaurien incorrigible," could hardly resemble. There were too many specific and undeniable facts about him and about the life that he had led for him to be pictured, reassuringly, as a fallen soul capable of redemption by a higher goodness. It was very difficult to see Villon as the "good" outlaw, and from 1828 to 1873 it never occurred to anyone to do so.

What did occur to someone was to make Villon not an outlaw but a bohemian. This was Murger's ploy in the *Préface* to his *Scènes de la vie de bohème* (1851). But he specified that "les bohèmes dont il est question n'ont aucun rapport avec . . . mille autres industriels mystérieux et vagues dont la principale industrie est de n'en point avoir, et qui sont toujours prêts à tout faire excepté le bien." His bohemians are neither "filous" nor "assassins"; they are the unfortunates of "tous les âges artistiques et littéraires."[25] For Murger, Villon sheds his criminal and scandalous aspects and becomes worthy of pity and admiration. Murger contradicts himself, of course, in including among his bohemians the "pauvre écolier," who stole as much through weakness of character as through necessity. In seeking to poeticize him, he forgets the crimes of the man for the magic of the poet.

But we have wandered pretty far from 1828, which goes to show how long we will have to wait, apart from the dangerous friendship of the classicist Nisard in 1844, to find a faithful, devoted, and even blind friend, who thinks that he is doing Villon a favor by eliminating the entire criminal side of his life. It also goes to show how awkward it must have been to befriend the "pauvre écolier."

In 1828, other objections were being readied. Sainte-Beuve pointed out drawbacks that were not to be remedied by the 1832 edition. These were "les difficultés et les obscurités du texte," in spite of which he would run the risk of quoting three ballads.[26] He also

[25]*Scènes de la vie de bohème* (Paris, 1851), p. 1.
[26]*Tableau*, p. 13.

pointed out the "mondain," "urbain," and anti-rustic style found in the *Testaments*: "voilà Villon qui mène tout d'abord les Muses au cabaret et presque à la potence."[27] It is true that Sainte-Beuve takes a lively tone here, but this did not prevent the nature-loving Romantics from taking him amiss. Gautier, in his important article, will not fail to point to Villon's "singulier mépris" of "la nature champêtre."[28] And Campaux, too, will admit reluctantly that "la dernière chose qu'il eût été capable de comprendre, c'eût été assurément la sublime et religieuse effusion de Martial d'Auvergne, remerciant le Créateur

> D'avoir veu ses œuvres tant belles,
> Le soleil, la lune et estoilles,
> Terre, elemens, fruitz, fleurs nouvelles.[29]

But here is something even more curious from the pen of Saint-Marc Girardin: "Telle est la tristesse de Villon. Ce n'est jamais une sombre rêverie ou une misanthropie mécontente. C'est plutôt par goût d'imagination que par réflexion chagrine qu'il moralise sur la mort."[30]

Here we have the young critic already announcing his hostility toward romanticism, which he takes this occasion to ridicule a little. Gautier will speak again of this "sombre rêverie" à la René or Don Juan, and Sainte-Beuve, having become hostile to the romantic school, will answer him.

In 1832, what impression could the memoirs of Abbé Prompsault have made on his readers? Villon, who was certainly a poor student, was, on the other hand, a past master of knavery. Speculation on the name of Villon or Willon, although inadmissible today, reinforces this impression. And, although the Abbé casts doubt on the Saint-Maixent episode, he appropriately remarks that it would have been characteristic of his protégé! But it goes farther than this. Lack of money was not the only cause of Villon's poverty: "un penchant violent pour le libertinage" and "la licence" also played a large part. Does he not regret having wasted his youth? Moreover, when he complains of being left in destitution by his close relatives, it is not solely "par faute d'un peu de chevance." The Abbé insists: "c'est encore à sa démoralisation plutôt qu'à sa misère qu'il faut attribuer la conduite de sa famille."[31]

---

[27]*Ibid.*, p. 14.

[28]*Les Grotesques* (Paris, 1897), p. 33.

[29]*F. Villon, sa vie et ses œuvres*, p. 322.

[30]*Tableau de la marche et des progrès de la littérature française* (Paris, 1828), p. 53.

[31]Cf. *Mémoire sur la vie de Villon*.

Prompsault argued, of course, that Villon had made an effort to better himself. And he did stress the poet's sharp native intelligence, the wit, grace, and naïveté of a style that prefigured Marot. But none of this really helped or mattered. His statement about Villon's "démoralisation" still rang in people's ears, and no one except Campaux and Nisard was to have the courage to contradict him directly.

It was during that same year, 1832, that Daunou published the article in the *Journal des Savants* mentioned earlier.[32] In this article he showed more scholarly caution than attachment to Villon. And—we might note in passing—he was sharp enough to ask to see the "lettres de grâce" that Longnon was to discover forty years later. To a certain extent he was sympathetic to the poet, whom he saw as driven to crime by his "extrême pénurie," and he believed him to be in the clutches of the hostile love that he complained of in the *Petit Testament*. Daunou considered his learning rather extensive for someone who had called himself a poor student. As for Villon's poems—at least those which he found intelligible—they interested him "par l'originalité des idées et par la vivacité de l'expression, par le caractère naïf et ingénieux du style." Daunou noted with satisfaction that Villon does not mix "les rimes masculines et féminines" and that "son grand mérite est de n'être jamais prosaïque." None of this, of course, was forgotten by Campaux. But he never said a word about other passages that have a very different overall tone. Villon's poetry, says Daunou, shares "la destinée de tous les ouvrages *qui ne sont pas des chefs-d'œuvre*, surtout de ceux qui appartiennent à un âge demi-barbare, à des siècles grossiers." This kind of comment could not be counted on to increase Villon's popularity. Daunou's conclusion, however, is a bit more enthusiastic: "Il nous semble que le progrès de l'art des vers sera toujours plus sensible dans Villon [than in Charles d'Orléans], parce qu'il exprime plus d'idées, qu'il a plus de saillies, des tours plus piquants, des formes plus diverses; qu'il ne demeure point resserré dans le genre érotique, dans les limites étroites de la galanterie chevaleresque. Du reste, nous avouerons qu'il est moins élégant, moins poli, moins clair que Charles d'Orléans."[33]

These compliments were probably all the less convincing because they were only relative, and based on a comparison with a poet who was surely not "très apprécié des Romantiques." This is important because most critics were interested in making this comparison. After Villemain and Chasles, who preferred Charles d'Orléans, the advantage will always go to Villon. In some cases, this favorable com-

[32]See above, n. 14.
[33]*Journal des Savants*, September 1832, pp. 562-63.

parison will undoubtedly be a kind of compensation for Villon's faults, which will never quite be forgotten. Critics will also tend to see in him the enemy of insipid chivalric gallantry. But is this directed against the insipidities of neoclassical or of troubadour poetry?

Two years later, Villon had the good fortune to find in Théophile Gautier a more sympathetic critic. He, too, notes in Villon's poetry the absence of "ces éternelles descriptions de printemps qui fleurissent dans les ballades et les fabliaux," of the "complaintes sur la cruauté de quelque belle dame qui refuse d'octroyer le don d'amoureuse merci" (the influence of these complaints on some passages of the *Testaments* is not noted). "C'est une poésie neuve, forte et naïve"—qualities of primitive freshness which would no doubt please the Romantics. Villon is also the only poet of his time "qui ait réellement des idées." Better yet, "c'est un poète égoïste: le *moi*, le *je* reviennent très souvent dans ses vers."[34]

By means of a tour de force, not found in any other critic, Villon is brought visibly closer to the Romantics: "Il disserte sur la mort, sur la vertu, sur tout; car le pauvre écolier a trouvé, sous Louis XI, la forme digressive du *Don Juan* de Byron. Comme le poème du noble lord, le testament du voleur roturier est en octaves; l'entrelacement des rimes est presque pareil; c'est le même mélange de sensibilité et de raillerie, d'enthousiasme et de prosaïsme." This Byronism is further evidenced in the medieval "enfant de Paris" by "le désenchantement amer de la vie, le coup d'œil moral et profond," "le regret du passé," "le sentiment du beau et du bon au fond de leur dégradation apparente," "la perte de toute illusion et la mélancolie désespérée qui en résulte." The *mal du siècle* was already taking shape in the fifteenth century: Villon was victim of a "destinée plus forte que lui."[35]

At a certain point in the essay, Gautier waxes a bit sentimental. Through an error in interpretation caused by the difficulty of the text and the subtlety of Villon's humor, he believed that the three orphans named in *huitains* 25-26 of the *Petit Testament* and who reappear in *huitains* 117-20 of the *Grand Testament* were actually protégés of Villon and needed his care. The robber-poet was thus not born "pour être un coupe-bourse; il avait une belle âme accessible à tous les bons sentiments"; he talked about his mother "avec un ton d'exquise sensibilité." Gautier soon returns, however, to his lighter style and observes that "Villon ne pèche pas du côté des belles maximes. Faites ce que je dis et non ce que je fais." He prefers to

[34]*Les Grotesques*, pp. 5, 13.
[35]*Ibid.*, pp. 13-14.

think that in another situation this "mauvais garnement" would have acted differently.[36]

Democratic romanticism also has its say: "Villon, tel qu'il nous apparaît dans son œuvre, est la personnification la plus complète du peuple à cette époque." What, then, was lacking in this poet "au teint de bohème," who had the great merit of hating "de bon cœur, les *bourgeois* et le guet"?[37]

In Gautier's portrait, Villon lacks more than anything else the dignity that we associate with poetic immortality. This essay, first published in *La France littéraire*, was reprinted as the preface to *Les Grotesques*. It is a well-known fact that the grotesque, even ugliness, was not repugnant to the romantic sensibility. But let us see what the creator of the "grimaçante" gallery thinks about it: "Nous avons choisi çà et là à différentes reprises et un peu au hasard de la lecture, quelques types qui nous ont paru amusants ou singuliers, et nous avons tâché de débarrasser du fatras les traits les plus caractéristiques d'écrivains tombés dans un oubli trop souvent légitime, et d'où personne ne s'avisera de les retirer." A little farther on, Gautier adds: "Ces écrivains dédaignés ont le mérite de reproduire la couleur de leur temps." And this is one of his principal motives in resurrecting "ces auteurs de troisième ordre." In the article on Villon proper, Gautier claims that this is why he is "aussi curieux pour l'érudit que pour le poète; il nous fait connaître une foule de petits usages et de façons d'être qu'on ne trouve nulle part ailleurs: lupanars, tavernes, jeux de paume, rôtisseries, bouges et repaires de toutes sortes, il nous conduit effrontément partout."[38]

Gautier's tone in discussing his *grotesques* is not the kind that one uses to exalt a poet. An element of friendly interest mixes with a note of jollity that often borders on the burlesque. What attracts him to these "pauvres diables" is surely not the admiration felt for a master. It is rather a taste for the curious, for those small surprising novelties that appeal to the dilettante, qualities that allow a facile and clever writer to indulge his verve and to play the protector's role.

As we reread the *Grotesques*, we are amused throughout by a style that is often comic, always charming. But this style is never powerful or pathetic. And we are struck by the mediocre company in which we find the author of the *Testaments*: Scalion de Virbluneau, Saint-Amant, and others who really deserve to be addressed in this manner: "Rentrez donc dans votre poussière, pauvres gloires éclopées, figures

[36]*Ibid.*, pp. 11, 13.
[37]*Ibid.*, pp. 19, 31.
[38]*Ibid.*, pp. vi, xiv, 35.

grimaçantes, illustrations ridicules—et que l'oubli vous soit léger!"[39] In this light, Gautier's praise, although far more favorable than that of the grave scholar Daunou, could not serve to enhance Villon's reputation. All that Gautier could do for Villon was to attract greater attention to him.

Even in this respect, however, he does not always draw attention to curious or romantic details. Villon took a sympathetic interest in prostitutes: "quatre siècles avant A. Dumas, il a presque littérale-ment trouvé les pauvres faibles femmes." True. But Gautier goes on to observe that Villon in no way tried to "elevate" them. On the contrary, he bequeaths to them "des préceptes pour plumer un homme au vif et mettre à profit [leur] jeunesse."[40]

Gautier's analysis of the *Ballade à la grosse Margot*, moreover, has little to recommend it to the reader's idealistic tendencies: "La hideur lascive ne peut être poussée plus loin, la nausée nous en vient. . . . Elle dit deux mots: l'un est un jurement par la mort de Jésus-Christ, l'autre une expression de tendresse ignoble à vous dégoûter des femmes pendant quinze jours."[41]

As for Villon's capacity for love, Gautier does not take it very seriously. In comparing it favorably to Panurge's "luxure de satyre," he seems inclined to believe that Villon was capable of real love. Else-where, however, after giving a physical description of the *pauvre écolier*, he concludes: "Ce ne devait pas faire un très agréable damoiseau. Aussi ses lamentations sont-elles fort comiques; il se dit martyr d'amour; il se compose une seconde épitaphe où il se pré-tend mis à mort par une des flèches de Cupidon."[42] Gautier's final remark is filled with the same skepticism: "l'écolier Villon est—mort d'amour, à ce qu'il dit, de faim, à ce que je crois."[43]

We have seen that Gautier was surprised by Villon's "singulier mépris" for nature. More than once he amuses himself by drawing up the list of his vices, the vices of a man devoted to the "bouteille," the "marmite." In his final paragraph, he enumerates Villon's disciples, all of them the least civilized habitués of the *Cour des Miracles*! His games "étaient piperies, voleries, repues franches."[44]

On the other hand, Gautier presented the public with a poet who was able to please by his earthiness, his Byronic melancholy, his sub-jectivity, and the "saillies" of his style. At the same time, however,

---

[39]*Ibid.*, p. xv.

[40]*Ibid.*, p. 27.

[41]*Ibid.*, p. 28-29.

[42]*Ibid.*, p. 30.

[43]*Ibid.*, p. 39.

[44]*Ibid.*, p. 8.

he cultivated his reader's indifference and distaste for Villon's vices, his absurdities, and his lack of feeling for nature. In this way, Gautier emphasizes those elements, both positive and negative, that would have interested the Romantics in Villon. Gautier's is undoubtedly the most important commentary on the poet before 1873; if he is not "exalted" here, will he be "exalted" elsewhere?

Certainly not by Michelet, who finally came to despise Villon— which goes to show that the Romantics did not always think in unison. According to Schnurer this attitude raises a problem which he himself, in my opinion, does not solve very well.[45] He alludes to two passages in Michelet, the first of which dates at the latest from 1833; there he sees a favorable appreciation of Villon, "enfant de Paris . . . , esprit universel, supérieur en cela."[46] But this does not jibe with another passage that figures in the introduction to the volume on the Renaissance (1855): "Des trentes poèmes épiques du XIIe siècle, imités de toute l'Europe, jusqu'à la platitude du *Roman de la Rose*, jusqu'aux tristes gaîtés de Villon, quel pas rétrograde!"[47]

Schnurer sees a paradox here. He explains it by recalling that for Michelet, *patriotisme*, *peuple*, and *morale* are a unified principle that he believed was incarnated in the medieval epic. For this reason, says Schnurer, Michelet prefers this genre to all others in the Middle Ages. But how should we understand his praise of Villon in 1833? Schnurer tells us that we must distinguish beween two attitudes in the historian, two autonomous tendencies: on the one hand, a nationalistic *passion* that condemns Villon's immorality and lack of patriotism; on the other, a certain *fantaisie*, an artistic concern that allows him to make an independent aesthetic judgment. Thus, in the first instance, Michelet had set aside morality while appreciating in Villon the poet of genius.

The subtlety of this distinction cannot conceal its defects, the first of which is to ascribe these two opinions to him without taking into consideration his intellectual development. In 1855 Michelet was simply not the same man as he was in 1833. Unchecked nationalistic fervor had begun to blunt his genius, and he was already on the way toward losing the historical talent that had still been real and firm in the first volumes of the *Histoire de France*. We are not dealing, then, with a simple and constant *dédoublement*, but with a separation of coexistent tendencies whose differences are accentuated by the gradual changes that Michelet's total outlook was to undergo.

---

[45]H. Schnurer, *Les Jugements littéraires de Michelet* (Paris, 1923), pp. 47-50.

[46]*Histoire de France*, 2: 176.

[47]*Ibid.*, 7: 32.

An even more serious fault on Schnurer's part is to quote only what is necessary in order to create an easily resolved paradox. "En Villon, en Boileau, en Molière, et Regnard, en Voltaire" (I reproduce the rest of Michelet's first passage, written in 1833), "on sent ce qu'il y a de plus général dans le génie français; ou, si l'on veut chercher quelque chose de local, on y distinguera tout au plus un reste de cette vieille sève d'esprit bourgeois, esprit moyen, moins étendu que judicieux, critique et moqueur, qui se forma de bonne humeur gauloise et d'amertume parlementaire entre le parvis de Notre-Dame et les degrés de la Sainte-Chapelle."

Michelet is making a distinction; alongside the French genius that Schnurer calls the "universal spirit," there is this "quelque chose de local," typically bourgeois, but which the historian attacks only mildly at this point. Later on, in *La Renaissance*, carried away by his acute disdain for bourgeois vulgarity, he will forget Villon's "universality" to attack the other element that has become more offensive. In a passage from the same book, which Schnurer relegates to the appendix, Michelet links Villon to that "société fondée sur l'imitation fidèle de Pathelin, de Grippeminaud, du procureur, du magistrat qui, le soir, mange avec les filles les épices du matin et les profits de la potence." Could he have read the *Repues franches*? And could he have attributed that book to the author of the *Testaments*? If so, it would seem that Michelet, who was already hostile to Villon, has simply credited him with the misdeeds on which Prompsault and Lacroix had cast doubt. If Michelet is not thinking of the *Repues franches*, it is easy to see his meaning: his poor opinion of Villon does not represent the paradoxical reversal of the praise voiced in 1833, but actually re-echoes and underscores an earlier reproach.

It is worth recalling that the change occurred in *La Renaissance*. What is Villon doing in a study of *that* period? His name turns up in the introduction, where Michelet expresses all the bitterness of a recent disillusionment. In two or three documents that he has recently discovered, the vice and corruption of the Middle Ages, especially right after the Hundred Years War, have become clear to him, and in a fit of spite, the disillusioned historian denies everything good that he had been able to say about this tarnished age. This is not the only time that he indulges in generalizations based on hasty perceptions. This time, however, there is not only a faulty method but also a change in taste; viewed through the Renaissance, which he has just discovered, the Middle Ages, and especially the fifteenth century, lose their appeal for him. He is scandalized by a seamy story which just happened to coincide with a general impression of his. And thereby Villon loses as much in Michelet's opinion as does the entire period to which he belongs.

Schnurer does not seem to have known another passage from this same sixth volume of the *Histoire de France*. After recounting the imprisonment of Charles d'Orléans, Michelet is offended that France, foundering in misery, should have so docilely adopted English customs: "Peut-être est-ce chose utile de réclamer en faveur de la vieille France qui s'en est allée. . . . Où est-elle, cette France du Moyen Age et de la Renaissance, de Charles d'Orléans, de Froissart? . . . Villon se le demandait déjà en vers plus mélancoliques qu'on n'eût attendu d'un si joyeux enfant de Paris," and he goes on to quote the *Ballade des dames du temps jadis*.[48]

These few lines are from the first edition of 1844. And the literary judgment that they contain is quite worthy of interest, for it marks an intermediate stage, both in meaning and in chronology, between the two judgments quoted by Schnurer. Michelet still admires the Middle Ages, which he has not yet abandoned for the Renaissance, but he has already forgotten the French genius of Villon, whom he does not mention, and he pays him a rather lefthanded compliment with the statement that he was surprised at his capacity for seriousness. In 1855 he will refuse him even this faint praise, a pale shadow of the favorable appreciation of 1833.

In comparison with other critics, Michelet's interpretation of the "vers mélancoliques" of the *Ballade des dames du temps jadis* as a lament for "la vieille France" is quite original; it is not unexpected, and can be explained by Michelet's natural romantic tendency.[49] This is, moreover, the only romantic trait, to my knowledge, that he attributed to Villon.

The "Romantics," however, are not of one mind concerning the *enfant de Paris*. Gautier, who certainly, at least at the beginning, belonged to the Romantic school, delights in Villon's tricks on the bourgeoisie. Michelet, who is also associated with the "Romantics," describes the bourgeoisie of the fifteenth century with hatred and makes it seem as if Villon were one of them!

Victor Hugo's silence is surprising. In *La Légende des siècles*, the Middle Ages unfold without the appearance of *maistre* François Villon; the poem on Montfaucon, where one would expect to run into him, deals with other medieval personages, and the description of the gallows, which Berret finds "plus réaliste" than in Villon, is taken from Sauval's *Histoire et recherches des antiquités de la vie de*

---

[48]*Ibid.*, 6: 44.

[49]This interpretation is found in a more expanded but more dangerous form in an English critic of the twentieth century: "Villon, while he revives one of the eternal commonplaces of all poetry, touches for the first time that modern chord of a nostalgic regret for the antiquity of the ancients, and because the past is past!" (F. Y. Eccles, *A Century of French Poets* [London, 1909], p. 11).

Paris.[50] Villon's absence is no less surprising in *Notre-Dame de Paris,* even if it can be explained in part by the fact that Hugo needed a character who he knew had produced plays. This is perhaps why he preferred Gringoire.[51]

Thuasne, it is true, felt obliged to point out in passing some possible analogies between Villon and that other *enfant de Paris* Alfred de Musset. He exercised the greatest prudence, nevertheless, in discussing the matter of influence and later, in 1931, in an article in the *Mercure de France* on the same subject, he reconsidered and recognized the impossibility of establishing any direct filiation between Villon and the author of the *Nuits.*

Neither Hugo, nor Musset, nor any other romantic *gros bonnet* went out of his way to celebrate Villon, whom Michelet disliked and Gautier looked upon as "curieux." Shall we view Murger, considered a realist, as a romantically inclined defender of Villon? It has already been pointed out that in speaking of his "bohemian" poet Murger remains on the defensive; he is too concerned with explaining the oblivion into which his protégé has fallen to think very energetically about reinstating him.

Will the works of Gérard de Nerval yield any clues? We know that around 1830 he wrote a melodrama entitled *Villon l'Ecolier* which, unfortunately, was never produced. Since Nerval promptly lost the manuscript, all we know of this play today is its title. In any event, he never takes up the theme again, and it is not until 1855, in *Les Poètes du XVIe siècle,*[52] that we find any further allusion to Villon, the French poet of primitive and popular origins.

Henri Martin, although not to be counted among the Romantics, does have some connection with them through the influence of Augustin Thierry and his philosophy of history. In Martin's *Histoire de France* we find this paragraph on Villon:

> Durant [les] progrès de l'érudition classique et [la] décadence de la scolastique, la littérature vulgaire n'était pas entièrement stérile: la France avait produit un poète; à Charles d'Orléans avait succédé Villon; au poète né sur les marches du trône, le poète né, non pas dans l'humble demeure du peuple, mais dans les bouges infects d'une

---

[50]P. Berret, *Le Moyen âge européen dans la "Légende des Siècles"* (Paris, 1911), p. 71.

[51]Note, however, that Hugo makes Villon's name rhyme with *vallon* in the *Chansons des rues et des bois* (1: iv). He points to him in passing as a representative of the *esprit gaulois,* and links him with Virgil, the representative of the Latin spirit! According to Emile Deschanel, in the *Romantisme des classiques,* Hugo admired him very much and in conversation often quoted from the *Ballade des pendus,* especially the line: "Plus becquetés d'oiseaux que dés à coudre."

[52]*La Bohème Galante,* No. 4, 1855.

populace sans nom, dans la fange de la *cour des miracles*. Cet homme, dont le nom même n'est qu'un sobriquet infamant [this is an echo of Prompsault], cet homme, qui végéta dans la misère et le vice, parmi les *truands* de Paris, entre l'hôpital et la potence, peut se poser hardiment en face de son rival fleurdelisé: il ne sera pas vaincu dans cette lutte poétique, il puise, dans sa vie de vagabond et de bohème, des inspirations d'une énergie étrange et inconnue: il balance au moins les grâces de Charles d'Orléans par l'éclat et l'originalité de son coloris, et parfois, d'entre ses chants de mauvais lieux, s'élèvent des cris de l'âme, des accents de profonde mélancolie, qu'égalent à peine les plaintes les plus touchantes du royal prisonnier d'Azincourt. Qui ne connaît cette ballade où Villon se demande ce que sont devenus les héros du temps passé:—*Où est le preux Charlemagne?*—*Où est Jeanne Darc?*— et répond, à chaque strophe qui évoque un souvenir glorieux, par ce double et triste refrain: *Mais où sont les neiges d'antan* (les neiges de l'an passé)?[53]

These last lines, which date from 1841, might tempt one to ask whether, in spite of the evidence adduced here, the poetry of Villon was not well known and highly prized during this period, at least in fragmentary fashion: "Qui ne connaît cette ballade," Martin asks confidently. The few quotations he gives, however, apparently to refresh his reader's memory, show quite clearly that he himself hardly knows the *ballade* at all, since he cites one line incorrectly ("*Où est Jeanne Darc?*") and another—also incorrectly cited—is actually the refrain from a different *ballade!* And if he were merely reminding the reader of a well-known poem, would he have had to translate "les neiges d'antan"?

Rather than insist on Martin's phraseology, which bogs down in confusion and internal contradiction, let us note the price that Villon paid for the preference given him over Charles d'Orléans. For Martin denies him the simplicity and the purity of the "peuple" and takes pains to emphasize what is most unattractive about him. If he praises him, notwithstanding, it may have been with a motive opposite to Villemain's. Martin seems to laud this *mauvais garnement*, principally in order to depreciate the poet-prince, who symbolized for him a royalist tradition that the entire evolution of French history will seek to destroy.[54] Given the brevity of this paragraph and its mixture

[53]Henri Martin, *Histoire de France* (Paris, 1841), 8: 181–82.

[54]It is interesting to note in this regard that in vol. 7 of the fourth edition of the *Histoire de France* (1860), this paragraph was slightly changed. We no longer read "Il balance au moins les grâces de Charles d'Orléans" but "il efface les grâces languissantes de Charles d'Orléans"; in the same way, it is no longer "qu'égalent à peine les plaintes" but "que n'égalent pas les plaintes." The desire to belittle Charles d'Orléans emerges clearly.

of favorable and adverse comments—this indecisiveness, probably because of Martin's popularity, was masked over by Campaux—we can hardly see here either an attempt to exalt Villon.

Villon's popularity among the Romantics, then, is a fiction that has remained alive simply because no one has ever thought to contradict Sainte-Beuve. His fortunes during the nineteenth century, having already followed a rather unexpected course, appear downright enigmatic when we note that in 1844 it remained for Nisard, a neoclassicist far removed from Romanticism, to praise Villon to the skies. And he comes close to exalting him. For example, he takes it upon himself to deny a crime that no one has ever hesitated to attribute to Villon. To excuse other acts that cannot be effaced, he evokes the poverty into which the poet was born, the "besoin" that reduced him to a disorderly life.[55] Nisard's praise is abundant and varied. "Villon n'imite pas le *Roman de la Rose*; il laisse ces froides allégories et ce savoir indigeste"; "presque toutes ses idées sortent de ses fonds"; "c'est un enfant du peuple, né poète, qui lit dans son cœur, qui tire ses images des fortes impressions qu'il recoit de son temps";[56] Villon "écrit le français du peuple de Paris," he is "novateur de forme," his style is "plus vrai, plus senti, plus français" (although less clear) than that of his contemporaries and predecessors; his poetry is filled with a "gaieté mélancolique" that does not seem to displease Nisard at all; finally, "le premier, il a créé des expressions vives, originales, durables. Charles d'Orléans clôt la liste des poètes de la société féodale; Villon est le poète de la vraie nation, laquelle commence sur les ruines de la féodalité qui finit."[57]

Such praise, coming from this critic, is rather surprising. And Thuasne's explanation is the only one that can account for Nisard's motives. Why did he assume a polemical style? Because the authority of Boileau was at stake. Champollion-Figeac, in his new edition of Charles d'Orléans, had put his poet in first place, assigning him the rank that Boileau had reserved for Villon. As we have already observed, that extremely important couplet from the *Art poétique* had to be saved; Boileau's prestige depended on it, and Nisard came swiftly to the rescue. We notice this concern near the end of his study, where he asks the reader whether there is really any point to questioning Boileau's opinion, in view of all the qualities of the poet who "sut le premier débrouiller l'art confus de nos vieux romanciers."

[55]*Histoire de la littérature française* (Paris, 1844), p. 218.

[56]*Ibid.*, p. 290.

[57]*Ibid.*, pp. 212, 216, 217.

He also relies on an opinion that belongs not to Boileau but to the Romantics. One of Villon's greatest merits is his proletarian origin, which is associated, in turn, with a kind of nationalism. For the glory of the poet rests on the very same foundations that had been laid for the French nation. Although he would have denied it, Nisard is obviously speaking the same language as the Romantics. It should be pointed out, however, that he remains faithful to a certain style of realism that is clearly found in Boileau, who, perhaps unknowingly, inherited it from Villon through Marot and Mathurin Régnier. This tendency does not reappear intact with Nisard, since he is inspired by an element of romantic idealism. But it is worth observing that, thanks to this example of realism in his model, the neoclassical critic found good reasons for pardoning the misdeeds of the poet-thief.

After a seven-year interval—during which F. Génin, in connection with a philological thesis,[58] is the only one besides Murger to speak of Villon—we come to two authors of literary histories: J. Demogeot, *Histoire de la littérature française* (1851), and Eugène Géruzez, *Histoire de la littérature française depuis ses origines jusqu'à la révolution* (1852). Whether or not they were influenced by Murger, both these commentators—and Demogeot, in particular—pleaded Villon's case by turning him into a bohemian. They begin by denying his guilt. "La détresse" says Demogeot, "poussa Villon au larcin"—a lovely euphemism!—"et presque au gibet." "Il est pécheur, il le sait bien; mais la pauvreté est coupable de tous les méfaits."

For proof of Villon's basic goodness, Demogeot turned to a story that, even in 1832, Prompsault had no longer believed: "Il alla finir tranquillement"—again, what a euphemism!—"sa vie en Poitou, à Saint-Maixent, auprès d'un homme de bien, abbé dudit lieu."[59] We find the same defensive tone in Géruzez: "Au reste, Villon s'est avili sans se dépraver; le fond généreux de sa nature subsiste sous les souillures"[60] (which recalls Gautier's amusing error). This "incorrigible vaurien," whose "repentir est sincère, comme sa faiblesse est incurable," is "un homme et un poète, homme de mauvaise compagnie, poète de bas étage, mais énergique et sincère"; elsewhere, Géruzez calls him a "véritable enfant de Paris, sans souci, sans scrupule," who "relève de lui-même et de l'esprit français, qu'il reproduit dans des conditions vulgaires, mais avec originalité."[61]

---

[58]In his *Des Variations du langage français depuis le XIIe siècle.*

[59]*Histoire de la littérature française* (Paris, 1851), pp. 252, 254.

[60]*Histoire de la littérature française* (Paris, 1852), p. 277.

[61]*Cours de littérature rédigé pour le baccalauréat-ès-lettres* (Paris, 1841); *Cours de littérature* (Paris, 1857), pp. 158–60.

Villon's misfortune, as he himself says, is not to have had a protector.[62]

Géruzez' use of the word "mais" is amusing—"poète de bas étage mais énergique et sincère"—and recalls Madariaga's ingenious remark on the "voix populaire" that tends to reduce national characteristics to two features: "un défaut et une qualité."[63] Géruzez follows a similar procedure: he cannot bring himself to accept Villon as he is, and, in order not to run him down too badly, he attaches attenuating circumstances and compensatory qualities to the liabilities that he finds in him. Although finicky and clumsy, Géruzez treats Villon generously. Unfortunately, however, during the course of his defense, he bogs down in self-contradiction. Villon was not after all, an "incorrigible vaurien" cursed by a "faiblesse incurable": his mistake was not to have had a protector.

This dangerous procedure, which Campaux once again interpreted favorably, is reinforced by a kind of poeticization somewhat in the manner of Murger. Villon becomes "l'écolier sans souci, sans vergogne, je ne dis pas sans reproches, mal en point, espèce de truand poétique."[64] According to Demogeot: "Il fut le premier qui saisit et dégagea la poésie que recèle la plus vulgaire et la plus misérable de toutes les conditions: il exprime la nature dans sa vérité la plus nue, et il se trouva que cette franche et grossière nature était souvent l'idéal même de l'art."[65] This last statement is not as close to Murger as the first. Elsewhere, however, Demogeot outdoes Géruzez. He quotes Villon incorrectly and sometimes uncomprehendingly. By weaving together threads and strands of verse, he creates a bohemian character, both comical and sad, who sings of his "misère, non pour nous apitoyer, mais parce qu'il est poète et que sa misère a un côté poétique."[66]

With Demogeot, we fall back into the comparison between Villon and Charles d'Orléans; it stops again in Géruzez, who does not care much for the "froides allégories" of the poet-prince; he prefers the "poésie moderne" of Villon, rooted in "la rue et les halles."[67] "Villon fait époque, parce qu'il tranche avec la poésie sentimentale, alambiquée et pédante qui avait précédé."[68] His "profonde sensibilité"

---

[62]*Histoire de la littérature française*, p. 283.

[63]Salvador de Madariaga, *Anglais, Français, Espagnols* (Paris, 1930), p. 11.

[64]*Ibid.*, p. 285.

[65]*Ibid.*, p. 252.

[66]*Ibid.*, pp. 250–51.

[67]*Ibid.*, p. 277.

[68]Géruzez, *Essais d'histoire littéraire* (Paris, 1853), p. viii.

and "vive imagination," his "âme" and his "esprit," his preoccupation with death—these are the grounds for his superiority. Demogeot says the same thing: his poetry "c'est sa vie, ce sont ses idées, ses émotions personnelles."[69] His digressions on mortality recall an oration by Bossuet, a scene from Shakespeare.[70]

Romantic love has its place in Villon's poetry as well: "Un beau jour, il quitte sa ville natale pour rompre une passion, ni plus ni moins que Saint-Preux ou Werther." Nostalgia for the past, Demogeot adds, finds expression in the ballad of the *Vieille heaulmière*.[71]

Géruzez still believed that Villon, "s'étant souvent mêlé à la Basoche et à la troupe des enfants sans-souci," was the actor-author of farces, among them, presumably, *La Farce de Maistre Pathelin*. So versatile is Villon's talent, in fact, that he is also credited with the authorship of the *Repues franches*.

All the critics studied here express particular admiration for the *Ballade des dames du temps jadis*. Although Gautier alludes to it only in passing, Demogeot and Géruzez, after Nisard, quote from it *in extenso*.

Géruzez was followed directly by Campaux, Villon's apologist. We should not, however, overlook Jean-Pierre Clément, who tends to echo Demogeot, especially in his pity for Villon, "livré de bonne heure à lui-même, entraîné fatalement dans le désordre." And, like Nisard, Clément considers Villon an innovator in poetic form.[72] We are all too familiar with what Campaux has to say; it is worth stressing, however, that his work was not very influential and that his neoromanticism, attacked by Sainte-Beuve, might have seemed dated.

For Campaux as well, "l'enfant du peuple"—whom he admires solely because he is "du peuple"—has the virtue of spontaneity. A stranger to the insipidities of a dying poetic idiom, Villon's characteristic is truth, sincerity of thought and feeling; he tells of himself, his miseries, his pains, his passions; "personne, pas même Charles d'Orléans, avec son art si consommé pour son époque, n'a su y mettre ce que Villon y a réuni de naturel, de sens, de passion, de vérité et de vie, toutes choses qui sont l'âme même du style et de la poésie."[73] The "sentiment profond du néant de l'homme," "de la grande égalité de tous devant la Mort," patriotism, filial gratitude, a

[69]*Histoire de la littérature française*, p. 252.

[70]*Ibid.*, p. 256.

[71]*Ibid.*, p. 253.

[72]*Jacques Cœur et Charles VII*, pp. 95, 99.

[73]*F. Villon*, p. 307.

knack for the *mot juste*, a French style that smacks of "le cru natal," all these qualities are described with the eloquence of a fervent admirer.

Campaux overcomes the hesitations in which his predecessors had bogged down. He admits at the outset that a reader who began with certain of Villon's cruder poems might be discouraged from going on. And having said this much, he proceeds to work out his protégé's defense: it is in Villon's other poems, where Campaux discovers many good and edifying qualities, that we will find the Christian, the good son, and the contemplative genius. No, we cannot deny that Villon had known love—"je veux dire celui qui intéresse le cœur au moins autant que le sens." No, we do not have the right, on the basis of two or three passages, to question Villon's religious faith. Can we doubt that this faith—Géruzez, too, judged it authentic—filled the poet with true and deep remorse? No, a son who loved his mother so much, who understood pity so well, who felt so great a debt to a man who was more than a father to him, such a man could not have been irreligious. And despite the self-depreciation and indifference towards nature that this good Romantic was forced to recognize in Villon, Campaux at long last effects the romantic spiritualization of a poet whose exoneration was far overdue.

Sic transit gloria mundi: in the same year, Villon sustained a new defeat at the hands of Sainte-Beuve. The author of the *Causeries*, while pointing out very real beauties in Villon, never tires of running him down.[74] He revises his more indulgent opinion of 1828 and now finds no more than "deux ou trois perles dans le fumier" of the *Testaments*. There are, moreover, two kinds of authors: those who benefit from the clarity of their work and others who benefit from its confusion. The legends that grow up around this second kind of writer feed on every obscurity in their writings. This is the case with Villon. His "ouvrage gothique bizarre" is not among the best; it was composed by one of those "natures d'abandon" who have no moral direction, although they are gifted—"porte-talents" but not real geniuses. This kind of poetry can give, at best, a certain "cachet" to the mock-will-and-testament genre. We may applaud Villon's aversion for "fadeurs pastorales," but it is absurd to admire his patriotism as much as people have—were it not for that, no element of decency would remain in his "vie de taverne et de crapule."

Je ne veux que mettre en garde sur un point: c'est de ne pas prêter à Villon plus de mélancolie qu'il n'en a eu, ni une tristesse plus amère.

[74]Krantz suggests that Sainte-Beuve, who did not pay much attention to Villon in the *Tableau de la poésie française*, was offended or alarmed that someone else had undertaken to re-establish the poet's importance (*Annales de l'Est* [Paris, 1905], p. 251.)

Ne venons pas prononcer, à son sujet, le nom de Bossuet, ni même celui de Byron et des Don Juan modernes. Villon a dit quelque part que *quand nous aimons ordure, elle nous aime* (c'est le sens) et que *quand nous fuyons honneur, il nous fuit*; mais il m'est impossible de découvrir là-dedans un cri *de damné.* Villon n'a pas de ces cris: il est de ce bon vieux temps où l'on s'accommodait mieux de son vice, et où on ne le portait pas avec de si grands airs, ni d'un front si orageux. Il n'est pas homme à s'écrier avec un poète moderne: "Je bois avec horreur le vin dont je m'enivre." Pour lui, je le crains fort, il but avec plaisir jusqu'à la fin le vin dont il s'enivrait.[75]

This passage has been quoted almost in its entirety to show just how Sainte-Beuve's attack confuses Villon and the Romantics. In two or three places he limits his mockery to the Romantics, and even gives Villon credit for not resembling them. But this advantage soon becomes a liability, since immorality—romantic or otherwise—remains immorality. Is Sainte-Beuve against Villon because of his "vie de crapule"? Or because he viewed him as the idol of the Romantics, whom he disliked? Both explanations are probably equally valid.

The last critic to be dealt with here is Théodore de Banville, author of the *Trente-six ballades joyeuses pour passer le temps, composées à la manière de F. Villon.* Some of these pieces are dated 1862, others 1869. The entire collection was published in 1873 and included two *dizains* written during that same year.

In one of these *dizains*, cited earlier, the line in which Villon is called a "vagabond dormant sous le ciel bleu" hardly suits him. Villon would not have cared for the verses all through these *ballades*, allegedly written in his style—some of them in fact quite pretty— where Banville speaks of *la belle nature*:

Au mois d'avril fumer près des lilas . . .	(VII)
Sucer le lait de la mère Nature . . .	(III)
Être ébloui par les bleus firmaments . . .	(III)
Rien n'est pareil à la gloire du lys . . .	(VII)
Au fond des bois chante le rossignol . . .	(XXVIII)
Sous le feuillage et sous l'antre secret	
Nous trouverons la ville hospitalière;	
Diane court dans la noire forêt . . .	(XVI)

But Banville is less interested in Villon than he is in the villonesque ballad. In his preface, he claims to have tried to "rendre à la France une des formes de poème les plus essentiellement françaises qui aient existé." A Parnassian predilection reinforces his nationalistic argument: "La Ballade a pour elle la clarté, la joie, l'harmonie

---

[75]*Causeries du lundi*, 14: 300-301.

chantante et rapide, et elle unit ces deux qualités maîtresses d'être facile à lire et *difficile à faire*."[76] In his eyes, "Villon, qui polit sa Ballade au temps jadis," is a hero of the Middle Ages—the medieval hero of the Parnassian, who is concerned above all with form and brilliant stylistic effects. He may very well maintain that "mon effort fût demeuré stérile si je n'eusse été de mon temps dans le cadre archaïque," but it is not *his* period that he describes any more than Villon's. The virtuosity of his rhyme schemes and dazzling description are prompted most often by his own caprices and fantasies and his personal bitterness against the prosaic bourgeois and the financier. In the *Ballade à la Sainte Vierge*, whose beginning is in itself significant—

> Vierge Marie! après ce bon rimeur
> François Villon, qui sut prier et croire,

there is one line that sums up Banville in a nutshell: "Dame des Cieux, dans l'azur plein d'étoiles!"

What a vast difference between the Virgin who shines in the firmament and Villon's Virgin, shrouded in a churchly aura, who exudes pure and simple faith! "Margot avec sa jupe rouge" does not conduct herself any better than the Grosse Margot of the *Grand Testament*. But, despite Banville's realism, how beautiful, seductive and—given her low station—how idealized she becomes!

The same is true for the other ballads which by their titles, and their titles only, recall passages from Villon: *Ballades à sa mère, Pour les Parisiennes, De Banville aux enfants perdus, En l'honneur de sa mie, De la bonne doctrine, De ses regrets*. Only Banville's rhyme system is reminiscent of Villon; his subject, never. Besides, Banville does not like Paris very much, and it is not by writing about "la gentille façon de rose" that he will win favor with the original *enfant de Paris*. Nor do I believe that Villon would have expected his admirer to show this kind of delicacy: "Il sied de boire en l'honneur des pucelles."

If we really search, we will find an occasional line that is not too far from Villon's style:

> Dormir son saoul sur un bon matelas,
> . . . .
> C'est le moyen d'avoir joie et soulas . . .   (III)

Such lines, however, are rare and they are lost among hundreds of verses completely opposed to the *Testaments* both in tone and in

---

[76]"*Avant-propos*," *Trente-six ballades joyeuses* (Paris, 1873), p. 1.

spirit. We need not blame Banville, who was not bound, after all, to write for anyone but himself. The fact remains, however, that mis-understandings could arise. When Banville says "à la manière de Villon" it should be understood that the *manière* is at odds with the *matière*. It was the formal difficulties and not the subject matter that attracted Banville to Villon.

III. CONCLUSION

Between 1828 and 1873 there is no justification for the claim, made by Sainte-Beuve and others, concerning Villon's great popu-larity among the Romantics. In examining the critical testimony of this period, we find that the many writers who tried to explain, conceal, or excuse the lack of interest in Villon's work actually con-tributed, by their defensive enthusiasm, to keeping their camp on the defensive. Most of them, whether Romantics or not, could not muster unqualified admiration for Villon. Their hesitation, already evident before the edition of 1832, stems from moralistic concerns which de-preciate the genius of the poet on account of the vices of the man. Nor did the obscurity of the text help to popularize his poetry. In short, only the neoclassical Nisard and the late Romantic and Parnassian Banville really celebrate Villon. Murger, who is called a realist, can hardly be ranked in this company. The Romantics, as a "school," were not interested in him, with the exception of Gautier, who turned him round and round like a curious and amusing object. Michelet, in the end, had no use for Villon whatever.

The general impression that we get from the variety of judgments on Villon is that he was often truly admired, rarely exalted, and al-most always the victim of his critics' moral scruples. This much might have been expected, since even today no one would be inclined to praise Villon's vices. But it was after 1828 that the Romantic school came into its own, and—if Sainte-Beuve and those who followed him were right—we would have expected the Romantics to appropriate this "grotesque" and "infortuné" personnage and set him up on a pedestal. But they did not, and if the obscurity of his texts is not a sufficient explanation, then it must be that this "gueux" did not lend himself to romantic rehabilitation.

Villon's fortunes must have suffered from a much more pervasive tendency. Before 1830, there was the desire to revisit the primitive and pure past of the nation. Later on, people were shocked to discover the immorality and the grossness of the Middle Ages, and since it is during and after the Hundred Years War, in particular, that such traits become most prominent, it was the fifteenth century that suffered most. In Michelet's view for example, Villon seems to have shared in the shame of his times.

This fact remains: until 1873 Villon did not enjoy any great popularity. After 1873, we have another subject and another story. This is not to imply that his fortunes underwent an abrupt change at that time. My study ends here, because this is the year when Longnon published his findings; it is also at about this time that Verlaine began to be known. If one were to study the question in the wake of this renewal of scholarly and poetic interest, a change in methods and reference would be required in order to follow the modern fortunes of "pauvre Villon."

A Scriptural Key to Villon's *Testament*

THE *Testament* OPENS with a vengeful, lethal curse. Many interpreters, slurring over it, do not integrate it into the structure and meaning of the whole. Yet this outcry is what the poet intended, with all the force of its position, as an introduction.

Villon inveighs against Thibault d'Aussigny, the bishop of Orléans in whose "dure prison de Mehun" he suffered torments in the summer of 1461—a few months before he undertook the composition of the *Testament*. "Tel luy soit Dieu qu'il m'a esté!" he begins. Feigning to yield to better sentiments, "Si prieray pour luy," he adds, but "ce sera donc par cuer," silently and privately, and in the fashion of the heretical Picards: hence no prayer at all. However, should the bishop wish actually to hear "qu'on prie pour luy," he shall not be disappointed. My text, Villon declares, will be verse 7 of the *Deus laudem meam* psalm.[1]

If the bishop ever bothered to check, this is what he may well have found: *Fiant dies eius pauci, et episcopatum eius accipiat alter* ("Let his days be few, and let another take his office"), a malediction upon the very life of the poet's former jailer, with, in Villon's true manner, a grim play on the word *episcopatum*. These words have occasioned a slight flurry of discussion; it has been objected, apparently on the

Originally published in *Modern Language Notes* 72 (1957): 345-51. © The Johns Hopkins University Press.

[1]CVIII in the Catholic psalter, CIX in the Hebrew and Protestant versions.

31

basis of modern texts of the Bible, that they were to be found in the eighth verse and that the seventh was in effect "When he shall be judged, let him be condemned, and let his prayer become sin."[2] Thuasne argued that he did have "Let his days be few" in mind, as verse 8, but intentionally misquoted it as the seventh, in order to demonstrate that he was indeed praying "par cuer"![3] But the point can be more soberly tested against the Biblical texts close to the poet's time, in medieval manuscripts and incunabula. When the verses of the psalms were numbered, "Let his days be few" in some texts was verse 8, as today, but in others was introduced as verse 7, and continued to be so designated in some editions of the sixteenth and seventeenth centuries.[4] In MS *A* of the *Testament*, Thuasne himself points out, a scribe inserted the *dies pauci* reference in full, as an explanatory note: in his old Bible or Psalter, this was verse 7, and so it may well have been in Villon's, without equivocation or confusion on his part.

But that is hardly the final question. Why does not Villon cite or translate the words? Is it only because his mock-prayer is too dangerous to spell out? He does very characteristically take precautions, though half in jest; he maintains that he prays "par cuer" because he is "fetart" or too lazy to read, and seems to hint that he has no psalm book before him from which to quote: if necessary he can always claim, of course, that he referred to the wrong verse. Yet Villon generally and almost automatically proceeds by antiphrasis and irony, and one could assume rather safely that here he really means: I have the book right before me, from which to pick a choice prayer for the bishop. When he says

> Le verselet escript septiesme
> Du psëaulme *Deus laudem* (vv. 47-48)

"escript" sounds superfluous and uncalled for—"le verselet septiesme" would have been normal and amply sufficient—unless the line is understood as "the verse *set down* [or *written in*] as the

---

[2]A. Guérinot, "Note sur une interprétation erronée du *Grand Testament* de Villon, St. 6," *Revue de Philologie Française et de Littérature*, 22 (1908): 221-24.

[3]François Villon, *Œuvres*, ed. Louis Thuasne (Paris, 1923), 2: 91.

[4]See, e.g., *Libri Psalmorum Versio Antiqua Gallica*, ed. Francisque Michel (Oxford, 1860); *Le Psaultier de Metz—texte du XIVe siècle*, ed. François Bonnardot (Paris, 1884); *Lothringischer Psalter*, ed. Friedrich Apfelstedt (Heilbronn, 1881); *Quincuplex Psalterium, Gallicum, Romanum, Hebraicum, Vetus, Conciliatum* (Paris, 1509), preface by Lefèvre d'Etaples. As it is not possible to know exactly what text Villon was quoting, Latin citations are given here from the Vulgate. A check with other versions shows that there are no variations of any importance for the present argument. Villon's *Testament* is quoted from the Longnon-Foulet edition.

seventh"; it suggests a strong or fresh visual impression. In any case, why this particular psalm, at this initial point? If Villon really refers to it "par cuer," why is this psalm the one to emerge from his memory, in this crisis of rancor and bitterness? Why has he been carrying it in his mind? Or if he has just read it, why did he stop at or pick out this very one? By his veiled yet extended presentation, not only does he set us wondering about the importance that the psalm holds for him, but he compels us to seek out the psalm ourselves in order to find the unquoted words, which certainly no reader could spot "par cuer"—in fact, there is in this a complicated prank, very typical of Villon: if you want to know what I mean, he implies, you must read the source and be either less "fetart" than I or as much of a cleric as I, according to your interpretation of my ambiguities!

"Je ris en pleurs," he might have interjected right here. A reading of the psalm, as a whole and not in one verse alone, is revealing. One perceives that it held up to Villon a likeness of himself that must have shaken him to his depths.

The psalm, like the *Testament*, opens with an ardent protest. The psalmist assails the wicked by whom he has been compassed about with words of hatred, and Villon with equal passion denounces the one who has been "dur et cruel" to him, "trop plus que cy ne le raconte" (vv. 25-26). And both retaliate with the most violent imprecations. The initial verses of protest, in the psalm, are aimed at an indefinite number of adversaries, and the maledictions at one. This has perplexed the commentators, of whom some believe that the curses are in fact those previously hurled by the adversaries at the psalmist and now indignantly quoted by him, as examples of their viciousness, while others argue—more convincingly, it would seem—that it is still the voice of the psalmist himself, who now gathers the full force of his imprecations upon the head of one adversary among the many. The latter interpretation, to Villon, must have been the obvious and only one. It is remarkable how in the *Testament*, a poem full of grievances against the many, all the onus of Villon's wrath similarly concentrates on the one hated man. At the age of thirty, "Que toutes mes hontes j'eus beues," he charges the bishop with all the "maintes peines" he has suffered,

> Lesquelles j'ay toutes receues
> Soubz la main Thibault d'Aussigny . . .   (vv. 5-6)

a furious, extravagant charge to make against any one man. After going on to consider at length his wasted youth, his poverty, his ill star, and his penchant for women as so many causes of his wretchedness, he concludes some seven hundred lines beyond by returning to Thibault and blaming him once again.

Among the numerous imprecations called out by the psalmist in fourteen relentless verses, some to Villon could have seemed as appropriate, for his purpose, as the *dies pauci* verse. For example: *Cum iudicatur exeat condemnatus* ("When he shall be judged let him be condemned"). If Thibault has shown me harshness and cruelty,

> Je vueil que le Dieu eternel
> Luy soit donc semblable a ce compte. (vv. 27–28)

He has not been "misericors" to me; he may be a bishop, but not mine; he may go about making the sign of the cross, but "moult me fut chiche" and all that I for my part received "soubz la main Thibault d'Aussigny" was "maintes peines": *Non sit illi adiutor* ("Let there be none to extend kindness unto him") . . . *pro eo quod non est recordatus facere misericordiam* ("because that he remembered not to shew mercy") . . . *noluit benedictionem et prolongabitur ab eo* ("as he delighted not in blessing, so let it be far from him").

But the psalmist out of his imprecations is moved to prayer. He implores the God of his praise (*Deus laudem meam . . .*) to protect and deliver him. In a development in many ways strikingly parallel, Villon, immediately after cursing Thibault, prays in that same vein, although his own deliverance (from the "dure prison" at any rate) is a matter of the past:

> Si prie au benoist fils de Dieu,
> Qu'a tous mes besoings je reclame,
> Que ma pauvre priere ait lieu
> Vers luy, de qui tiens corps et ame,
> Qui m'a preservé de maint blasme
> Et franchy de ville puissance.
> Loué soit il. . . . (vv. 49–55)

This is in part a prayer in support of the previous "povre priere," the curse invoked against Thibault. So the psalmist had pleaded that his words of malediction be fulfilled. Why then was this a *"povre priere"*? Not because of its vindictiveness. This did not trouble the psalmist, and Villon could not have asked the "benoist fils de Dieu" to receive a prayer manifestly poor as a prayer. There is a hint of irony: the prayer was "povre" because offered by one allegedly "fetart" in his reading of Scriptures. But in Villon's language the word "povre" is also a complex note of humility, self-depreciation, and self-pity, in tune with preachings of those mendicants so loathed and yet so popular at that time. It could grow into an expression of feeling for others: his mother, for example, "ma povre mere . . . la povre femme," "femme je suis povrette et ancïenne"; or the "povre viellart"; or those "povres vielles sotes," "ces povres fameletes" like the "belle Heaulmiere," "povre, seiche, megre, menue." Constantly, the word recurs to label Villon himself: "le povre Villon," "vostre povre escolier Françoys," "povre je suis," "povre de sens et de savoir," "se pitié de nous povres avez." In earnest or in jest, he is forever belittling his own figure, setting off his own insignificance, inadequacy, or misfortune.[5] "Povreté" which has trailed and pursued his family "de petite extrace"—"Povreté tous nous suit et trace" (v. 277)—becomes, one might say, the *condition villonesque*, by which the *povre escolier* interprets to himself and may even be tempted to explain away his woes, and by extension the woes of others: "pitié de nous povres." *Ma povre priere* is the prayer of "one such as me— le povre Villon"—a humble prayer in its way, though ferocious, very much as in the psalm.

The poor, in the psalm as well, occupy a central position. The psalmist is one of them. He laments his waning strength, in words that apply all too well to Villon himself: "My knees are weak through fasting [*ieiunio*]; and my flesh faileth of fatness [*oleum*]." But that is not the essence of his condition. "I became also a reproach [*opprobrium*] unto them," he says; "I am poor and needy [*egenus et pauper*] and my heart is wounded within me [*conturbatum est intra me*]"; the wicked man persecuted the poor and needy [*inopem et mendicum*] that he might even slay the broken in heart [*compunctum corde*]." The prayer rises to its height in the last two verses, where the psalmist "among the multitude" praises the Lord: "For he shall stand at the right hand of the poor [*pauperis*], to save him from those that condemn his soul"—or *"my* soul" (*persequentibus animam meam*), as Villon could have seen in the Latin. The psalmist does not pray that his body may be replenished or healed, but only that he may be delivered from persecutions of the soul. Villon does at times regret the comforts and joys of the body, but the prayer that grows out of his curse is addressed to a Savior "Qu'a tous mes besoings je reclame" and "de qui tiens corps et ame." "Loué soit-il," he exclaims like the psalmist, for He has preserved me "de maint blasme [reproach, blasphematory injury, *opprobrium*]/Et franchy de ville puissance." Here too the curse is prelude to a prayer about deliverance and redemption from debasing oppression. Immediately after the "benoist fils de Dieu," he praises "Nostre Dame," and then Louis XI, his royal savior: "le bon roy me delivra" (v. 82). "Dieu vit," he says a little further; "au plus fort de mes maulx," He showed me a city of hope, in the land of Bourbon (XIII, XIV).

---

[5]Italo Siciliano has already brought out the significance of this note in Villon; see his *François Villon et les thèmes poétiques du moyen âge* (Paris, 1934), pp. 96, 517-18.

More significantly perhaps than appears in Italo Siciliano's discussion,[6] the *Testament* is patterned after the *Lais*, a poem of mockliberation. The second poem also opens as an escape, not from an alleged martyrdom of love but from the traumatic nightmare of Thibault's oppression. The bishop, no doubt, subjected Villon to harsh physical punishment, mentioned in the poem, but that alone does not account for the virulence and finality of the malediction Villon hurls back at the bishop, or for his reluctance to tell everything ("dur et cruel/Trop plus que cy ne le raconte"). The rancor went deep, to levels plumbed by the psalmist's words: "Let this be the reward of mine adversaries [*qui detrahunt mihi*: who humiliate or calumniate me] and of them that speak evil against my soul [*qui loquuntur mala adversus animam meam*]." Villon would have hoped that the bishop, of all men, might show him "misericorde." Thibault, instead, not only failed to grant it, but he failed to hear, understand, or believe the voice of a Villon speaking of regeneration. He was the most formidable of those "qui me font telle presse" and "en meurté ne me vouldroient veoir" (vv. 119–20). Such an encounter in Villon's life, as Louis Cons forcefully argued,[7] could have been a moral revelation and catastrophe for him, and may disclose the sense of the whole work as a reaction to this experience. Even as he vindictively celebrates his liberation from the unspeakably "dure prison," Villon suggests that he remains in a pitiful state, and has not escaped. He regrets that he did not encounter on his way, like Diomedès, "Ung autre piteux Alixandre," who might have saved him (XVII–XXI).

It is also evident that this encounter with Thibault acquainted Villon with the terrifying prospect of death. That is implicit in the very death curse, called down upon Thibault as Villon elaborately protests that he asks for no more than exact retribution. In liberating him, he tells us, Louis XI "vie me recouvra" (v. 84), and more than once, later, he speaks like one arguing against a death sentence that has hung over him (vv. 106, 121ff., 136, 165). In the "dure prison," he must have faced the dread penalty. In this sense, too, the curse is followed by a celebration of deliverance. But the experience has left its mark. After the release of that opening outburst of protest and liberation, his imagination insistently fastens upon visions of death, a disintegration of life that he often comes to visualize not only as inevitable but as final. "A la mort tout s'assouvit" (v. 224).

This kind of ironic retort to the outcry of deliverance, to be sure, is not to be found in the psalm, also silent on other themes important to Villon, among which "le temps de ma jeunesse," women and, of

[6]*Ibid.*, pp. 467–68.

[7]*État présent des études sur Villon* (Paris, 1936), pp. 139ff.

course, "Saturne." But the psalm is a revealing companion piece to the *Testament*, providing a context for the introductory curse. The poet does everything to invite us to probe the meaning of that mock-prayer, even repeating it, much later, just before the second part of the poem, which contains the distribution of legacies. There the bishop reappears and stands, a privileged legatee, in advance and outside of the formal testament, to receive a second malediction, couched once more in bitterly veiled terms implying a settling of accounts (LXXIII). The importance of the reiterated curse calls attention to its source, intimated on the first occasion, and its amplest explanation lies in the psalm read in its full sweep as it turns from imprecations against the cruel to a prayer for the destitute wounded in heart and soul, and ends with praises to the God who protects and liberates. It contains in a given balance major themes that Viilon will maintain in a similar balance, with ironic extensions of his own. It was present in the poet's mind as he constructed his opening stanzas and looked ahead. Against that Scriptural background, the passionate outburst against Thibault d'Aussigny is fraught with meaning, and what follows is commentary, development, and repercussion.

The Unity of Villon's *Testament*

THERE IS A POWERFUL UNITY in Villon's work which does not come through in the samples displayed by anthologies. These, understandably, all include poems like the *Ballade* to the Ladies of Long Ago. But those are fragments and snatches; however outstanding, they remain incomplete, impoverished, when detached from the whole body of Villon's poetry. For that is the collection in which they truly belong. Villon's *Testament* as total unit is the poet's most intense, sustained creation, providing a context for every part inserted.

Another context, both illuminating and mystifying, is the poet's life. The *Testament* itself, though poetically a personal document, is not an itemized account of confidences. It reveals very little about the incidents of his life. On that score, the chief sources of information have turned out to be the fifteenth-century police records of Paris and of the provinces. These, unhappily, abound in precise particulars: association with notorious gangs, homicide, robbery, flight from justice, imprisonment, appeals, capital punishment barely averted. Villon is reticent about this record; the *Testament* is not like a criminal's private diary. But the record is always there, like an underlying assumption.

For example, in 1456, when he was twenty-five years old, he wrote a first short poem of 320 lines entitled *Le Lais*. The title itself is a play on words: one of its meanings is legacy, or things bequeathed, and

Not previously published.

most of the poem is in fact a series of mock-gifts distributed to all and sundry. Another possible meaning is that of *lai* as poetic narrative or plaintive tale of love. Villon relates that he is running away from Paris to escape the rigors of unrequited love; hence, on the eve of a long journey, and uncertain of the future, he disposes of his belongings. But that is a *lai*, a tale, not to be taken literally. With accomplices, Villon had just perpetrated a sensational robbery, and to cover his flight, cautiously and yet ironically, he wrote his poem of self-exile and mock-distribution of personal wealth. For all the layers of meaning and tone commingled in the title and in every stanza, this early poem does not as yet grow very deep. But the manner, if not the substance, of Villon is already there—his allusive manner of referring to events never explicitly recorded and described, a manner which may be at first only a precautionary measure against the police, but which grows into a silence pregnant with meaning. It is as if he were writing not so much for a private purpose but for a private public of informed readers and friends. To follow him as far as he will go, it is imperative to become one of his intimates and to be, as it were, in the know.

The major work, the *Testament*, is a complex poem of over two thousand lines, distributed in stanzas or *laisses* of eight lines, among which are inserted pieces of special form, particularly the celebrated *ballades*. On the surface—and some critics have stopped there—it may meet the eye as a rambling, confused medley of jests and confessions. But it has a definite shape, which grows more and more discernible to the eye and becomes one of the enigmas of the work, although it is of elementary simplicity.

The poem is divided into two almost equal parts. The second is like a development of the *Lais* of 1456. Again, but with greater profusion, we have a racy succession of mock-bequests. One of the best examples is Villon's concern, expressed both in *Le Lais* (XXV, 196) and *Le Testament* (CXXVII, 1275) over "trois petis enfans tous nus, trois povres orphelins," whom literal-minded critics, not long ago, compassionately took to their hearts.[1] It is my will, says Villon, that they be provided for, so that they may survive this winter. I'll see that they go to a good school. And I order that my long coat be rent in two, that one half be sold and that the proceeds of the sale be used to buy these youngsters some pastry, "car jeunesse est ung peu friande" (CXXIX, 1297)! Investigation reveals, however, that these legatees, whom Villon names, were not three babes but three old men, not destitute but wealthy, aggressive, and greedy. The jest is typical, and we learn gradually to gather the opposite of what Villon declares.

[1]All quotations are taken from Villon's *Œuvres*, ed. A. Longnon and L. Foulet (Paris, 1932).

The bequests are trivial, imaginary, grotesque, worthless, and usually ironic, serving to characterize and satirize the legatees. To three rich, rapacious speculators who fight like dogs, for example, he leaves a maddening bone of contention: something like four little pennies to be divided equally. To the religious, who are supposed to maintain an ascetic life, he liberally bequeaths the choicest morsels and all the resources of his imaginary kitchen and cellar. Thus everyone is stamped, and the jest often serves the purpose of turning individuals and types inside out. On a rare occasion, a cherished legatee will receive a real, direct, and priceless bequest. Villon's mother, for example, receives one of the flowers of her son's poetry, a *ballade* to pray in her own simple fashion to the Holy Virgin. But Villon remembers legions of heirs among the ruffians, the police, the ladies, the clergy, the merchants, the financiers and government officials. He had a wide acquaintance with all strata of society and apparently enjoyed a certain renown in his own lifetime. And one of the obvious facts about him is that he never got around to making use of his connections in the upper strata to achieve a peaceful and comfortable position in life. Almost all his heirs are victims and not beneficiaries of his bequests. The dominant note in this second part of this criminal's *Testament* is that of a mocking settling of accounts with the respected, who at heart are evil, and especially those—women or men—who withheld the love or the assistance with which they might have endowed him. Many of his bequests carry this feeling of regret, reproach, and reprisal.

And that is one meaning of the title, *Le Testament*. The first part, of equal length, is like a long introduction, to tell us why he has been moved to write a testament—that is, why in his thoughts he is on the verge of death. He is now thirty years old. In the medieval scheme of things, this means that he is barely approaching what would be the end of youth. And yet, he says, he is already like an old man, shattered and worn out. I regret, he says in dead earnest, I regret the time of my youth—"je plains le temps de ma jeunesse" (XXII, 169). It has left me, without warning. Not as one would leave, at a walk or at a gallop. How then? Alas! of a sudden it has flown away and has left behind no gift for me:

> Il ne s'en est a pié allé
> N'a cheval: helas! comment don?
> Soudainement s'en est vollé
> Et ne m'a laissié quelque don.   (XXII, 173-76)

The time of my youth has gone away, and I remain, doleful, fallen, darker than a berry, and despised even by my own.

Why has youth left me without any blessing? Villon, at such moments, can find the reason within himself. Oh, if only I had studied in the time of my mad, foolish youth and had applied myself to good ways of life.

> Hé! Dieu, se j'eusse estudié
> Ou temps de ma jeunesse folle
> Et a bonnes meurs dedié. (XXVI, 201-3)

But what did I do? I would shun my school, as the bad child will do. In writing these words, my heart all but breaks:

> Mais quoi? je fuyoie l'escolle,
> Comme fait le mauvais enfant.
> En escripvant ceste parolle,
> A peu que le cuer ne me fent. (XXVI, 205-8)

That is but one of the many notes that give the first part of the *Testament*, in general, a tone distinctly grave, inward and tragic. It is like a confession, soul-searching in quality, and strikingly different from the second part. For that reason, it may seem at first that the two parts are alien to one another. But Villon knew that he was putting them together and we cannot lightly suppose that to him they had no connection.

He put the *Testament* together after suffering an overwhelming shock. Following his flight from Paris in 1456, he had wandered round and about for over four years, and in the summer of 1461 found himself in Meun-sur-Loire, in a prison-dungeon of Thibault d'Aussigny, bishop of Orléans. We don't know why he was there. On this, perhaps the most crucial moment of Villon's life, we have as yet no official documentation. This time—very exceptionally— most of what we know comes from the poet himself. It is a most significant exception, for Villon in the *Testament* never refers directly to any other prison he has inhabited. This one, which he names openly, was apparently, among all jails, the harsh prison—"la dure prison" (XI, 83), as he calls it. Yet, he too tells us nothing of the crime, the charges, the sentence. All we know is that Villon had a narrow escape: Louis XI, newly crowned king of France, stopped in his travels in the town of Meun, and by virtue of an old custom, which granted amnesty to all prisoners held in any locality on the occasion of the king's first visit to the town, Villon was freed, on October 20, 1461. And in the months that followed, Villon composed the *Testament*.

Directly, immediately, impatiently, the *Testament* opens with a vengeful, vehement, lethal curse against Thibault d'Aussigny. Most interpreters, roaming up and down the poem for a key, and fastening on one favorite fragment or another, have slurred over these opening stanzas and have not integrated them into the structure and meaning of the whole. Yet this outcry is what the poet, visibly, intended to be at the very head. With all the force of its initial position, it is like an introduction and keynote to the whole.

Poetically, it is appropriate and fortunate that here we have no police document. The outburst remains mysterious and disturbing, like a passion arising from the depths of Villon, never to be fully probed even by an intimate reader, or, for that matter, never to be fully fathomed by the poet himself. It is powerfully disturbing also, because nowhere else in his works does the poet invoke any such curse on anyone, whatever his grudge. Invoking against his adversary one of the psalms, in which the psalmist did the same, Villon calls down upon his former jailer the most hating malediction of all: he passionately prays for the death of Thibault d'Aussigny.

I am thirty years old, Villon says in the very first line. I have drunk down all my shame and humiliation; I am not all foolish or all wise, for all the pain I have received at the hands of Thibault d'Aussigny. He may be a bishop, blessing everyone in the street, but no bishop to me. He has not shown me *misericors* (III, 22). Villon does not protest that he was innocent. He protests against an unspeakably harsh punishment:

> Je suis pecheur, je le scay bien;
> Pourtant ne veult pas Dieu ma mort,
> Mais convertisse et vive en bien.   (XIV, 105-7)

I, he adds, and all others bitten by sin. Although, in sin, I am like one dead, I know that God lives, and His *miséricorde* (XIV, 110), if I am remorseful, by His grace will grant me pardon. However base the sinner, He hates only perseverance in sin:

> Combien que le pecheur soit ville,
> Riens ne hayt que perseverance.   (XIII, 103-4)

And that is the *miséricorde* that Thibault must have withheld. The bishop, says Villon, has been to me "dur et cruel" (IV, 25). "Trop plus que cy ne le raconte" (IV, 26), he adds, grimly, in his characteristically allusive manner. There is an anguish in his loathing of Thibault which cannot be explained in terms of any physical punishment, however harsh, that he may have suffered in his dungeon. It would not account for the virulence and finality of the death curse. Any such physical pain was past; he had been liberated from it. Yet anguish remained very live in Villon. He had not gotten over his meeting with Thibault. He had hoped that the bishop, of all men, might show him *miséricorde*; Thibault, of all men, did not grant it, did not believe in his chances for regeneration. Thibault, of all men, had crossed his path and stood before him as the most formidable of those who, as he says, "me font telle presse" (XV, 119) that "en meurté ne me vouldroient veoir" (XV, 120). Such an encounter in Villon's life could have been a moral revelation and catastrophe. I feel that it discloses the sense of the whole work as a reaction to this experience.

How does the *Testament* work itself out? Like the short *Lais*, it may be read in part like a poem of escape, not mock-escape this time, but liberation in grim, dead earnest. After hurling imprecations at Thibault, Villon celebrates all those, in heaven and on earth, who have been his liberators: God, Jesus, "benoist fils de Dieu," the Holy Virgin, and Louis XI (VII, 49–56); also, the duke of Bourbon, who had shown him kindness after his release.

Yet one of the deepest ironies of all in Villon is that, after having been released from prison, he was not yet liberated from his encounter with Thibault—hence the vehement outcry against him, at the head of a poem written in days of freedom. Throughout, he shows that he has remained aware of his wretched self—he has not really escaped Thibault.

Immediately after celebrating his release, Villon goes into a long search into his own past and the condition of all human beings. We sense that it is an explanation—a reproach and an atonement, as it were—addressed to the bishop.

Who am I, he says, to be so pursued and harried? I am but one of the poor, "le povre Villon," as he calls himself,

> Povre je suis de ma jeunesse
> De povre et de petite extrace
> . . . .
> Povreté tous nous suit et trace. (XXV, 273–74, 277)

Poverty not simply in a pecuniary sense. The word "povre" in Villon's language becomes a complex note of humility, self-depreciation and pity—pity for all, not only himself. It echoes the preachings of the mendicant orders of his day. It is one of the most constant words in his vocabulary. He is forever applying it to himself and, in earnest or in jest, forever belittling his own figure, setting off his own insignificance, inadequacy, or misfortune. "Povreté," in this sense, becomes the essential *condition villonesque*, by which he is tempted to interpret and explain away his woes.

For what course is open to one born in *povreté*? Virtue comes from wellbeing and good fortune. Necessity incites us to evil actions, and hunger emboldens the wolf to rush out of the woods. This had been the case, so argues Villon, of that pirate in the days of Alexander. But the emperor, far from putting him to death, changed his lot to a fortunate one, and the pirate became a good man! If only God had granted that I meet "ung autre piteux Alixandre" (XXI, 162)! So Villon is lured, as he argues against the sternness of Thibault, into thinking that the blind, unpredictable, uncontrollable force of fortune, outside of himself, has driven him into *povreté*, and under the laws of *nécessité*. That was one possibility.

Yet, he goes on, how I regret the time of my youth! Time squandered, during which I might have made something of my life. If I had pursued my studies, I should not now be "povre de sens et de savoir" (XXIII, 178). Villon, in fact, had succeeded in becoming a master of arts at the age of twenty-one and was officially a cleric, entitled to a cleric's position. But he had not pursued this course. He remained forever conscious of the cleric he might have been, and often quotes the Bible and the learned sources. Seriously or jokingly, he is constantly striking the pose of a preacher, and at times argues a point of doctrine. He reminds us, or rather himself, that he could do it! But he has cast himself out of that way of life and has come to naught. If youth has departed, leaving nothing behind, it is then because he has himself thrown its possible gifts away. Villon is drawn into feeling, very deeply, his own responsibility toward himself. And that was another possibility that opened up, in the dialectic of his search, regret, and remorse.

Around these two themes of fatality and responsibility, Villon groups his reminiscences, which include recollections of the fatal force of *feminine nature*, which has abused and deceived him, and has also been responsible for reducing him to naught. One of the most somber pictures in the *Testament*, relegated to the second part, is the *ballade* in which he describes, frankly and graphically, his union with *la grosse Margot*. It is a picture of utter degradation. But whence the degradation? Who has degraded whom? Is he really here the victim of *la nature feminine*? Desperately, Villon displays himself in the most stark and ruthless light and assumes a fearful responsibility:

> Je suis paillart, la paillarde me suit.
> Lequel vault mieulx? Chascun bien s'entresuit.
> L'ung vault l'autre; c'est a mau rat mau chat.
> Ordure amons, ordure nous assuit;
> Nous deffuyons onneur, il nous deffuit. (1622–26)

Villon's encounter with the bishop has made him look intently within himself, and he has come to know both the need to believe that it has not all been his fault, and the necessity to bear all the burden.

But that encounter has opened another perspective. He had not had, previously, to face the possibility of death. There had been no direct threat of capital punishment. But it is rather clear that Thibault d'Aussigny, on this occasion, had condemned him to death. In calling down the malediction of death upon Thibault, Villon hints that he is only repaying him in kind. Louis XI, he says, saved his life. So, in many other ways, he indicates indirectly that he has known in the bishop's prison the terrifying prospect of the dread penalty. In this sense, too, the outcry against Thibault and what follows is a celebration of deliverance. But again, an ironic deliverance. The dread experience has left its mark. Villon has been delivered from immediate death only to contemplate the prospect of the impending death that is inevitable, that has become familiar to his innermost thought. After the release of the initial outburst of liberation, his imagination persistently fastens upon visions of death, a disintegration that he often comes to visualize not only as inevitable but as final. In the text and in his thoughts, that is the full meaning of the beautiful *ballade* to the Ladies of Long Ago. There, and in other meditations on the dead, he rises to a high sense of the passing of all things and of the vanity of vanities. "Car à la mort tout s'assouvit" (XVIII, 224).

But by this appeasement, he needs to quiet and to resolve the terrors of his soul, the terror of envisaging the physical end of being, which he describes more than once. The terror of having come so suddenly, so prematurely, to the end of his own strength and vitality, and the terror of being in the vicinity of death. But, because of that, the terror also of spiritual and moral death, the hopelessness of recovering all that had been lost after the time of youth had flown away. For, to him, his encounter with the bishop was a revelation of the double and joint prospect of physical and spiritual disintegration.

He cannot get the bishop out of his thoughts. It is a gripping experience to see, in the first part of the *Testament*, how Villon, by the force of his inner search, strays from Thibault; how he struggles to find the cause in himself, and yet to locate it in inevitable forces outside of himself; and how, in bringing the first part to a conclusion with one more portrait of a *povre Villon* worn out with premature old age, suddenly, without having directly referred to him for some seven hundred lines, Villon again, irrepressibly, cries out: "I owe this all to Thibault" (LXXIII, 737)! Here the bishop reappears, springing out of the depths, and stands outside and in advance of the formal testament in the second part, a first, special, privileged legatee, to receive a second, resounding malediction, a startling echo of the first. The whole first part of the *Testament*, in which Villon grapples with himself, is framed between these two outcries against Thibault—for Thibault it was who set off the whole painful search.

A vivid light is thrown on this encounter between Villon and the bishop by one of the few pieces that the poet left out of the *Testament*. Some of these were written well after the *Testament*, but not this one. Villon, here too, says that he is thirty years old; many other signs indicate that, in fact, he wrote this poem in Thibault's prison. Why then did he not include it in the *Testament*?

It is entitled *Le Débat du cuer et du corps de Villon*. It is the Body that first, spontaneously, awakens to the presence of the Soul, and not the Soul that first cries out to be recognized—a searching and touching introduction to a fateful debate. The Soul is distressed to see him so alone, crouching like an animal in his hole, and tries to get to the bottom of his unhappiness. You have spent yourself in mad revelries. You are lost. "Rien ne cognois" (l. 15). If you were a moron, you would have the semblance of an excuse. But you have no case. All to you is one, the beautiful and the ugly: "Si n'as tu soing, tout t'est ung, bel ou let" (l. 24).

But the Soul makes no headway at first. The Soul dwells on past errors and their consequences in the present—and all that, which already is, cannot be made to have been otherwise. Words of recrimination cannot move Villon, the Body. They can only make him face a prospect of doom, and the poet, with honesty and realism, makes the Body answer all these observations evasively, flippantly, cynically. And when the Soul asks the Body, "dont vient ce mal?" the Body replies, "il vient de mon malheur" (l. 31), from Saturn, which burdened me with this destiny. The Soul is outraged, but he persists. Such as the planets have caused me to be, so I will be; this is my creed.

But the Soul finally asks the telling, regenerating question, not about the past or the present, but about the future: "Veulx tu vivre" (l. 41)? "Will you have life?" "God give me that power!" cry out the Body and Villon. "Then," the Soul drives home, "you must . . ." "What?" asks Villon. "Remorseful in your conscience, you must 'Lire sans fin.'—'En quoy?'—'Lire en science' " (l.43). This, to the poet, was the culmination of a *Débat du cuer et du corps de Villon*.

Thibault d'Aussigny here is not mentioned, not held responsible for torments suffered by Villon. The *miséricorde*, of God or of men, here is not invoked. Villon must face Villon, must come to self-knowledge, to moral self-rediscovery. It is the higher study that will give him life, continued life, and with it the renewed chance of having life that will sustain him in reading without end.

It is clear why this poem could not fit into the *Testament*. The *Testament* was also to be a death-or-life debate, but the outcome of the earlier poem, written while Villon was still in prison, had been hopeful. It sounds like the poem of a lost cleric who, with frankness and delicacy, with realism and depth, relates how he has found himself again and rediscovered that the good life is the life of study without end. It is a poem of regeneration—not only the promise but the realization of regeneration.

And Thibault failed to hear, understand or believe. Villon was coping with Villon, but surely it was meant to be in the sight of Thibault. His intimate reader, this time, was surely meant to be this high cleric, who might have comprehended in the lost cleric the regenerating power of that need to study without end. There was as yet no trace of any rancor against Thibault—only ruthless self-analysis, and determination, and hope. But Thibault, we know from elsewhere, was of a stern, legalistic disposition. Evidently he discounted and rejected Villon's inner debate and plunged Villon into a traumatic nightmare. That is why the *Testament*, shortly after, emerges as a rewritten and expanded *Débat du cuer et du corps de Villon*, and Thibault emerges as the formidable adversary, bearing the responsibility not so much for having made Villon what he is, but for having made him desperately aware of what he is.

It is still like a long inner debate, in which the Soul perceives the possibility of utmost personal responsibility and the Body is tempted to blame the stars, Fortune, or any exterior force. But now the Soul and the Body, too close to death, and without the prospect of renewed, prolonged life, seem condemned, in a fallen state. And that seems to be the tragedy of Villon, against which he struggles, and because of which he cries out against Thibault: that in coming to know himself, he loses himself. That is another meaning of the *Testament*: so close to the death which awaits him, Villon leaves Thibault what is both a curse and a confession.

All stems, like an evolving network of interrelated themes, from the initial outburst. So does the second part of the *Testament*, where he speaks of others who have failed him, others who have failed themselves and followed the way of the Body, and not known any inner debate. It is a series of grotesque caricatures, which comes to a climax against himself in the gruesome *ballade* to *La Grosse Margot*. It seems to be there to testify to the opening stanza of the first part, where he says right off:

> En l'an de mon trentiesme aage,
> Que toutes mes hontes j'eus beues. . . .   (I, 1-2)

The second part is a general tableau of the fallen condition of men, which has absorbed the poet himself, where Thibault resolved to let him stay. In the second part, which thus is drawn into satire, the voice of Villon turns to laughter, always native and irrepressible in him, but it often resumes the grave tone of the first part—which itself anticipates the second and at times yields to laughter. All is intermingled. The grimmest jest of the *Testament* is the whole second part, like a retaliation against Thibault, to whom he seems to say: "See, then, where you have left me and see how those are who remain uncondemned." On reading the *Testament* as a whole, one feels such a unity among the parts—a unity not distinctly of structure but of feeling. All is repercussion and retort to the passionate outburst at the start. So much so that the last image in the *Testament* reflects the first image, bearing to it the same tonal relationship as the whole second part to the first. In the closing *ballade*, of which the refrain speaks laughingly but disturbingly of the possibility of suicide, Villon's last word is this:

> Sachiez qu'il fist au departir:
> Ung traict but de vin morillon,
> Quand de ce monde voult partir.   (2021-23)

This is a closing echo to the opening display of all shames and humilitations drunk down.

Villon has been called the first modern French poet, the first to have asked himself, poignantly, "What am I?" To the modern reader he is indeed a kindred soul for the complexity, the contradictions, and the diversity of tones with which he expresses a feeling that is one.

Villon's *Epitaphe*:
A Reading

LET US LEAVE the title behind; it is probably no more than a scribe's notation on the manuscript. This is an *épitaphe*, surely, but not Villon's alone. Let us also leave behind the criminal archives of the period, although they may indicate certain specific circumstances that gave Villon cause to fear the agony of the gallows; the ballad does not single out a particular incident any more than it identifies a particular individual. Nor does Villon relate the experience of the condemned, anticipating or undergoing their agony. And yet, to him and to his contemporaries who were haunted by the *Danse Macabre*, a dying man's ordeal seemed horrible (*Testament*, vv. 313-28). But they never discuss the horror that the hanged have already lived through.

The voice that we hear comes from the gallows itself—"vous nous voiez cy attachez"—before it can return to earth from some place beyond, and this is a collective voice. This is no longer the *je* of the *Testament*; it is *nous*; all the way through, it is *nous*—at the very outset it is *nous*, the hanged. This voice, which speaks for *nous*, addresses itself relentlessly, almost uninterruptedly, to *vous*—named, from the beginning, "frères humains." This must be emphasized. Heavenly arbiters are invoked; yet the gesture that gives the poem its movement goes from *nous* to *vous*, from men to men.

Originally published as "Explication de texte de François Villon," in *Explication de texte*, 2d ed., Jean Sareil (Englewood Cliffs, N.J., 1967), 1: 3-11. © 1970. Translated by Jules Brody and Kathleen Duda by permission of Prentice-Hall, Inc., Englewood Cliffs, N.J.

The movement develops progressively, a first time, in one strophe. An entreaty seems to come through (vv. 1-4): "N'ayez les cuers contre nous endurcis." Then a reproach (vv. 5-8): "Vous nous voiez cy attachez . . . nous, les os." We never hear a direct response from *vous*, as though the "cuers contre nous endurcis" had hardly listened or had understood nothing; but they are there, and what we may be hearing is their laughter. After the reproach, a warning (v. 9): "De nostre mal personne ne s'en rie," which prepares the refrain, where an inversion takes place (v. 10): "Mais priez Dieu que tous nous vueille absouldre." *Nous* and *vous* are brought together. The voice still speaking in the name of *nous* finds itself speaking, however, of a larger collectivity, a *nous* that has been universalized by the *tous* preceding it. Thus, in the final analysis, *vous* is named by its inclusion in the *nous*. The voice becomes prophetic.

The same movement is taken up again and extended by the ballad in its totality. The refrain closes each strophe and concludes the poem, and a line that runs in front each time, by means of a new transition, according to the orientation of the passage, comes to redirect the development toward this refrain. Following the first strophe, the second one resumes the entreaty on a broader scale, and the third one, piling on description, takes up again the tableau of "nous, les os," in the same order. This amplification marks the powerlessness of the appeal or the reproach, even when repeated insistently, to awaken fraternal feelings; it heightens the tension, the ordeal which the refrain will resolve. For we notice that the mockers are still there and that they answer not a word. The estrangement of *vous* and the isolation of *nous* are aggravated by the absence of all dialogue. What has become of the first word in the poem, "frères"? Reintroduced at the beginning of the second strophe, but preceded by a *si*, it must now be examined, justified—

> Se frères vous clamons, pas n'en devez
> Avoir desdaing   (vv. 11-12)

and it does not appear again for a last time until the end of the third strophe, where it seems to lose itself, to dissolve into pleasantry: "Ne soiez donc de nostre confrairie" (v. 29). Then, the word disappears for good; it is finally suppressed. As far as the hanged men are concerned, "frères" in the first line had been the name of their fellow men, "humains" had been a modifier. In the final apostrophe—"hommes"—the only word to leave a trace is "humains," an adjective recast into a substantive and new general noun; instead of "frères," we have simply "hommes," without any suggestion of fraternity. The rhythm leans and lingers an instant on this word, stripped of all modifiers, making it function like a target, and drawing to it all the accumulated force of the final refrain.

Without playing with the words too much (but how can we deny a poet like Villon, who delights in double and often multiple meanings, ambiguities, and ironies, his humor and even his puns?), we see that even though they scotch the word "frères," the hanged men actually hang on it or come back to it, and thus redefine in what sense *nous* and *tous* belong to the same family. This painful but necessary discovery of a more truthful meaning is inherent in the nature of the tragic reversal. Still, the substitution of "hommes" for "frères"—the sudden absorption of *vous* into *nous*, raised to the power of *tous*—also has something of the twist of a good joke, so to speak, that has been played on *vous*. The refrain, pressing though it may be, retains a touch of the "last laugh" attitude so characteristic of many of the bequests in the *Testament*.

Let us follow the sinuousities of this continuous, fluid, but undulating movement. At first, the hanged men seem to imply that the condition of brotherliness consists in interdependence, compassion, and succor. But they seem to sense at the same time that they are deluding themselves. From the beginning, in contrast with the initial "frères humains," a feeling of division is brought out by means of four successive inversions in four lines, detaching *nous* from *vous* and pitting them against each other. The same inversions bring about the antithetical rhyme "endurcis–mercis" and, by interrupting the direct order, they emphasize further the words neighboring on *nous* and *vous*, such as "pitié" and "mercis," which are thus separated from the verb *avoir*. "Endurcis" stands out at the end of the line both by its position and by the "contre nous" that precedes and qualifies it: the hardening of brother against brother. This second line is also characteristic in that it introduces into the ballad a means of describing *vous* by negation, the plea for reverse behavior: "ne soyez pas ainsi, n'agissez pas de la sorte envers nous": let no one among you laugh at our misfortune (v. 9), do not torment us (v. 19); you must not scorn us for calling you our brothers (vv. 11–12); finally, "icy n'a point de mocquerie" (v. 34) is yet another reproach. In the third line "se pitié de nous povres avez" raises the question in context: will you have pity on us? Lines 3–4 prepare a hint of caution, and they still retain a *car*, a *se*, from the rhetoric of entreaty, the promise of a reward that will be forthcoming "plus tost."

In trying to persuade and soften the "cuers endurcis," the entreaty describes them. The picture which the hanged men later paint of themselves is done with a merciless realism. What does this mean? Is this how they hope to awaken pity in the *"endurcis?"* It is a nuance in the picture: you see us, *nous povres*, putrified cadavers. But why recapitulate something that in any event is abundantly clear to the *vous* who are there? They seem to want to emphasize, in particular, the way in which *vous* see *nous, les os.* The context and the style would seem to uphold this progression: don't harden your hearts against us; consider the way you look at us; don't laugh at our misfortune. The passage is brief, dense, like a rapid glance, a sketch in three or four strokes. Eyes are immediately fastened on the skeletons firmly held by the rope. You see us, they say, "cy attachez," not "attachez icy," which would center attention on "icy" (in this place, at this point); the gaze emanates, on the contrary, from "cy," which by condensing itself and by coming first, leads directly to the bodies tied at a fixed point, and places the main emphasis on "attachez"— an ungracious, grotesque posture. "Jamais nul temps nous ne sommes assis," the hanged men will add at line 25. This incongruous, ludicrous remark, while humorously suggesting that the hanged men, incorrigibly, still are speaking the language of the living, transmits at the same time a mocking tone, which perhaps typifies their facetiousness. Hanged men, securely attached, not content to remain motionless in the air, who sway back and forth. "Vous nous voiez cy attachez cinq, six": the rhythm reflects the movement of skeletons at times swinging in cadence, at other times abrupt and jostling, as in the echo at lines 26-27:

> Puis ça, puis la, comme le vent varie,
> A son plaisir sans cesser nous charie,

with a preponderance in both passages of spirant, sibilant, and blowing consonants, and from time to time a more abrupt *k, p,* or *t* in support. All that the mockers see is this weird dance at the end of a rope; the number of unrecognizable dancers (*cinq, six*) is not clearly given. They have lost all their individuality. "Quant de la chair, que trop avons nourrie" (v. 6): the hanged men judge themselves, moralize, and explain why the flesh, "elle est pieça devorée et pourrie" (v. 7). The irony pokes through for anyone who is familiar with Villon, the great observer of the gluttonous and the famished: gluttons, *nous povres,* more or less like the next man, but not just anyone can be a glutton, without a penny, without a cent. These lines cannot be taken quite literally. We can almost hear—as if a kind of dialogue with the crowd were going on—the amused and sardonic comment of the bystanders: "chair nourrie, chair pourrie": the devourers have been devoured; all's right with the world.

After the flesh is gone nothing is left but "nous, les os, [qui] devenons cendre et pouldre" (v. 8); and in the third strophe this phenomenon will be examined in a more leisurely fashion. We still see the hanged men "ci-attachés," struggling against the elements; now they make us think of hanging laundry as often "debuez et lavez" by the rain as "dessechiez, noircis" by the sun. Or they may remind us of scarecrows;

> Pies, corbeaulx nous ont les yeux cavez,
> Et arrachié la barbe et les sourcis.   (vv. 23-24)

But "jamais nul temps . . . assis," there they are dancing again, totally disfigured, "plus becquetez d'oiseaulx que dez a couldre" (vv. 25-28). Strung up, exposed to outrage, they are not a pretty picture, and yet they describe themselves without exaggerating the horror: they do not try to make themselves repugnant. The first part of the tableau relates past violences, visible only in the traces that they have left. The metaphors at the beginning and at the end that are borrowed, simply and humorously, from the hard chores of family life and the resumption of the round by dancers who cannot sit down lend a touch of humor to the macabre scene. The hanged men poke fun at *nous povres*, sadly but without sentimentality, impelled as they are by a complex sense—resigned and at the same time indignant, humble but clairvoyant, ironic—of the inconsistency typical of *povre Villon* himself, when he is a character in the *Testament* (e.g., *laisses* 33-36). They continue at the same time to describe not only what can be seen, but the way in which *vous* details one by one the indignities done to "nous . . . cy attachez." While they reproach those who mock them for their laughter, they indulge in it themselves: very well then, they seem to agree, since this is what has happened to us, "ne soiez donc de nostre confrairie" (of the hanged). We understand also from the same line (v. 29), after the shift from "frères humains" to "se frères vous clamons": very well then, do not be part of our (human) brotherhood, but (at the refrain), you will be part of it anyway. This is a diversely nuanced voice whose facetious ironic twists can be heard, for example, in the quatrain, "je suis Françoys," another sketch of a man dangling from a rope—François himself this time:

> Et de la corde d'un toise
> Sçaura mon col que mon cul poise.

The hanged men turn and respond to this horrible insensitivity, the encircling laughter of the crowd that has thronged to the gallows, which is not the invention of a morbid imagination but a reality. History tells us that people went to executions as they did to fairs. In describing the harshness of the assembled multitude, Villon makes it into a scene from the *Danse Macabre*, but after his own fashion. Death, having become a terrifying obsession, in spite of traditional religious faith, is ritualized into a hideous spectacle of jesting, grimacing, prancing cadavers—into a vision stripped of compassion or consolation. At the cemetery of the Innocents, a popular meeting place that Villon had seen, in paintings accompanied by verse each cadaver of the procession shows to the living person whom he drags along against his will his future condition, his posthumous identity. Villon retains the image of dancing skeletons and the image of the equality in death, often preached and forgotten, but we hear a new note—the note of pity for *nous povres* and *nous tous* that Villon sought to express in the dance, while still sustaining all its rigor.

What is "nostre mal" that should not be laughed at? The dead address themselves to those "qui après nous vivez" (v. 1): not "qui vivez après nous," but "après nous," further emphasized by the inversion, followed by this "vivez"—present, actual, surviving. "Veulx tu vivre?" asks Villon's heart in "Le Débat," and this was the decisive point; the body replied: "Dieu m'en doint [donne] la puissance." The terrifying mystery was the harsh necessity of not being alive one day, a mystery whose harshness he was able to appease (in the ballad of the snows of yesteryear), and which he could even flaunt if need be (in the ballad on his funeral), but which haunted him in his work and made him speak disconsolately of the dissolution and the obliteration of earthly life as if he were speaking of an everlasting disappearance, with no further thought at all of life eternal. These various images of disappearance do not usually try to portray the act of dying itself, most often unobservable or unnoticed ("le temps de ma jeunesse," for example); it is the mental state of someone who has already passed on—rather than of a person who is on the way—that he suddenly perceives. In "L'Epitaphe," the voice of the hanged men still "cy attachez" even tries to describe the feelings of a dying man, and the insensitivity, the indifference of those "qui après nous vivez" and "voiez."

"Pitié de nous povres." We cease to be, this is "nostre mal"; it is no laughing matter. The hanged men, finally united in death, address themselves still to their fellow men, hoping at least not to disappear from their memory, and they appeal to their conscience, their charity. They, in their state at any rate, cannot but think at the same time of the hereafter, which they know awaits them—infernal or otherwise. It should be noted to what extent this preoccupation is still aimed at *vous*. In the second strophe, which resumes the entreaty, there is a prayer, but the hanged men do not address it directly to Jesus. They would like to have prayers from the "cuers contre nous endurcis." Do not disdain this name of brother, "quoy que fusmes occis / Par justice" (vv. 12–13), they tell them; "puis que sommes transsis" (v. 15), help us ("Excusez nous . . . / Envers le fils de la Vierge Marie"). They in no way try to deny that justice has been done, but they seek mercy. Although they are outlaws, they should not for that reason be cut off from humanity, nor are they necessarily excluded from grace: "vous sçavez/Que tous hommes n'ont pas bon sens rassis" (stable judgment), that they do not act rationally. They would say like the author of the *Testament* (vv. 105–12): "Je suis pecheur, je le sçay bien," but

> Dieu vit, et sa misericorde,
> Se conscience me remort,
> Par sa grace pardon m'accorde.

The striking thing here is that the hanged men ask for divine mercy through human mediation; they beseech other men to plead for God's mercy on their behalf—a sign of fraternity in spite of their conviction ("Excusez nous . . . [pour] Que sa grace ne soit pour nous tarie"). Be then our mediators with the Mediator. The line that follows and ends the phrase ("Nous preservant de l'infernale fouldre") is directly related to the grace of Jesus and from a distance rejoins "excusez nous."

In vain do they address themselves to men. "Nous sommes mors," must they repeat, "ame ne nous harie" (v. 19). The envoi, which appears to prolong the entreaty, terminates the appeal addressed to fellow men. We hear the voice turn from them and speak directly to "Prince Jhesus, qui sur tous a maistrie" (v. 31). With this word—derived from *maistre*, which is linked with *seigneurie* (v. 32) by its meaning and rhyme—signifying authority, or more precisely, in the medieval-feudal style, suzerainty, they affirm their desire not to be remanded to the power of Hell, but to remain under the dependency and protection of Jesus, the ultimate and now, without intermediaries, the sole mediator-judge before God. At this point, this act of faith and submission is also the gesture with which they renounce the assistance of their brethren. But as they turn their voice away, do not the hanged men still remain in the presence of men? Although "Prince Jhesus" is clearly in the vocative, the verb *avoir* is in the third and not the second person. This is not an oversight, since usage at that time allowed both constructions and both are present in Villon; but this *a* (if it is really Villon's choice and not the copyist's) is it, like an echo of the refrain, intended once again for the ears of the men "qui sur tous a maistrie"? Or is it rather—or simultaneously—a nuance of reserve or caution, the awareness of the great distance to be covered to reach Jesus? But do we know at this point whether or not the voice still comes from the gallows? The hanged men ask that in Hell "n'ayons que faire ne que souldre" (v. 33). Where are they then, if they are still awaiting judgment? "Hommes"—the voice turns again toward them—"icy n'a point de mocquerie" (v. 34). "Icy"? The word carries different meanings, all of them possible. Here, before the gallows. Here, in Hell. Here, once and for all, in this refrain.

Initially, we might miss the meaning of the "mais" in the refrain, and understand it the first time as meaning: instead of laughing at us, pray God, rather, that he pardon *nous povres*, all of us who are hanging here. The second time as well: instead of tormenting us. But for those who have any understanding—for all except the mockers— the ambiguity is cleared up: pray, rather, that God pardon each and every one of us; we all need succor and mercy. And if the entreaty does not get to them, then the third time the somber jest will. At the envoi, the refrain is addressed to "hommes," without any further possible ambiguity. To those who have refused them fraternity, help, and mercy, the hanged men reaffirm that, if it was an illusion to call them brothers, it was—"icy n'a point de mocquerie"—reckless insensitivity and fearful pride on their part—on the part of mortal men—to forget that, by our common nature and destiny, we are all only too much alike. "Mais," in this instance, warns them and im-plores them to pray. The subjunctive "vueille" recalls both their common danger and their common hope. To have ended with "prions Dieu," however, would have implied a completely different ballad; for, in this one, the essential movement is to end, specifically, with "priez"—you are the ones who must pray; "icy n'a point de moc-querie," unless it be the supreme irony of the poem that the hanged men, they who are the most reviled of all, should have pity on the rest of mankind.

The sound pattern in the poem blends into this general develop-ment, without becoming simply its musical equivalent, and works into it its own undulating but continuous and steady movement of *reprises* that is favored by the *ballade* form. Like most of Villon's decasyllabic ballads, this one is composed of ten-line strophes, fol-lowed here by a five-line envoi—thirty-five lines, following a pre-established rhyme scheme: three strophes in *a b a b b c c d c d*, then the envoi *c c d c d*. To the eye, this scheme would seem to divide each strophe into two parts of equal length; however, the meaning of each strophe develops, rather, in three stages, by grouping the lines in a 4/4/2 pattern. To the ear, the disposition of the rhymes, far from interrupting this progression, actually keep it going: *a b a b —b c c d — c d* links the first to the second group, and the second to the third. The ear, in the rhyme series *-vez, -sis, -vez, -sis, -sis, -rie, -rie, -oudre, -rie, -oudre*, hears the predominance of the *i* sound which the rhyme introduces in the second line, brings back four times in a row in the middle part, and repeats again before the refrain. The ear remembers Villon's visit to the cemetery of the Innocents (*Testament, laisses* 162-64), the many rhymes in *i* (*-dire, -dire; -vies, -vies, -vies, -vies;* especially *pourris, nourris, riz,* and *ris* closed in by *pouldre* and *absouldre*), and hears in the *ballade* this same funereal tone, a concentrated resonance in *-ie* and *-oudre* at the envoi. The most constant rhythm, the one in the first line, for example ("frères humains qui après nous vivez"), condenses and slackens the movement a bit at the beginning, only to start it up again with growing momentum. This rhythm can change, as in lines 11–13, emphasizing the liveliness of the reply, or it may vary with four- and six-syllable measures, as we might have noticed in the earlier examples. But, in general, this rhythm predominates, slowing down and finally stopping at the refrain. If we invert the rhythm (------'/----'), or if we merely read it this way: ----'/--'/----', the final accent is heard, still leaning on *tous*, and by the silence that will ensue leaves us wondering whether *les hommes* will ever get around to answering.

The Early Uses of
Medium Aevum,
Moyen Age, Middle Ages

OF OLD EXPRESSIONS like "the middle ages" and "le moyen âge" there remains only the form. Their original meaning is no longer appropriate, for we cannot view the medieval period as an enormous, intermediate gap, abruptly severing modern times from Antiquity. In former centuries, indeed, classical and humanistic innovators thought that they had suddenly cleared such an abyss, thick with the "fogs" and "swamps" of "dark ages"; "middle times" very aptly expressed their outlook on the past.

But the powerful sense of revival and rediscovery came early; in France, it appeared definitely in the sixteenth century, and manifested itself much earlier in Italy, where Petrarch felt it. How far back, then, can we trace its characteristic vocabulary?

A preliminary glance at the early uses of the word "Renaissance" can give us a hint as to what may be expected. To be sure, scholars have shown that even ancient and medieval writers had visions of regeneration, in divers forms;[1] but we need not go so far afield, for, after serving various purposes, the traditional image definitely took

Originally published in *Romanic Review* 29 (1938): 3–25.

[1]Cf. Karl Borinski, "Die Weltwiedergeburtsidee in den neueren Zeiten," *Sitzungsberichte der Bayerische Akademie der Wissenschaften (Philosophisch-philologische und historische Klasse)* (Munich, 1919), pp. 34–119; Konrad Burdach, *Reformation, Renaissance, Humanismus* (Berlin-Leipzig, 1926), 1st ed. 1918, pp. 1–84; Percy Ernst Schramm, *Kaiser, Rom und Renovatio* (Berlin-Leipzig, 1929).

on the historical aspect which it still retains, and which has made of it an inseparable complement of "moyen âge": this interesting phase of the development is what concerns us directly.

Very naturally, the starting point is in Italy, where Vasari, in his *Vitte de' più eccellenti pittori, scultori, ed architettori* (1550), wrote the history of Italian art "della *rinascita* di queste arti sino al secolo che noi vivamo," from Giotto's and Cimabue's period to his own.[2] "Rinascita," the first noun form to appear, singled out one trend in the general movement; it had been preceded by several forms of the Latin and Italian verbs, "renasci" and "rinascere," but these too had restricted meanings, such as religious reformation or resurrection, renovation of the state, revival of empire.[3] It was from these fragmentary beginnings that the more comprehensive, modern word was derived.

In French, the verb also seems to have preceded the noun: Amyot, dedicating *Les Vies des hommes illustres* (1559) to Henri II, recalls how "ce grand Roy François vostre feu pere avoit heureusement fondé et commencé de faire renaistre et florir en ce noble Royaume les bonnes lettres."[4] M. Plattard,[5] who does not mention the Latin and Italian verbs, has noted, however, that a number of other terms, both Latin and French, referred to the renewal of the humanities as a restitution or return from exile; observing that none of them, "renaistre" least of all, prevailed in the sixteenth century, he adds that Amyot's infinitive did not produce a substantive with the same meaning before the *Dictionnaire de Trévoux* (1704): "*Renaissance* des beaux-arts." But we need not wait so long, for Littré found "la *renaissance* des lettres humaines dans ce royaume" in Bouhours' *Remarques* (1675); and to that we may add a passage written forty-five years earlier by Gabriel Naudé: "deduisant l'estat de la barbarie qui commença soubs Theodoric Roy des Gots, je viendray de siècle en siècle jusques à celuy de nostre Louis XI. auquel je pretends monstrer qu'il faut establir la renaissance et restablissement des lettres, non seulement en cette Université [Paris?], mais aussi par toute l'Europe."[6]

Here, then, is a neat outline of history, with the "renaissance" cutting off the reign of barbarity. Naudé did not call the latter a "middle" era, but others had learned to do so long before 1630—indeed, before the discovery of America, that familiar terminus of the

[2]Burdach, *Reformation,* p. 4.

[3]Borinski, "Die Weltwiedergeburtsidee," pp. 34ff.

[4]*Ibid.,* p. 80.

[5]" 'Restitution des bonnes lettres' et 'Renaissance,' " in *Mélanges offerts par ses amis et ses élèves à M. Gustave Lanson* (Paris, 1922), pp. 128-31.

[6]*Addition à l'histoire de Louis XI* (Paris, 1630), p. 138.

Middle Ages! Various expressions had been put in circulation during the sixteenth century and several were introduced later, by contemporaries of Shakespeare and Molière.

Although this terminology has not attracted as much attention as "Renaissance," part of it has already been traced to the literature of that time.[7] The Latin texts particularly have yielded numerous items, interesting for their early date. "Media tempestas," found once in 1469,[8] was soon followed by "media aetas" (1518) and "media antiquitas" (1519), "media tempora" (1531) and "medium tempus" (1534), "medium aevum" (1604), "intermedia tempora" (1620), "medium seculum" and "media secula" (1625), "inter media aetas" (1639). After their first appearance, most of these terms were used again—some with considerable frequency, after 1600; in the latter half of the seventeenth century, "media aetas" and "medium aevum" began to predominate.[9]

The list published in Professor Gordon's tract constitutes a very handy and detailed summary of all these findings; as it stands, however, it is not entirely accurate. One passage, for example, is wrongly attributed to Vossius. It is true that to a certain extent the error was brought about by Du Cange, who, after citing a few lines from the grammarian's *De Vitiis Sermonis* (1645), adds the following words within the same quotation marks: "Saepe accidit, ut qui in probis Auctoribus scioli sibi videntur, incipiant rursus esse discipuli in iis quae *mediae aetatis* appellamus."[10] But in the margin, this is marked "S. Hier. [St. Jerome] *Praefat. in Daniel.*"; in reality, it is merely Du Cange's paraphrase of a sentence found in the Church Father's *Praefatio*: "qui mihi videbar inter Hebraeos, coepi rursus esse discipulus Chaldaicus";[11] its purpose is to enlarge on the passage drawn

---

[7]Valuable contributions have been made by Professor Paul Lehmann, "Vom Mittelalter und von der lateinischen Philologie des Mittelalters," *Quellen und Untersuchungen zur lateinischen Philologie des Mittelalters* (Munich, 1914) vol. 5, no. 1, and by Professor George S. Gordon, *Medium Aevum and the Middle Age*, tract no. 19 in a series published by the Society for Pure English (London, 1925).

[8]It occurs in a description of Cardinal Cusa worth citing at greater length: "Vir ipse, quod rarum est in germanis, supra opinionem eloquens et latinus; historias idem omnis non priscas modo, sed *medie tempestatis*, tum veteres, tum recentiores; usque ad nostra tempora retinebat," in a letter of Giovanni Andrea printed at the head of the Rome edition of Apuleius.

[9]The authors and editors who made use of these various forms were, besides Giovanni Andrea: Joachim von Watt (Vadianus), Beatus Rhenanus, Joannes Herwagen, Joannes Oporinus, Hadrianus Junius, Marcus Welser, Henricus Canisius, Melchior Goldast, Joseph J. Scaliger, Friedrich Taubmann, Jacques Sirmond, F. Bacon, Sir Henry Spelman, Charles Spelman, Gerhard J. Vossius, Rausin, Gisbert Voet (Voetius), Stephanus J. Stephanius, Georg Horn, Christoph Keller (Cellarius), Charles Du Cange.

[10]In Du Cange's preface to his glossary, sec. 66.

[11]S. *Hieronymi Stridonensis Opera Omnia* (Frankfurt, 1684), 3: 19.

from *De Vitiis Sermonis*. Professor Gordon, who apparently did not examine this work, was misled by Du Cange's punctuation and assigned this "media aetas" to Vossius; obviously, it must be transferred to the French savant, and the date shifted from 1645 to 1678.[12]

In addition to the citations compiled thus far, several more can be pointed out, and some in texts already investigated. Our list will help to show how frequently the Latin terms were used, even in their early stages:

1469—Giovanni Andrea, in the letter already cited (n. 8), speaks of Plato, "quem prisci omnes, quem veteres, quem *medie tempestatis* homines, quem nostre etatis maximi, quem greci, quem barbari, quem christiani, omnes eruditissimi, oraculi vice colunt." This is to be seen a few lines beyond the passage mentioned by Professors Lehmann and Gordon.

Before 1551—Joachim von Watt, in *De collegiis monasteriisque Germaniae veteribus*, published in Melchior Goldast's *Alamannicarum Rerum*: "Sed jam ad exempla donationum et chartarum *mediae antiquitatis* veniendum";[13] "Neque ignorant vel *mediae aetatis* temporum periti";[14] "Constanter autem produnt *mediae aetatis* Chronica nostratia circiter excessum Imperatoris Hainrici Tertii."[15] In the *Praefatio* to *In Farraginem Antiquitatum de Collegiis et Monasteriis Germaniae Veteribus*: "*mediae* illi *antiquitati*, tot incommodis obrutae et destitutae."[16]

1590 (1586?)—William Camden, in *Britannia, sive Florentissimorum Regnorum, Angliae, Scotiae, Hiberniae*, p. 68: "non falso cecinerit ille *medii temporis* Poëta"; p. 123: "Extant etiam versus, in nescio quo *medii temporis* poëta, de Cambala cruore effuso inundante." These expressions could probably be found in the first edition of *Britannia*, which appeared in 1586.

1610—John Selden, in *Jani Anglorum Facies Altera*, "Ad Lectorem," 5th page: "qui sunt *aevi medii*"; p. 49: "Minime aliud *aevo* hoc *medio* aestimet quis patibulum a furca."

1623—Valerius Andreas, in *Bibliotheca belgica*, p. 373: "Henricus Canisius . . . Historiam *medii aevi* omnem in numerato habebat"; concerning the same, p. 374: "ad historiam *mediae aetatis* illustrandam"

---

[12]It must also be noted that the expression "densas *Antiquitatis mediae* tenebras," appearing in the dedication of the *Glossarium Archaiologicum*, 1664, should not be attributed to Sir Henry Spelman, the author of that work. The dedication is signed by Charles Spelman, his grandson; moreover, it is dated 1663, and Sir Henry died in 1641.

[13](Frankfurt, 1730), 3: 36.

[14]*Ibid.*, p. 64.

[15]*Ibid.*, p. 72.

[16]*Ibid.*, p. 4.

this is a reproduction of Canisius' expression on the title page of his *Antiquae Lectiones*. In the second edition of the *Bibl. belgica* (1643), only the second citation appears again.

1626—Sir Henry Spelman, in *Archaeologicus, in modum glosarii*, p. 299: "Qui duo [modi musici] *mediae aetatis* Musicis ignoti"; p. 352: "Authoribus *medii temporis*"; p. 364, a strange passage, concerning the words "Hostis, Hostium": "Saepe in Conciliis, LL. antiqq. et mediastinis Authorib."; "mediastinus" apparently means "medieval," but this is a strange meaning for the old adjective; perhaps it is used for its derogatory implication.

Before 1641—Sir Henry Spelman, again, in *Icenia*, p. 136: "sed Normanni postea [Hidam] Carucatam appellarunt, Scriptores *medii seculi* Coloniam, et Romani olim Villam Rusticam."[17]

1628—Franciscus Sweertius, in *Athenae Belgicae*, p. 324: "ad Historiam *mediae aetatis* illustrandam," again a reproduction of Canisius' expression.

1649—Joannes de Laet, in a Latin translation of Wotton's work, *Elementa Architectura*, preface, p. 1: "(quas calamitates tumultus *medii aevi* conturbarant)."

1661—Philippe Labbe, in the *Thesaurus epitaphiorum veterum ac recentium selectorum*, at the end (pages unnumbered): "Index copiosissimus poetarum Graecorum ac Latinorum, aliorumque scriptorum veteris *mediae* ac recentioris *aetatis*." The same is to be found in the table of contents at the beginning of the work.

1678—Charles Du Cange, in his *Glossarium ad Scriptores Mediae et Infimae Latinitatis*, title page: "complures *aevi medii* Ritus et Mores"; *Index seu Nomenclator Scriptorum Mediae et Infimae Latinitatis* (1: lxxvii of the *Glossarium*): "*mediae aetatis* latinos scriptores"; *Praefatio* to the *Glossarium*, sec. 23: "*aetatis mediae* Scriptoribus"; sec. 38: "apud Latinos *aevi medii* Scriptores"; sec. 56: "veterum ac *aevi medii* auctorum lectionem"; sec. 62: "hanc esse complurium *mediae aetatis* Scriptorum scribendi rationem"; sec. 66: "*medii* et infimi *aevi* Scriptores," and the passage attributed by Professor Gordon to Vossius; sec. 77: "Scriptoribus *mediae aetatis*"; sec. 82: "Huc accedit, quod *mediae* etiam *aetatis* mores, ritusque persaepe enucleantur."[18]

1683—Joh. Jacobus Hoffmann, in *Lexici universalis historico-geographico-chronologico-poetico-philologici Continuatio*, vol. 1, title page: ". . . historiam . . . in omni Aetate, Sexu, Conditione, *Aevo*, recentiori, *medio*, veteri . . ."; preface: "omnis *aevi*, citerioris, *medii*, veteris."

---

[17]*Icenia* was published, from manuscripts in the Bodleian Library, in the *English Works of Sir Henry Spelman Kt.* (London, 1727) pt. 2. It remained undated.

[18]Professors Lehmann and Gordon, of course, refer to these terms in Du Cange's work, but give no specific references.

1685—"[ei] qui in *mediae* et infimae *aetatis* Historia satis nondum versati sunt," quoted by Adrien Baillet[19] from the catalogue of de Lamoignon's library.

Numerous and varied, these Latin citations become especially significant when compared with lists of similar terms in two modern languages.

The English expression, for example, coming much later than "media tempestas," seems to be limited to the seventeenth century. Professor Gordon has recorded six uses of it, distributed over a period of 126 years; the first is in Thomas James' *Treatise of the Corruptions of Scripture, Councils, and Fathers* (1611): "auncient, middle-aged, or moderne writers";[20] then comes the noun "middle age," in 1621, 1624, 1649, 1710–1714 ("middle ages"), 1727. The citations that follow will show some earlier examples, a greater number of forms, and a far greater frequency:

1605—William Camden, in *Remaines of a Greater Work, Concerning Britaine, the Inhabitants thereof, their Languages, Names, Surnames, Empreses, Wise Speeches, Poësies, and Epitaphes,* ch. 1: "I will bring you in some poets, to speake in this behalfe for mee and will beginne with olde Alfred of Beverlie, who made this for Britaine in generall, which you must not reade with a censorious eye; for it is, as the rest I will cite, of the *middle age*"; ch. 2: "and first this Latine Rythme of the *middle time*[21] in praise of the English Nation"; ch. on *Poems:* "I will only give you a taste of some poets of *middle age,* which was so overcast with darke clouds, . . . that every little sparke of liberall Learning seemed wonderfull."

1610—William Camden or Philémon Holland, in *Britain* (an English translation of Camden's Latin work already cited), p. 131: "a Poet of the *middle time* sung not untunably in this manner"; p. 194: "an unknowen Poet living in the *middle time.*" Holland's translation was revised by Camden, so that it is hard to say which one of the two wrote in this term.

1611—Thomas James, in the advertisement to *A Treatise of the Corruptions of Scripture, Councils and Fathers* already cited, p. xxxv (J. E. Cox ed., 1843): "I thought good to adjoin unto these some few texts corrupted of later and *middle-aged* writers."

[19]*Jugemens des Sçavans* (Paris, 1685), vol. 2, at the end of "Critiques Historiques" (pages unnumbered).

[20]"Advertisement to the Christian Reader," sec. 3.

[21]1605 is then the first known date for both "middle age" and "middle time." The latter will be found again in the seventeenth century. There are 1614, 1623, 1629, 1636, 1637, and 1657 editions of this work; I have seen those of 1636, 1637, and 1657, where the same citations are to be found.

1612—John Speed, in *The Kingdome of Ireland*, p. 138: "But from these ancient and barbarous maners [sic], let us come to the conditions of their [Irishmen's] *middle time*."[22]

1614—John Selden, in the 1st edition of *Titles of Honor*, preface: "Stories . . . of the *Midle* and Ancient *times*,"[23] and "the *Midle times*, when Ignorance rode in Triumph"; 1: 21: "as . . . they have been in *middle times* often titled"; 1: 52: "mongst Writers of *middle times*"; 1: 99: "the *middle* Grecians" (an expression rarely used) and 1: 100: "(saith Theophanes a Chronologer of *middle times* in Greece)"; 1: 112: "another of them in the *middle times*"; 2: 243: "a very ancient Writer, of the *midle times*"; 2: 354: "the Grecians of *Midle times*."

1618—John Selden, in *The Historie of Tithes*, p. iii: "in the *midle times*," p. 211: "in those *midle times*"; p. 44: "Those kinds of Acts and Legends of Popes and others, are indeed usually stufft with falshoods, as being bred in the *midle ages*[24] among idle Monks."

1631—John Selden, in the 2d edition of *Titles of Honor*, 1: 104: the two expressions found in the 1st edition (pp. 99, 100); 1: 109: "Autors of the *middle time*"; 1: 135: "the *midle ages* of Christianitie," "in the examples of those *midle times*," "in the *middle times* as also in the more ancient"; 1: 164: "another and an ancient (though of the *midle times*)"; 2: 380: "*Praetorium* and *Palatium* being especially in the *midle times*, meerly Synonymies"; 2: 863: "in the Latine of the *middle times*."[25]

1639—Sir Henry Spelman, in *The Original, Growth, Propagation and Condition of Feuds and Tenures by Knight-Service in England*,[26] ch. 10: "All the foresaid words being of the *middle-age*-dialect, not appropriated to the feodal Language."

1659—Peter Heylyn, in *Examen Historicum*, pp. 9–10: "first we finde it in the monuments of the elder times. . . . And secondly for the *middle times* we have the like story"; p. 11: "the *middle* and darker *times*."

1662—Thomas Fuller, in *The History of the Worthies of England*, p. 44: ". . . the shrievalty in ancient times was *honos sine onere*, in the *middle times honos cum onere*, and in our days little better than *onus sine honore*." This is repeated in the *Anglorum Speculum* of 1684 (p. 16), an abridged edition of the *Worthies of England*.

---

[22]*The Kingdome of Ireland*, although the fourth book of a larger work, *The Theater of the Empire of Great Britaine* (London, 1611), is marked 1612 on the title page.

[23]The first known use of the plural form in English.

[24]The first known use of the modern form.

[25]These citations will be found also in a 1672 edition.

[26]In *The English Works of Sir Henry Spelman Kt.* The author of the preface says this work is marked 1639 on the manuscript in the Bodleian Library, which squares with the internal evidence.

1682—Redman Westcott, in an English translation of Selden's Latin work already quoted, *The Reverse or Back-face of English Janus,* "The Author's Preface to the Reader," 3d page: "unless it be from them of the *middle age,* many times sufficiently barbarous"; pp. 37-38: "in this *middle age.*"

1695—Edmund Gibson, in an English translation of Camden's work already quoted, *Britannia,* col. 126: "so that the *middle-age* Poet is probably right"; col. 2: "There are also extant some verses of a *middle-age* poet about Camel's running with blood."

1727 (1723)—Edmund Gibson, in *The Life of Sir Henry Spelman Kt.*: "as many of the *middle-age* Historians as he could meet with."[27]

As for the French expressions, Professor Gordon cites one seventeenth-century example, drawn from the first edition of the *Dictionnaire de l'Académie* (1694): "On appelle, *Autheur du moyen âge,* Les Autheurs qui ont écrit depuis la decadence de l'Empire Romain jusques vers le dixiesme siecle, ou environ." In later editions: "jusque vers la fin du dixième siècle, ou environ." But "moyen âge," sufficiently current in 1694 to be listed in the Dictionary, had appeared long before that time:

1657—Charles Du Cange, in the preface to the 2d part of his *Histoire de l'Empire de Constantinople sous les Empereurs François,* 6th page: "Et comme il est malaisé de travailler à l'Histoire du *Moyen-temps*[28] sans ce secours"; in the preface to the 1st part, last page: "divers passages des Ecrivains François et Latins du *moyen âge*"; in his *Observations sur l'Histoire de Geoffroy de Ville-Hardouin,* p. 289: "Guillaume de Tyr, Albert d'Aix, Jacques de Vitry, et autres Escrivains du *moyen temps*"; p. 292: "dans les Autheurs Grecs et Latins du *moyen âge*"; p. 302: "chez les Grecs du *moyen âge*"; p. 310: "dans les Autheurs Latins et François du *moyen âge*"; in his *Glossaire* for *L'Histoire de l'Empire de Constantinople* (pp. 354-70): three times "Escrivains Latins du *moyen âge,*" twice "Autheurs Latins du *moyen âge,*" three times "Autheurs du *moyen âge,*" once "Poëtes François du *moyen temps.*"

1668—Du Cange, in his *Dissertations ou Réflexions sur l'Histoire de Saint Louys;*[29] p. 1: "quelques auteurs grecs du *moyen temps*"; p. 16: "Un poëte *du moyen temps*"; p. 53: "les histoires du *moyen temps*"; p. 66: "les auteurs du *moyen temps*"; p. 71, the same; p. 122: "les

---

[27]At the end of the work cited above, n. 26. The latter, however, was first published in 1723, and is known to have contained this same *Life* of Spelman.

[28]The French expression, then, has also more than one form, and both appear in 1657.

[29]The following citations are taken from the *Dissertations* as published in the *Glossarium ad Scriptores mediae et infimae Latinitatis* (Paris, 1850), vol. 7, as no first edition of the *Dissertations* is available.

auteurs latins du *moyen temps.*" In his *Observations sur l'Histoire de Saint Louys,*[30] pp. 346, 355, 359: "les auteurs latins du *moyen temps*"; p. 349: "qui semble être tiré des jurisconsultes du *moyen temps*"; p. 357: "Les Grecs du *moyen temps*"; pp. 350, 356: "les auteurs du *moyen temps.*"

1678—Journal des Sçavans, August 15, p. 335: "la difficulté d'entendre et d'expliquer les Auteurs du *moyen temps*"; p. 339: "quoyque les Auteurs du *moyen temps* n'ayent pas écrit purement"; September 5, p. 376: "les Auteurs des *moyens-temps.*"[31]

1685—Adrien Baillet, in his *Jugemens des Sçavans,* vol. 3, sec. 414: "la connaissance des Auteurs de *moyen aage,*[32] et de la basse Latinité"; sec. 449: "Auteurs qui ont vécu pour la pluspart dans le *moyen âge*"; sec. 575: "les Auteurs de *moyen âge*"; sec. 577: "la connaissance des siècles du *moyen âge*"; sec. 690: "les Auteurs Grecs du *moyen* et du bas *âge*"; vol. 4, sec. 612: "Il y en a même qui sentent le *moyen âge*" (talking about notes to inscriptions).

1690—Antoine Furetière, in his *Dictionnaire Universel,* vol. 2: "On dit . . . qu'un auteur est du *moyen âge,* pour dire qu'il n'est ni ancien, ni nouveau."

1719—Jacob le Long, in his *Bibliothèque historique de la France* (posthumous work—le Long died in 1709), headings of divisions in ch. 1: "Article I—Geographie ancienne des Gaules, et celle du *moïen âge.* 1. Geographie ancienne. 2. Geographie du *moïen âge* de la France." These indications will be found also in the table of contents.

1727—In the 1727 edition of Furetière's *Dict. Universel,* vol. 3: "On appelle Auteurs du *moyen âge,* les Auteurs qui ne sont ni anciens ni nouveaux; qui ont écrit depuis la decadence de l'Empire Romain, jusques vers la fin du dixiéme siècle ou environ"—a definition which assimilates that of the Academy.

1657, then, is the earliest date we can show for the French term; this is already surprisingly early if we recall that Bloch's *Dictionnaire étymologique* does not trace it further back than the late eighteenth century;[33] but so much is clear: "moyen âge," and "middle age" as well, lag far behind their Latin prototypes. The latter have almost one

---

[30]The following citations are taken from *Extraits des Observations,* published in the *Glossarium.* The references will be to the 1850 edition, vol. 7.

[31]Note the plural form. Professor Gordon, on the basis of his data, believed this was peculiar to the English and Latin terms.

[32]Note the absence of the article in this form.

[33]It may very well be that earlier examples exist, for Du Cange used "moyen âge" and "moyen temps" very often, as though these expressions were not new. We have searched, but in vain, through a wide range of likely sources.

hundred and fifty years to themselves.[34] During this period, they are to be found chiefly in the works of humanist-scholars and only once in the writings of an historian—a capital fact, which clearly reveals the source of our terminology.

Besides the threefold question of origin, frequency, and dates, which can be answered by simple enumeration, there is the more intricate problem of meaning. How many of our terms coincided with modern usage? How much agreement may we expect to find among the various forms listed together? As scholars of varying points of view began to adopt the new words in the seventeenth century, a certain variety of interpretations, at so early a time, can hardly be surprising. The constant, in all these expressions, was an adjective which could be applied to any one of several "intermediary" periods; the many nouns attached to it could add nothing in the way of precision.[35]

In certain cases the author himself indicates the span of his "middle age." Others, alluding to many writers, works, sovereigns and institutions, indirectly reveal what period they had in mind. Some, it is true, yield only one reference, or give no clues whatever; but fortunately, the more informative passages abound.

Thus far, resorting to offhand generalizations, investigators have neglected these valuable indications. Although equipped with an amazingly small number of facts, Godefroid Kurth, in *Qu'est-ce que le moyen âge?*, evolved a comprehensive theory whereby it would appear that all expressions centering about "medium aevum" were derived from an erroneous philological concept, unfortunately adopted by the historians. Professor Lehmann[36] then attempted to refute this theory by reversing it; historians, he said, had used these terms in a general historical sense before philologists had thought of a restricted meaning; he gives, however, only one example, Canisius, who indeed, in 1601, was thinking of "historiam mediae aetatis." It was mainly Vossius, and Du Cange at times, who later viewed the centuries in terms of linguistic development—pure Latin in Antiquity,

---

[34]It would be interesting to know what other languages might reveal. Professor Lehmann pointed out in passing a German expression used by Joachim von Watt (who also used "media aetas" and "media antiquitas"): "frankischen chroniken *mitler jaren*," "*mitteljärigen* chroniksschreibern" ("Von dem mönchsstand," 1: 69, 101, in *Deutsche historische Schriften*, Götzinger edition, 1875). To this we may add a work by Christian Juncker, *Anleitung zu der Geographie der mitlern Zeiten* (Jena, 1712). Nothing else has been found between these two dates, so that our Latin forms predominate in the sixteenth century.

[35]Cf. Du Cange, Spelman, Selden, Camden, Goldast, Andreas, and von Watt, who readily interchanged them.

[36]"Vom Mittelalter und von der lateinischen Philologie des Mittelalters," passim.

Latin already corrupted in the "media aetas" (from the fourth or fifth century to Charlemagne), and Latin at its worst in the "infima aetas." But Professor Lehmann, rightly so, associates Marcus Welser with Vossius and Du Cange[37]—and his citation is dated 1600. To add to our confusion, Welser is as much an historian as a philologist! Be that as it may, the historians would seem to have preceded the philologists, although Professor Lehmann himself makes a supposition which appears very plausible: "media aetas" and other Latin expressions came into use especially after the writings of Rhenanus and von Watt, who were known to those who followed them, and who thus must have transmitted the term. Rhenanus, however, was primarily a humanist, and von Watt, a Swiss savant, scarcely a specialized historian.

Professor Gordon, though possessing more facts than his predecessors, continues and complicates this theory.[38] Not only are there historical and philological uses of the term, but also a third use, that of Latin purists, who named the Republican age "prima aetas," the Imperial times "media aetas" and the period after Claudian "postrema" or "infima aetas." Why, we may ask, should this be condemned by Professor Gordon? At a time when general usage had not yet determined the meaning of "media aetas," it was natural enough for a group of specialists to adapt this symbol to a concept of their own.

But it is Du Cange, a philologist and not a purist, who suffers most at the hands of Professor Gordon. In his work, confusion holds its sway. He took a perfectly good expression and spoiled it, philologically. At times—Prof. Lehmann also grants this—he used "scriptores medii aevi" to encompass all the Middle Ages. Unfortunately, he also wrote "scriptores medii et infimi aevi" for exactly the same period, with "medium aevum" then reduced, as a subdivision of the historical "medium aevum," to the *earlier* Middle Ages—namely, the span of "media Latinitas"; what is worse, it is claimed that he wrote "medii aevi" and "medii et infimi aevi" in consecutive sentences. On the other hand—what is still worse—whenever he wrote "infimi aevi" alone, he meant by it again the whole span of the Middle Ages, but when the phrase came together with "medii" it was also shrunk by a half, to mean the *latter* part of the medieval period. In fact, so chaotic was this terminology that even "inferius aevum," which at first represented the Middle Ages as a whole, shrank as "infimum aevum" did,

[37]Professor Gordon, here, will make a distinction based on the word "antiquitas" (*media, propre infima antiquitas*), observing that Welser is considering only the past and is not dividing time into ancient, middle, and modern periods. But this would involve "media" in another confusion.

[38]*Medium Aevum*, pp. 16–22.

by association. All this disturbed, it would seem, the comprehensiveness of the historians' term. Although Welser, J. J. Scaliger,[39] and Vossius were, before Du Cange, guilty of this—in the sense that the purists were guilty—the French savant was especially dangerous because of his prestige.[40]

Who then was right? Vaguely, and without examples, the historians and antiquaries; but very clearly, the English. It will be interesting, later, to examine this claim. But what have we in French? Apparently, a deplorable confusion from the outset, and that owing partly to Du Cange's Latin terms. The first use of "moyen âge" known to Professor Gordon is in the definition given by the Academy —a period extending from the fall of the Roman Empire to the tenth century. Why, he asks, the tenth century? Because the French must have seen, in Du Cange's preface to his *Glossarium,* the title of section 29, which speaks of corrupted Latin in Carolingian times; as the author does not indicate definitely where the break between "media" and "infima Latinitas" occurred, this, says the English scholar, is what was seized upon—with a slight manipulation of dates. And where the "media Latinitas" ends, there the "moyen âge" must end. Aside from the fact that this is a mere assumption, Professor Gordon overlooks section 33, where a revival of learning is justly accredited to Charlemagne: certainly, this could not be the beginning of an "infimum" or lowest "aevum." We may add that the first edition of the *Glossarium* had no section headings; the title which is supposed to have had so much importance was inserted in subsequent editions.[41]

A more plausible explanation of the Academy's term lies in the fact that the tenth century "was regarded as pre-eminently the 'Dark' century . . . and as the close of a millennium. . . ."[42] The savants probably knew that those of the tenth century had looked forward to the year 1000 with apprehension.

Explain it as one may, the definition is not "correct." How slow and traditional are the French! We must wait until 1798 before the Academy declares the Renaissance to be the upper limit of the Middle Ages: "History had asserted itself and put philology in its place."[43] But this is not all; the French term has another weakness. It does not

---

[39]*Scaligerana* (The Hague, 1666), s.v. "Cujacius."

[40]Gordon, *Medium Aevum,* pp. 16–17. (Cf. also p. 16, n. 1; p. 17, n. 1.)

[41]It should also be noted that the Academy's Dictionary gave a clear definition of "moyenne Latinité," which extended "depuis environ le temps de Severe jusque vers la decadence de l'Empire."

[42]Gordon, *Medium Aevum,* p. 21.

[43]*Ibid.,* p. 20.

appear "independently," "in its own right";[44] it is used only in phrases like "auteurs du moyen âge." Not until 1835 does the Academy's Dictionary say "l'histoire du moyen âge"; and very significantly, the earliest example of such freedom is in this title: *Histoire litté-raire du moyen âge*, Paris, 1785, which, be it noted, is a translation from an English work by James Harris! "Auteurs du moyen âge" is not acceptable because some have used "scriptores medii aevi" in Latin, and the French expression looks like an imitation of it. Why it is more original to say "the history of the middle ages" when there are Latin authorities for "historia mediae aetatis" is a question that Professor Gordon does not raise. To conclude, he affirms: "It seems highly possible that our long and unbroken tradition of an historical "Middle Age" may have helped the French language to widen the meaning of its term and to disencumber it of philological associations."[45]

That "author of the middle ages" should have been used so frequently—in all the three languages—is not astonishing; it is readily perceived that anyone citing references could say, quite naturally: "as may be seen in this or that author of the middle ages," without needing a Latin model. In historical or philological criticism, this would seem to be a very useful phrase: how else explain its frequency in Latin, which had no model? But Professor Gordon's aversion for it is so strong that it leads him to reject even von Watt's German expressions; he calls them "premature,"[46] and, because they refer to "chronicles," labels them "an accident of translation" from the Latin![47] Why not scorn, then, the earliest English term known to Professor Gordon, the "middle-aged . . . *writers*" of Thomas James? And did not Camden use "medium tempus" before "middle time"?

Let us see what can really be found in the French expressions; and since Du Cange is first in line, let us clarify his stand by looking more closely at both his French and Latin. The first obvious fact is that, far from anteceding "moyen âge" and influencing it nefariously, Du Cange's "medium aevum" is long preceded by his own French term. How does he use it? Most of the time, to be sure, he says "poëtes," "auteurs," or "écrivains du moyen âge" or "du moyen temps"; but here, at the very outset, we also meet: "Histoire du Moyen-temps." In 1668: "jurisconsultes du moyen temps," "les Grecs du moyen

[44]*Ibid.*
[45]*Ibid.*, p. 22.
[46]*Ibid.*, p. 24.
[47]*Ibid.*, p. 23. Professor Gordon does not indicate the Latin models.

âge" or "du moyen temps." Never, besides, does he write "du moyen et du bas âge." Is there any chance that nevertheless "moyen âge" means the earlier philological middle age? In his *Observations sur l'Histoire de Ville-Hardouin* (p. 289), Du Cange writes: "Guillaume de Tyr [1130?-1190?], Albert d'Aix [1060-1120], Jacques de Vitry [d. 1240], et autres Escrivains du moyen temps," citing, then, authors of the eleventh, twelfth, and thirteenth centuries—a period that would belong to the alleged philological "infima aetas"; similarly (p. 292), listed after "les Autheurs Grecs et Latins du moyen âge," we find Cedrenus and the *Chronicon Alexandrinum* (eleventh century); better still (p. 302), the following have noticed a certain word among "les Grecs du moyen âge": Tudebodus (twelfth century), J. de Vitry, G. de Tyr, Sanutus (probably Marino Sanudo il Vecchio—d. post 1334), Pope Alexander IV (1254-1261), Codinus (end of fifteenth century). In the *Glossaire* for *L'Histoire de l'Empire de Constantinople,* these "escrivains Latins du moyen âge" (pp. 355, 369), philologically, would have to be separated into the two groups of "media" and "infima aetas": S. Maximus (580-662), Anastase Bibliothécaire (d. 886), Arnolfus (eleventh century), *Acta (Gesta) Innocenti III* (ca. 1208), J. de Vitry. And so Du Cange goes on, including among the writers and works of the middle ages: Modestus (275 A.D.), Vegetius (fourth-fifth century), the *Chronicon Fontanellense,*[48] Fulcher de Chartres (1059-ca. 1130), Hariulfus (before 1075-1143), Metellus (1160), Tzetzes (twelfth century), Jean de Meung, Philippes Mouskes, Oliverius Scholasticus, Rolandin, "Jean de Genes, ou de Juana"—Joannes Januensis, Matthew Paris, a title of the duke Eudes de Bourgogne (all of the thirteenth century), the *Chronique de Flandres,*[49] the Concilium Senonense A. 1346.[50]

The French term, in its earliest uses known to us, is free, then, from what Professor Gordon calls a confusion. And this in Du Cange! An analysis of his Latin term becomes the more interesting.

Let us grant that very frequently he repeats "*scriptores* medii aevi." This is obvious. Yet, no one has pointed out that on the very title page of the *Glossarium ad Scriptores Mediae et Infimae Latinitatis* there appears an expression far removed from "authors" and philology: Du Cange announces as an enrichment of his glossary "Complures aevi medii Ritus et Mores." In the preface (section 82), he elaborates on these "mediae aetatis mores ritusque." The history

---

[48]Begun in the ninth century, and continued to 1053.

[49]The one known to Du Cange under this title was probably that running from 792 to 1384, continued to 1435, and published by Denis Sauvage, Lyon, 1561-62.

[50]Du Cange also cites a Concil. I Salisburg., but there is more than one similarly designated, with dates differing widely.

of language in itself was not his only preoccupation; he set as one of his important tasks to analyze the customs and institutions listed in the glossary. This side of the Du Cange who wrote learned historical observations and dissertations is apparently forgotten.

His attitude is clearly summarized in a passage of the *Index seu Nomenclator Scriptorum Mediae et Infimae Latinitatis*[51] which has been overlooked: "Nominatos enim fere duntaxat inveniet [lector], neque omnes tamen, etsi plerosque, mediae aetatis latinos scriptores, adjunctis annorum quibus vixere characterismis, sumptoque initio a collabente Latinitate, quod circa Antoninorum AA. tempora accidisse constat, ad medium usque quintum decimum saeculum, quo studiosorum opera rursum Latini eloquii splendor effloruit." Here, to be sure, lies a strongly philological understructure; but a good deal of historical research is based on it.

As for the many uses of "medium aevum" and "media aetas" in the preface to the glossary, none of them gives definite indications that these terms designate only a philological or shorter age within the middle era. The same may generally be said of the "infimum" or "inferius" age.[52] In the *De Imperatorum Constantinopolitanorum seu de Inferioris aevi, vel Imperii, uti vocant, Numismatibus Dissertatio*, on the other hand, Du Cange shows that he means to include the early Middle Ages, especially after Heraclium;[53] he repeats this, though less precisely, in the preface of the glossary.[54] He cannot be accused, therefore, of having imagined a "lower" age restricted to the later medieval times.

This reproach becomes the less justifiable when Professor Gordon's other arguments are analyzed. It is especially the term "medii et infimi aevi" that he blames. One would gather, from the accusation, that this phrase was habitual with Du Cange; but I find it only once in the long preface;[55] one could also imagine, as we have seen, that it was used very indiscriminately, right along with "medii aevi," thus creating a double and confusing terminology: but one of the "consecutive sentences" in which Professor Gordon found these two expressions is not in the first edition; it is the heading of section 66, and like all the section headings, it was added in later editions; that passage shows "medii et infimi aevi" used alone.

---

[51]In the *Glossarium* of Paris, 1678, 1: lxxvii-lxxviii.

[52]In sec. 61, Du Cange cites, for "Scriptor aevi inferioris," the *Chronicon Montis Sereni*, which runs from 1124 to 1225. In sec. 68 there is also "Poëta inferioris aevi, Leonius Presbyter," who is of the twelfth century. But isolated cases do not indicate the span in which they belong.

[53]In the *Glossarium* of Paris, 1678, pt. 3, sec. 1, p. 1.

[54]Sec. 82.

[55]Sec. 66.

Professor Gordon adds: "It is perhaps worth observing that Du Cange, in his Preface, says nothing of *infimum aevum,* and is perfectly consistent in his use of *medium* and *inferius,* until he reaches sect. LXIV [read 65], and records a wish of Scaliger for 'infimi seculi Glossaria.'[56] From that moment, as if by some infection, *infimum aevum* commands and confounds his terminology."[57]

Where, after section 65, does "infimum aevum" appear, let alone command? It seems rather to disappear, after section 66, where we find the "medii et infimi" expression; "inferius aevum," on the other hand, is not confounded or undone, but used twice again (sections 67, 82).[58] Moreover, Du Cange does not need to quote Scaliger to bethink himself of "infimum": ". . . a nescio quo Poëta *infimi aevi* MS." comes from section 46. What is there, indeed, in Scaliger's vague term[59] that could have suddenly inspired Du Cange to use it in so precise a way?

The term "medii et infimi aevi," therefore, does not find itself at a crucial turning-point in Du Cange's vocabulary. This dissipates much of the importance that has been granted it. Consider, besides, that it occurs but once, whereas "medii aevi" and "mediae aetatis" will be found at least seven times, and the "infimum" or "inferius" age twelve times: can it be argued that this lone expression, lost among others used so much more often, will have had a drastic influence on the French term? Our facts have already shown the unreality of this conjecture. Needless to deny that, thinking of linguistic development, Du Cange found a "media" and an "infima Latinitas"; but let us stress the significance of the passage drawn from the *Index Scriptorum,* where "Scriptorum mediae et infimae Latinitatis" is parallel with "mediae aetatis latinos scriptores": the "media" and "infima Latinitas" are contained in the "media aetas." In our view, when Du Cange uses "medium" alone with the noun "aevum" or "aetas," it covers the whole of the Middle Ages; when "infimum" or "inferius" is thus used alone, the same is true; when both "media" and "infima" are used, it is with "Latinitas" and consequently in a distinctly philological sense. Only once do they appear together with "aevum"; and there we may consider the "medium aevum" as a shorter period than the usual middle age[60]—without exag-

---

[56]*Scaligerana,* s.v. "Glossaria." The text is somewhat different: "Qui feroit un glossaire des Autheurs infimi seculi, feroit bien."

[57]*Medium Aevum,* p. 17, n. 1.

[58]It is used also in the *Dissertatio* on numismatics: e.g., secs. 20, 25. Here, it is changed to "inferioris aetatis."

[59]Cf. n. 56.

[60]It would not be impossible to explain this expression differently, by suggesting that, since "medium" and "infimum" mean the same thing when used separately with

gerating the importance of this one singularity. The French use of "moyen âge" by Du Cange confirms this interpretation.

This was the vocabulary of the writer who, to our best knowledge, first used the French term. After him, the *Journal des Savants*, writing about the *Glossarium*, used "moyen temps" three times, but gave no clues as to the span of the term. We may infer that the authors were reproducing Du Cange's expression.

Baillet reserves a little surprise for us, in 1685, when he says: "Il y en a même qui sentent le moyen âge"—here is certainly a very "independent" phrase! Unfortunately, we cannot tell very clearly the limits of this "moyen âge." The beginning, at least, appears to be the decadence of the Roman Empire.[61]

On two occasions, Baillet's citations raise an interesting question: Pithou, says he (vol. 3, sec. 414), "étoit le plus docte . . . dans la connaissance des Auteurs de moyen aage, et de la basse Latinité"; and Du Cange's Greek glossary, says he elsewhere (vol. 3, sec. 690), "servira pour avoir une intelligence parfaite de tous les Auteurs Grecs du moyen et du bas âge." Again, the problem of that "infima aetas." Did Du Cange's alleged confusion finally find a victim? Not yet, for Baillet has another meaning for "bas âge" and "basse Latinité." When speaking of Pithou, he is referring directly to J. J. Scaliger's description of him: "F. Pithoeus doctus in *medii aevi* scriptoribus,"[62] where there is no mention of "infima Latinitas"; Baillet adds "basse Latinité," and we must suppose he does it to explain the other expression. Indeed, Colomiès, to whom Baillet also refers, simply substituted "Auteurs de la basse Latinité"[63] for the "medii aevi scriptoribus" of Scaliger. Here is something even clearer: Scaliger said of Jean Savaron: "Savaro omnia digessit ad Sidonium, doctus in infimi aevi Scriptoribus";[64] Baillet repeats: "Scaliger remarque qu'il étoit habile dans l'intelligence des Auteurs de la basse Latinité, c'est-à-dire de ceux qui ont écrit depuis la décadence de l'Empire Romain en Occident, et que ses Commentaires sur Sidoine Apollinaire . . . en font foi."[65] With such references, there can be no question of an exclusively post-Carolingian period; the "basse Latinité" becomes the Latin of what we generally call the Middle

---

"aevum," "infimum" here may be added to strengthen the idea of a culturally lower age.

[61]*Jugemens des Sçavans*, vol. 3, sec. 449.

[62]*Scaligerana*, s.v. "Pithoeus."

[63]*Bibliothèque Choisie* (Paris, 1731), p. 229. The first edition was published in La Rochelle, 1682.

[64]*Scaligerana*, s.v. "Savaro."

[65]*Jugemens des Sçavans*, vol. 3, sec. 467.

Ages. The same may be said of "bas âge." "Leunclavius . . . ," said
Scaliger, "bene intellixit Graeca Constantinopolitana et inferioris
aevi";[66] "Scaliger témoigne," as Baillet understands it, "qu'il étoit
fort entendu dans la lecture des Auteurs Grecs du Bas âge, c'est-à-
dire, de l'Empire de Constantinople."[67] Obviously, "le bas âge" is
not a limited "infimum aevum," but a synonym of "le moyen âge."
When, in one case, Baillet wrote "du moyen et du bas âge," he was
straying from his usual practice, probably to imitate the title of the
work which he was discussing, the *Glossarium ad Scriptores Mediae
et Infimae Graecitatis.*

With Jacob le Long's posthumous work, the French term appears
once again "independently," in the "geographie du moïen âge."
This period stands between "modern" and "ancient" times, with
Clovis at the lower limit.

As we turn to our first English expressions, shall we find them
used "in their own right"? Not by Camden. He—an historian—speaks
of *poets* "of middle age," a *"Latine Rythme* of the middle time,"
and *poems* "of the middle age"! In 1610, again "a *Poet* of the middle
time" and a *"Poet* living in the middle time." Nothing could be more
natural, but Professor Gordon would be forced to scorn all this,
smacking as it does of the Latin.

In two instances, Camden gives copious references. "Some poets of
middle age" are Joseph of Excester (second half of twelfth century),
Foelix, monk of Crowland (fl. 1281), John Havill (fl. 1200), Gaulfrid
(second half of twelfth century). The poems "of the middle age"[68]
are from Henry of Huntingdon (1080 or 1090-?), Hildebertus (ca.
1055-1133), Alfred of Beverley (first half of twelfth century), Walter
Mapes (twelfth century), Matthew Paris (?-1259), Pope Innocent IV
(1243-1254), Michael Blaunpayn (fl. 1240-1250), Robert of Glou-
cester (ca. 1300). Nothing, then, below the eleventh or above the
early fourteenth century. But in the chapter on *Poems,* where he distinguishes the poets "of middle age" from those of earlier times and
those "of this our Learned Age," he cites for the former Claudia
Rufina (fl. 100-110), Gildas (516?-570), Caedmon (ca. 680) and a
Claudius Clemens who flourished in 820: if the ninth century be
taken, then, as Camden's lower medieval boundary, what a strange
reversal presents itself! With Charlemagne's time apparently in mind

[66]*Ibid.,* s.v. "Leunclavius."

[67]*Jugemens des Sçavans,* vol. 3, sec. 409.

[68]*Remaines of a Greater Work, Concerning Britaine, the Inhabitants thereof, their
Languages, Names, Surnames, Empreses, Wise Speeches, Poësies, and Epitaphes*
(London, 1605), ch. 1.

as a dividing line, the English historian outlines a "middle age" which is almost equivalent to the supposedly shorter "infimum aevum."

The limits that John Selden assigns to his "middle times" are altogether different. At the lower end we find Cassiodorus (1: 52),[69] Theophylactus Simocatta (1: 112) and Jornandès (1631 edition, 1: 164), all of the sixth century; this is probably the boundary, although elsewhere (1631 edition, 1: 135), speaking of the "middle ages of Christianitie," our author enumerates some writers of the "elder ages of Christianitie," among whom are Pope Symmachus, who borders on the sixth century, and Saint Gregory, who is definitely of that age.[70] Is he thinking of a separate "middle age" for the Church? It hardly seems plausible, for in the same passage, alluding to both ecclesiastical and secular sources—Boniface of Mainz (680-754), Hincmar (ca. 805-882), Petrus Blesensis (ca. 1135-ca. 1205), Anselm (eleventh-twelfth centuries); Alfonso II (830), Otto III (980-1002)—he fuses them together as "examples of those midle times," apparently not differentiating between them. *The Historie of Tithes* adds another complication by stating definitely that the "Consecrations, Appropriations and Infeodations" of Tithes "in the midle times" took place "twixt about DCCC and MCC from Christ."[71] The starting point may shift, then, from the sixth century to the eighth or even the ninth.

As may be gathered from the last quotation, the upper limit is the year 1200, and here Selden is consistent, for not one of his references goes beyond the early thirteenth century. In the passage already cited concerning "the middle ages of Christianitie," he calls the remaining centuries "later times," indicating that they began approximately "CCCC years since"—consequently, from about 1200 to 1215. Why such a terminus for the middle age? Did the end of Richard I's reign seem like the threshold of a new period? Here Selden gives no hint.

Sir Henry Spelman is far more explicit. For him, the feudal period, beginning with William the Conqueror, is preceded by a Saxon or intermediary era. The "middle-age-dialect" is Saxon.[72] In *Icenia*[73] he again makes a distinction between the "Normanni" and the "Scriptores medii seculi."

---

[69]This and the following references, unless otherwise specified, will be to the 1614 edition of *Titles of Honor*.

[70]Selden alludes to *Epistles* of St. Gregory, and as there are no specifications, those may be the *Epistles* of St. Gregory of Nyssa (ca. 331-ca. 396). However, the case of Pope Symmachus remains.

[71]Pp. iii, 69-70.

[72]*The Original, Growth, Propagation and Condition of Feuds and Tenures by Knight-Service in England*, ch. 10, in *The English Works of Sir Henry Spelman Kt.*

[73]*Ibid.*, p. 136.

A similar division of time may have been in the mind of Peter Heylyn,[74] who alludes only to Aethelstan, Melkinus Avalonis (fl. 560), Gildas Albanius (d. 512). Nothing, at least, can show that he may have thought of the later centuries.

The greatest puzzle lies in Thomas Fuller's two passages. With "the Greeks of that middle age,"[75] he would seem to associate Constantine Porphyrogenetus (905-959); yet, in *The History of the Worthies of England,*[76] "the middle times" extend from King Edward III (1327-1377) "till within our remembrance"! Why the "middle times" should begin just then is hard enough to say; but why this inconsistency? If absent-mindedness seems too simple an explanation, then we must infer, until other and clearer examples may be found, that Fuller thought of unrelated historical sequences, each with its own middle age.

The obvious conclusion is that uniformity is not the outstanding quality of our English terms. Different points of view determine their meaning. Add the fact that after Camden, Thomas James says "middle-aged *writers*"; Selden, "*Authors* of the middle time," "the *Latine* of the middle times," "a *Chronologer* of the middle times in Greece";[77] Spelman, "middle-age-*dialect*," "*Scriptores* medii seculi," "*Authoribus* medii temporis"; add that all of these writers—like most of the others in the English list[78]—were nevertheless historians, antiquaries, or at least, like the librarian Thomas James, scholars whose writings often contributed to history; add all this, and what remains of Professor Gordon's statement, on the basis of his own criteria? "Our English practice has been simple and consistent. We had *Middle Age* early, probably first of the vernaculars, and we had it from the historians in its original comprehensive sense."[79]

In the English texts, we are furthest removed from the Renaissance meaning of earlier Latin expressions; we have an intermediary period, but the idea that this is a lapse between ancient and modern civilization has been lost. Camden, perhaps, retained something of it, for he found in writers up to Claudius Clemens a certain polish and refinement; Charlemagne's revival of learning probably seemed to him the last flash of Antiquity.

---

[74]*Examen Historicon* (London, 1659), pp. 9-10, 11.

[75]Thomas Fuller, *The Church History of Britain: From the Birth of Jesus Christ until the Year MDCXLVIII* (London, 1656), vol. 1, century 4, p. 16.

[76]P. 44.

[77]Cf. von Watt's German term.

[78]In Professor Gordon's list of four seventeenth-century authors, only two may be considered historians or antiquaries.

[79]*Medium Aevum,* p. 19.

Among the Latin authors, the humanist-bishop Giovanni Andrea still heads the list. It may be futile to look for an earlier reference, but when we consider that, in 1469, "media tempestas" is used twice in the same letter, apparently without the slightest hesitation, it seems plausible to imagine that the term was not entirely new, even then. Of course, triparted divisions had been common before Andrea's time, but what we have in mind is the special way in which he used such an outline: an intermediary period between Antiquity and his own modern time. In this, "media tempestas" is original, and very close to the "Middle Ages" of today.[80]

It is possible that Joachim von Watt's expressions did not cover as large a span; all we can gather is that the "media aetatis autor non ignobilis" was Walahfried Strabo (d. 849); that the "exempla donationum et chartarum mediae antiquitatis" began with Theodoric III,[81] going on beyond Charlemagne; and that the "mediae aetatis Chronica" are of the time of Henry III's death (1056). Marcus Welser, cited by Professor Gordon, yields even less, for if a fourteenth-fifteenth-century codex helps to date his "infima antiquitas," it leaves the "media" without specifications.[82] In Canisius' work, where the earliest writer to be used "ad historiam mediae aetatis illustrandam" is S. Hippolytus (280), the lower limit is clear enough; the upper terminus is not as definite, as the latest work cited (Joannes Malanus, *Catalogus scriptorum, qui contra Judaeos scripserunt*, 1580) comes up to Canisius' own time. As for Jacques Sirmond, who cites one reference (Sidonius), his "media aetas" is that of the purists.[83] Bacon's expression, though much broader, is also subject to reservations: as history becomes a succession of rare revivals of learning, with long periods of ignorance ("media mundi tempora") interposed between these renaissances, it happens that the intermediary era between the Roman civilization and Bacon's own time—one of the barbarous interims—coincides with what we call the Middle Ages.[84] This more restricted concept is found in Georg Horn's *Arca Noae* (1666) and *Orbis Politicus* (1667), where the "medium aevum" encompasses a span of twelve centuries, from about 300 to 1500.[85]

---

[80]Borinski ("Die Weltwiedergeburtsidee," pp. 112-13), who knew only Andrea's first passage, asserted that "media tempestas" stood for the Christian interim as defined by Cusa: an era extending from the time of Christ to the Day of Judgment. His argument, based on "recentiores usque ad nostra tempora" (and helped by an incorrect punctuation of these words), is not confirmed by our second passage, which is very clearly worded.

[81]This is Thierry III (d. 691), son of Childéric II.

[82]*Opera historica et philologica, sacra et profana* (Nuremberg, 1682), p. 794.

[83]Professor Gordon has shown this clearly: *Medium Aevum*, p. 17, n. 2.

[84]A demonstration of this point may be found in *ibid.*, pp. 12-13.

[85]Cf. *ibid.*, p. 4.

Our best example of the philological term is in Vossius, who announces, when writing of "medii aevi" poets: "continebo me intra Latinos: quos a Severi temporibus [193–211] ordiar."[86] He begins, indeed, with Tertullian (ca. 155–ca. 222), and going on through Sidonius Apollinaris, Ausonius, Prudentius, Prosper, Arator, Corippus and others, he ends with Petrus Apollonius Collatius, of the seventh century; this seems like the upper limit, for he concludes: "Adderem et alia de proximorum temporum poetis."[87] As Vossius is a grammarian, small wonder that his middle age fails to correspond to the more usual "medium aevum"; be it noted that, running from the second to the seventh century, it also fails to correspond to the span (fourth–fifth century to Charlemagne) assigned to it by Professor Lehmann.

Some authors changed the meaning of their term. For example, Voetius at first divided the "inter media aetas" into two definite parts —the first running from 600 to the tenth century, the second from the tenth century to 1517 (a Protestant terminus); later, he fused the two parts into one "intermedia aetas" of Church history.[88] Here again, through a specialized view of the centuries, the author finds a middle age that coincides closely with the general concept. An even greater change comes over Cellarius' "middle age": the full title of his 1676 work was *Nucleus Historiae inter Antiquam et Novam Mediae, hoc est, ab Augusto Caesare ad Carolum Magnum in Occidente, et ad captam a Turcis Constantinopolim in Oriente productae*; this division between Occidental and Oriental history produced a shorter middle age in the West; but in the *Historia Medii Aevi* (1688) and the *Historia Nova* (1696), where this distinction no longer exists, the difference between the two middle ages disappears, leaving only one with the capture of Constantinople as the terminus. The lower boundary also underwent a decided shift: in the first edition of the *Historia Antiqua* (1675), ancient history ends at the birth of Christ, and in the 1685 edition, it is prolonged to the age of Constantine.[89]

The other Latin writers do not give sufficient indications. Johannes J. Hoffmann, like Hadrianus Junius[90] and Philippe Labbe,

[86]*De arte grammatica* (Amsterdam, 1635), p. 302.

[87]*Ibid.*, p. 309.

[88]Gijsbert Voet, *Selectae Disputationes Theologicae*, 1639 (published in 1648), 2: 737; *Exercitia et bibliothecae studiosi theologicae*, 3d ed. (Utrecht, 1685), pp. 200, 316, 830ff. It is to be noted that Giovanni Andrea divided the "historias medie tempestatis" into "veteres" and "recentiores"; and that, in the French Academy's definition of 1694, the "moyen âge" also came to an end in the tenth century.

[89]Cf. Gordon, *Medium Aevum*, p. 15, n. 3.

[90]In the dedication (dated 1575) of his *Batavia* (Leyden, 1588): "vasto illo et immenso veterum, recentiorum, mediaeque aetatis scriptorum oceano." His meaning is the same, although the wording is somewhat different from that of the other two.

merely names three periods: the ancient, middle, and "more recent" times. This mode of expression, however, is not without interest, as it might lead us to believe that the modern or contemporary times were excluded from the general outlook.[91] But without definite dates or some line of demarcation, nothing seems to prove that, to our authors, the "more recent" times represented a period different from their own. Labbe certainly had no such distinction in mind; in his *Index copiosissimus poetarum Graecorum ac Latinorum, aliorumque scriptorum veteris mediae ac recentioris aetatis*, the latest writers mentioned are presumably those of the "recentioris aetatis"; and we find, among the latter, F. Pithou, S. Sweertius, J. Sirmond, and none other than Labbe himself! The same is true of "media antiquitas";[92] Rhenanus merely adds a "prisca antiquitas," and we may assume that these two, together, make up the whole of the past, leading up directly to modern times; though "antiquitas" does not mean "tempus" or "aevum", it may be considered here as a substitute that does not change the meaning of the whole term.[93]

For Rhenanus as for the others, we may conclude, then, that the adjective was the essential word, and the only constant in all our citations; even when "media" changed to "intermedia," the significant idea was not modified, but stressed.

When the Latin and French terms revealed a definite span of time, we found, more than once, that their meaning was very close to that which still prevails; and when writers simply put the "middle" age between Antiquity and modern times, without further indications, they too may be said to have anticipated a general and vague manner in which we use the same expression today. As might have been expected, others, at the beginning, interpreted these new symbols in their own special way; but it cannot be shown that the "philologists" were particularly responsible for the several variations; on the contrary, it was the historians and antiquaries—especially those among the great English scholars of the seventeenth century—who used "middle age" and "middle time" with little or no uniformity. We must, therefore, reverse Professor Gordon's conclusions, which were all too favorable to the historians; in reality, the philologist-

---

[91]Selden does something of this kind by ending the "middle times" at the thirteenth century, before the "later times."

[92]Cf. Rhenanus, von Watt, Welser, Taubmann, Goldast, Spelman.

[93]Welser, it is true, added an "infimam antiquitatem," but von Watt before him and Taubmann, Goldast, and Spelman after him do not seem to have needed such a term. Moreover, von Watt, Goldast, and Spelman used "media antiquitas" along with "media aetas," "medium aevum" and "medium seculum," without making any apparent distinction.

historian distinction was unnecessary and misleading, for some of the great men we cited were active in both fields; besides Du Cange, there is Sir Henry Spelman, for example, whom history led ever so often into linguistic inquiry.

At any rate, even when "medium aevum," "moyen âge," and "middle age" had limited meanings, they referred to times which, as it happens, can be incorporated into the more recent conception of the Middle Ages.

All these general and restricted terms appeared very frequently in the seventeenth century, but the Latin forms arose much earlier, in the wake of the Renaissance spirit. Of course, other expressions existed at the same time: how much more often did the authors of those centuries inveigh against the "misty," the "dark," the "ignorant," the "barbarous," the "monkish," or the "Gothic" age! These were more vehement and polemical phrases—some of which, in passing, were not too strong for the anticlerical Michelet, even in times of romanticism and medievalism! But they did not join to the idea of barbarity that view and interpretation of history which is all contained in the words "medium," "moyen," and "middle."

Other Early Uses of
Moyen Age
and *Moyen Temps*

IN A SURVEY dealing with various early uses of "medium aevum," "middle ages" and "moyen âge,"[1] we found that the Latin expression "media tempestas" came first, in 1469, to be followed by "middle age" and "middle time" in 1605. "Moyen âge," together with its variant "moyen temps," came later, appearing only in 1657, in the works of Du Cange. But the latter made such frequent and unhesitating use of these two forms that it seemed to attest earlier occurrences of the French term, and a greater frequency than that already shown. Indeed, many new authors can now be added to those previously listed; of these, three preceded Du Cange.

As early as 1640, Pierre de Marca speaks of "les Coustumes du moyen temps," "les Auteurs du moyen temps," "cet escrivain du moyen aage" (Alanus de Insulis), "les Auteurs Grecs et Latins du moyen aage," "les auteurs du moyen aage," and "les Annales du moyen temps."[2] Here again, "moyen âge" and "moyen temps" appear together. The very next year, Pierre de Caseneuve uses the latter

---

Originally published in *Romanic Review* 30 (1939): 327–30.

[1]"The Early Uses of *Medium Aevum, Moyen Age, Middle Ages*," *Romanic Review* 29 (1938): 3–25. See pp. 000–00 above.

[2]*Histoire de Bearn, contenant l'origine des Rois de Navarre, des Ducs de Gascogne, Marquis de Gothie, Princes de Bearn, Comtes de Carcassone, de Foix et de Bigorre* (Paris, 1640), "Au lecteur" (3d page) and pp. 26, 254, 510, 684.

alone: "ceux [les auteurs] du tems moïen";[3] and again, nine times, in his *Origines de la langue françoise*, printed in 1694 but written and consulted before 1650.[4] Finally, in 1656, Pierre-François Chifflet refers to "les anciennes histoires des siècles metoyens."[5]

Besides these writers who preceded Du Cange, there are several more who immediately followed. Jean-Jacques Chifflet, Pierre-François' brother, used "les siècles mitoyens" twice again, in 1659;[6] this is an interesting plural variant which Jean Scholastique Pitton repeated in 1668, in a somewhat different form: "siècles moyens."[7] As for "moyen âge" itself, it reappears eleven times in Philippe Labbe's *Etymologies*, in 1661,[8] and some twenty years later in another work of Pitton,[9] to be used once again by Galaup in 1704.[10] Some cling to the variant "moyen temps," which we find once in 1659,[11] twice in 1687,[12]

---

[3]*Instructions pour le Franc-Alleu de la Province de Languedoc* (Toulouse, [1641]), p. 215. The catalogue of the Bibliothèque Nationale gives 1640 instead of 1641 as the date, but one copy of this treatise states at the end that it was printed "conformement à la Déliberation de Messeigneurs des Trois Estats de ladite Province, faite en l'Assemblée du xii. Novembre, de l'an M.DCXL."; it is hardly possible, then, that the work was put out in the remaining seven weeks of 1640. Le Long and Vaissette also prefer 1641.

In the *Indice* to this work, de Caseneuve uses the Latin expression "Scriptores [or "Authores"] mediae aetatis" five times. All of these, together with the French term, appear again in a second edition, in 1645.

[4]This work was published by H. P. Simon de Val-Hébert in Gilles Ménage's *Dictionnaire étymologique* (Paris, 1694), pp. 8, 35, 40, 41, 42, 45, 92, 93, 97. De Val-Hébert, in his preface to *Les Origines*, cites a letter of de Caseneuve, dated November 18, 1650, in which the latter states that he began this treatise "il y a quelques années."

[5]*Lettre touchant Beatrix Comtesse de Chalon* (Dijon, 1656), p. 5.

[6]*Le Faux Childebrand relégué aux Fables* (n.p., 1659), pp. 88, 95. This same writer used "media saecula" and "medium aevum" in his Latin works, *Vindiciae Hispanicae* (Antwerp, 1645), pp. 181, 187, and *Verum Stemma Childebrandinum* (n.p., 1656), pp. 13, 25. Marc-Antoine Dominicy, in his point for point refutation of the *Vindiciae*, *Assertor Gallicus* (Paris, 1646), p. 199, also used "media tempora." We may add one more use of the Latin expression "media aetas" in Medon's Life of P. de Caseneuve, in *L'Origine des Jeux-Fleureaux de Toulouse par feu Mr. de Caseneuve* (Toulouse, 1659), p. 4, where it occurs twice.

[7]*Dissertations historiques pour la Sainte Eglise d'Aix* (Lyon, 1668), p. xxi.

[8]*Les Etymologies de plusieurs mots François, contre les abus de la Secte des Hellénistes du Port-Royal* (Paris, 1661), pt. 1, pp. 30, 63-64, 65, 69-70, 90, 232, 260, 305, 324, 328; pt. 2, p. 56.

[9]*Sentimens sur les historiens de Provence* (Aix, 1682), p. 29.

[10]Pierre de Galaup de Chasteuil, *Apologie des anciens historiens, et des troubadours, ou poétes provençaux. Servant de réponse aux Dissertations de Pierre Joseph, sur divers points de l'histoire de Provence* (Avignon, 1704), p. 51.

[11]In the *Epistre aux Capitouls de Toulouse de l'an 1659*, by one Tornier, at the head of *L'Origine des Jeux-Fleureaux de Toulouse*.

[12]Germain de Lafaille, *Annales de la Ville de Toulouse* (Toulouse, 1687), p. 63; "Abrégé de l'Ancienne Histoire de la Ville de Toulouse" (in the same work), p. 60.

twice in 1704,[13] and twice in 1711.[14]

What makes these citations significant, when we add them to those already known,[15] is partly the fact that they more than double the frequency of our term and almost triple the number of authors who used it in the seventeenth century. Moreover, with the appearance of new forms like "siècles mitoyens" and "siècles moyens," and with the recurrence of "moyen temps," it also becomes more evident that the scholars and historians of that time had not yet found one common, definite expression; usage was not yet uniform. If that is so, do these new texts also reveal a diversity of meanings?

We found it difficult, in our previous analysis, to draw sufficient indications from some of the passages cited, and the same problem arises now. Pitton, for example, gives scarcely a hint: who are, exactly, "les Escrivains du moyen âge"?[16] And if "les siècles moyens" are distinguished from the "premiers"[17] (of the Christian era), how broad a span do they cover? De Haitze seems to include the tenth, eleventh, and twelfth centuries in his "moïen tems,"[18] but nothing shows that this excluded others. Lafaille views "l'origine et la décadence de la Poësie Provençale" âs part of "l'Histoire du moyen tems," which also takes in Nithard (ninth century),[19] but leaves us without further specifications. P.-F. Chifflet merely quotes documents of the thirteenth century.[20]

But others are more explicit. J.-J. Chifflet's references, at least, are more numerous, and place Saint Isidore of Seville (ca. 570–636) at the head of the "siècles mitoyens."[21] By means of Chifflet's Latin works, we can follow the "media saecula" up to the thirteenth century,[22] and in *Le Faux Childebrand*, where he speaks of "quelques Escrivains modernes du XVI. et XVII. siecle,"[23] we may wonder whether the fifteenth is not already considered the last medieval century. De Marca would seem to go beyond Saint Isidore, to begin his

---

[13]Pierre Joseph de Haitze, *Dissertations de Pierre Joseph sur divers points de l'histoire de Provence* (Anvers, 1704), pp. 40–41, 44.

[14]Pierre Joseph de Haitze, *Apologétique de la religion des Provençaux au sujet de Ste. Madeleine* (Aix, 1711), p. 32, 66.

[15]Adrien Baillet, one of those authors previously cited (see p. 000 above), used "moyen âge" twice in his *Jugemens des Sçavans* (Paris, 1685), pt. 3, pp. 44, 166.

[16]*Sentimens sur les historiens de Provence*, p. 29.

[17]*Dissertations historiques pour la Sainte Eglise d'Aix*, p. xxi.

[18]*Dissertations de Pierre Joseph*, pp. 40–41.

[19]*Annales de la Ville de Toulouse*, pp. 63, 60.

[20]*Lettre touchant Beatrix*, p. 5.

[21]*Le Faux Childebrand relégué aux Fables*, p. 95.

[22]*Vindiciae Hispanicae*, p. 190.

[23]P. 72.

"moyen âge" at the time of Clovis;[24] his latest reference is Alain des Isles (twelfth century),[25] but as *L'Histoire de Bearn* stops short in the thirteenth century, we cannot know whether this was intended as the upper terminus of the Middle Ages.[26] The canons of the Synod of Laodicea (fourth century), confirmed by the Council of Chalcedon (fifth century), are Labbe's earliest reference, which is followed by many others throughout the centuries, up to Steron (Stereon—thirteenth-fourteenth centuries).[27] As for de Caseneuve's "tems moïen," it includes as early a writer as Ennodius (474–521),[28] with authors of every century as far as Matthew Paris[29] of the thirteenth.

The upper limit of the "moyen âge" is not easily discernible in most of these texts; and whenever we try to determine it, it seems to fall somewhat short of our modern notion of it. Our authors, however, may have thought of a longer span without chancing to use "moyen âge" in connection with specific fourteenth- or fifteenth-century documents. At any rate, whenever indications are not lacking, the lower limits correspond more closely to those established by usage.

We may conclude then that the diversity of forms was not symptomatic of a diversity of meanings. Where our terms yield some kind of definition, they cover, more or less, the same centuries, and most of those included in the Middle Ages today. This but confirms our earlier conclusion that the French term was not confined to a philological meaning, as is further proved by expressions like "la Provence dans le moyen tems,"[30] "les Coustumes du moyen temps,"[31] and "l'histoire du moyen temps."[32]

[24]*Histoire de Bearn*, p. 684.

[25]*Ibid.*, p. 254.

[26]A MS bringing the work up to 1620 was known to exist, but it has disappeared.

[27]*Les Etymologies de plusieurs mots François*, pp. 65, 30.

[28]*Instructions pour le Franc-Alleu de la Province de Languedoc*, p. 215.

[29]*Les Origines de la langue francoise*, p. 97.

[30]P. J. de Haitze, *Dissertations de Pierre Joseph*, p. 44.

[31]Pierre de Marca, *Histoire de Bearn*, "Au lecteur."

[32]P. J. de Haitze, *Dissertations de Pierre Joseph*, pp. 40–41; Tornier, *Epistre aux Capitouls de Toulouse*; G. de Lafaille, *Annales de la Ville de Toulouse*, pp. 60, 63.

The Case against
Gothicism

THE NEWCOMERS of the Renaissance in France came into a world that
remained Gothic and Romanesque all about them. Even after this
world had been altered in its general aspect by a wide assortment of
new styles, it remained strewn with vestiges of the Middle Ages.
Some of those imbued with the new spirit resented the enduring
presence of these monuments, which they judged antithetical to good
taste. In this they do not voice the general opinion of their time, but
they challenge it, and help to bring it into focus. Their case against
gothicism is more worthy of interest than one is usually led to believe.

Much of their case is concentrated in the term "gothique" itself,
which belongs to the language that gave us "moyen âge" with its
twin term "renaissance." In England, it takes on a special polemical
sense in the seventeenth century, when the Parliamentarians, in their
search for slogans and doctrines to oppose to monarchical absolutism,
with the help of antiquarians discovered in the Goths a freedom-
loving folk of high moral purity, and set them up as ancestors of the
English; simultaneously, the word Gothic carried the familiar meaning, far from laudatory.[1] No such ambiguity, but only a long evolution, is discernible in the usage of Latin countries. In medieval times,
the Goths were already designated as "barbarians" but, it would

Not previously published.
[1]See Samuel Kliger, *The Goths in England: a Study in Seventeenth- and Eighteenth-
Century Thought* (Cambridge, Mass., 1952).

seem, purely in the sense that they were not a Latin-speaking nation. They begin to look "barbarous," crude, and cruel when a desolate middle era is marked out between Antiquity and modern times, and they, with the Vandals and others, are charged with the fall of Rome. The ogival style, for a long time called French ("opus francigenum"), is later called German in Italy, where the epithet has the meaning and ring of Gothic: Raphael speaks in the same context of "architectura Tedescha" and "edifici poi del tempo delli Gotti"; Vasari likewise speaks of "i Gotti" and "edifizi che oggi da noi son chiamati Tedeschi." Palladio seems to be the first to attach the word "Gottica" directly to architecture.[2]

In sixteenth-century France, the idea of "gothique" early makes its way. Gargantua describes to Pantagruel the days of his own youth: "Le temps estoit encores tenebreux et sentant l'infelicité et calamité des Gothz, qui avoient mis à destruction toute bonne litterature."[3] Ronsard's friend, the poet Jean-Antoine de Baïf, spells it out in his own way: "Donk le Gotisme, je lêss é je pran lêz êrres de sês vieus Grés é Latins."[4] Of trials by duel the conteur Noël du Fail writes: "telle façon de faire de gothique avoit été ostée et abolie."[5]

The actual Goths of history recede into a vague, general background of barbarity. Their name, a residue of tradition, becomes one of the stigmas conventionally attached to all that is held uncouth, uncivilized, brutal; it is not geographically localized, like "Tedeschi"; "gothique" is a close equivalent to "médiéval," in a general and hostile sense, at a time when this adjective, far behind "moyen âge," has not yet emerged. The Norman invaders are themselves described in a text of 1521 as "Gotz."[6]

The cliché spreads, and can be used in any style. For irony: "O le bel ouvrage gothique!"[7] To ridicule Ronsard's old-fashioned "vers plats et grossiers":

---

[2]Cf. ibid., pp. 66-70; John Britton, The Architectural Antiquities of Great Britain (London, 1807-26), 5: 33; Ernest Renan, "L'Art du moyen âge et les causes de sa décadence," Revue des Deux Mondes 40 (1862): 209-10; Louis Courajod, Leçons professées à l'Ecole du Louvre, 1887-1896 (Paris, 1899-1903), 1: 145, 420-21; Camille Enlart, Manuel d'archéologie française (Paris, 1902-16), 1: xxxv, 466.

[3]Pantagruel, ed. Jean Plattard, p. 41. Cf. "Prologue," Le Cinquiesme Livre, p. 5: "peu de reliques restent de capharderie et siècle Gottis"; letter of 1532 to Tiraqueau: "E densa illa gothici temporis caligine plus quam Cimmeria," quoted by Gustave Cohen, Ronsard (Paris, 1924), p. 3, n. 3.

[4]Oeuvres en rime, ed. Ch. Marty-Laveaux (Paris, 1881-90), 5: 300.

[5]Oeuvres facétieuses, ed. J. Assézat (Paris, 1874), 1: 241.

[6]Du Cange, Glossarium mediae et infimae latinitatis, ed. Faure, 4: 89, s.v. "Goti."

[7]Marc-Antoine, Sieur de Saint-Amant, Dernier recueil des oeuvres, Oeuvres complètes, ed. Charles Livet (Paris, 1855), 2: 58.

On dirait que Ronsard sur ses pipeaux rustiques,
Vient encor fredonner ses Idylles Gothiques.[8]

For mock-heroism, in describing the "fureur Gothique" of a grotesque Battle of the Books.[9] Or to protest in 1652 against the dispersal of Mazarin's library: "certes les Vandales et les Goths n'ont rien fait autrefois de plus barbare, ni de plus rude que cela"—with a more direct reference to the historical Goths.[10] Petrarch, says Du Cange, first brought literature "ex Gothicis tenebris."[11] In the French vernacular, we hear in a defense of the use of Latin for inscriptions, there are remnants "de la barbarie Gotique."[12] Empty-headed scribblers could provoke "des desordres plus que Gotiques."[13] "Manière barbare et Gothique" is a phrase registered and consecrated by Furetière's *Dictionnaire universel* (1690).

"Gothique" is current, and may even find its way into a bold anachronism like François Blondel's, in his description of certain mouldings of rather bad taste "qui sont d'un Dorique Gothique."[14] Antoine de Baïf's "Gothisme" recurs.[15] But, particularly with reference to architecture, this vocabulary comes into confusing competition with one of the extensions of "moderne." Usage has it that "un basti-ment moderne" refers to a building in the new manner. The Academy Dictionary recognizes that at the same time, however, "Les Archi-tectes appellent, *Architecture moderne*, toutes les manières d'Archi-tecture qui ont été en usage en Europe depuis les Anciens Grecs et Romains, comme l'Architecture gothique, et autres. Ainsi en parlant des édifices gothiques, on dit, que *C'est une moderne*; et mesme quand on parle de quelque ancien édifice gothique, on dit, *c'est une vieille gothique*."[16] Furetière would seem to disagree, opposing the modern to the Gothic, but the Academy is right; various authors con-firm its report, among them, in 1678, the members of the Royal Academy of Architecture.[17] Henri Sauval displays the flexibility, or

---

[8]Boileau, *L'Art poétique*, 2: 21.

[9]Boileau, *Lutrin*, 5: 146.

[10]Michel de Marolles, *Mémoires* (1755), 1: 366. Cf. François Ogier, *Apologie pour Monsieur de Balzac* (1627), p. 38, for his comparison of a harsh style to the effect of "quelque invasion des Gotz et des Vandales."

[11]*Glossarium*, preface, sec. 52.

[12]François Blondel, *Cours d'architecture* (1675-85), pt. 4 (1683), p. 610.

[13]Gabriel Guéret, *Le Parnasse reformé* (1668), p. 128.

[14]*Cours d'architecture*, p. 605.

[15]Jean Chapelain, *De la lecture des vieux romans* (1647), ed. A. Feillet (1870), p. 4.

[16]*Dictionnaire de l'Académie Française* (1694), s.v. "Moderne."

[17]Etienne Pasquier, *Lettres*, in *Oeuvres* (1723 ed.), 2: 192; André Duchesne, *Les An-tiquitez et recherches . . .* (1637 ed.), p. 85; François Derand, *L'Architecture des*

ambiguity, of this terminology; in architecture the medieval is modern, and yet in woodwork there is a certain Italian manner which the connoisseurs, he says, call modern to distinguish it from the Gothic.[18] In centuries when not one but several quarrels of Ancients and Moderns turned the word "moderne," like "ancien," into a battlecry, it is possible that the Gothic reaped the benefits of falling into the one camp, as it incurred the disadvantages of falling out of the other. But the Middle Ages in general, "les siècles passés," while called "modernes" were also at times called "anciens." There is a zone, which would deserve further study, in which confusion is due chiefly to indistinct, unsettled usage, and has as yet little to do with the misunderstanding and cross-purposes of the two factions.[19]

Basically, "gothique" is a term of condemnation, in the general sense that was noted, but especially with reference to art. Painting has its own "manière ordinaire, gothique et barbare."[20] But medieval architecture above all bears the brunt of the criticism. Nowhere is it more brutally attacked than in the anonymous *Chasse au vieil grognard de l'antiquité*, a pamphlet published in 1622 (perhaps earlier, in 1619) by a bilious champion of modern times. He will tolerate no remembrance of centuries past, and with sustained crudeness mangles every image of medieval life. "Et des bastiments des anciens roys, quoy?" Cheap old castles like Saint-Ouen near Saint-Denis, Bicêtre, and Vauvert (not a word about others, like the Palais and its Sainte Chapelle). And what of those wretched city dwellings of old? "Les architectres estoient de venerables ingenieurs pour bastir force nids à rats."[21] Indifference, perhaps, is worse than such hostility, even when expressed with the breezy verve that blows in the *Voyage d'Encausse*, where Chapelle and Bachaumont, describing Narbonne, summarily bypass the cathedral—these *beaux esprits*, however, more gaily still brush aside the Venetian Sebastiano del Piombo's painting of Lazarus arising from the tomb, a prized showpiece of the town.[22]

---

voûtes (1643), pp. 9, 392; *Procès-verbaux de l'Académie Royale d'Architecture* (1671-1793), 1: 180.

[18]*Histoire et recherches des antiquités de la ville de Paris* (1724), 1: 295, 2: 4.

[19]For further details, see N. Edelman, *Attitudes of Seventeenth-Century France toward the Middle Ages* (New York, 1946), pp. 11-12, 18-19. On the early uses of "gothique," see Renan, "L'Art du moyen âge"; Raoul Rosières, "L'Architecture dite gothique doit-elle être ainsi dénommée?" *Revue Archéologique*, 3d ser., 19 (1892): 348-62; Courajod, *Leçons*; Ferdinand Brunot, *Histoire de la langue française*, 6 vols. (Paris, 1966-72), 6: 685; Denyse Métrat, *Blaise de Vigenère, archéologue et critique d'art* (Paris, 1939), pp. 103-4.

[20]Nicolas Poussin, letter of June 16, 1641, in *Lettres* (Paris, 1929), p. 38.

[21]In Edouard Fournier, *Variétés historiques et littéraires* (1855-56), 3: 31-33, 58.

[22]*Voyage d'Encausse faict par Messieurs Chapelle et Bachaumont* (1663), ed. M. Souriau, pp. 97-99.

More sober critics afford us some insight into their point of view. The Gothic, it is charged, suffers from a lack of proportion. A "Colomne Gothique," for example, is a round pillar too short or too slight for its height, and without the necessary entasis: "il est fait sans règles et n'a rien qui approche des proportions antiques."[23] The Gothic, in addition, is too daring. "Nos aïeux," wrote Louis Racine, "élevoient de très-hauts bâtimens dont la hardiesse étonnante leur paroissoit une beauté admirable. Nous avons méprisé cette architecture, lorsque nous avons reconnu qu'elle étoit contraire à la simplicité de la nature." We may still be struck with wonder at the boldness of this Gothic architecture; but we no longer call it beautiful: "nous disons seulement qu'elle est hardie."[24]

The Gothic is barbarous, finally, in its low taste—"le mauvais goust des Goths"[25]—which offends particularly in the realm of decorative art. That would seem to be Molière's chief objection. In La Gloire du Val-de-Grâce (1669), a poem in honor of Pierre Mignard's painting for the dome of the modern church, he hails the artist's group of figures harmoniously ordered in a "beau tout-ensemble," where all is seen

> Assaisonné du sel de nos grâces antiques,
> Et non du fade goût des ornements gothiques,
> Ces monstres odieux des siècles ignorants,
> Que de la barbarie ont produits les torrents,
> Quand leur cours, inondant presque toute la terre,
> Fit à la politesse une mortelle guerre,
> Et de la grande Rome abattant les remparts,
> Vint, avec son empire, étouffer les beaux-arts.

A resounding condemnation. But what importance are we to attach to it? Written by the comic poet on matters in which he had no special competence, and concerning which his contemporaries would not normally turn to him for a judgment (despite Boileau's admiration for the poem), these lines are still significant to us, but only as the opinion of one honnête homme among a multitude; they are not the verdict of a whole age. They do not bear the stamp of Molière's genius for zestful, irreversible statement. This is not the place to take

---

[23]Cf. Thomas Corneille, Le Dictionnaire des arts et aes sciences (1694), 1: 498.

[24]Réflexions sur la poésie, in Oeuvres, 2: 447, 309; cf. 1747 ed., 4: 168, 3: 252. Cf. Daniel Mornet, who in citing only part of Louis Racine's statement makes it sound more hostile than it is: Le Romantisme en France au XVIIIe siècle (1912), pp. 61, 280.

[25]René Rapin, Les Comparaisons des grands hommes de l'antiquité, qui ont le plus excellé dans les belles lettres (1684), 1: 285. (1st ed. 1671)

part elaborately in the old dispute concerning the merits of *La Gloire du Val-de-Grâce*, but some measure of disappointment may be registered in passing. It has been suggested that Molière may have written this poem to support his friend Mignard in a struggle against the painter Le Brun and the latter's own poet-champion, Charles Perrault. However that may be, it is at least clear that Molière imitated or reproduced at numerous points Charles Alphonse du Fresnoy's *De arte graphica*, published posthumously in 1668 by Mignard, possibly as a retort to Perrault's *La Peinture* of the same year. *La Gloire du Val-de-Grâce* at times is inspired, but between these high spots does little honor to Molière; one senses a perfunctory effort at translating another's formulas, as in the lines quoted above, where he unloads the whole stock of clichés about the "siècles ignorants," the reign of barbarity, the monsters, the torrents, the flood, Rome, and the throttled fine arts, most of which were already on display in Du Fresnoy's Latin verse.[26] Molière assuredly was no admirer of the Gothic, but the expression of his sentiment, if not indeed the sentiment itself, was borrowed.

Roger de Piles, in his French translation of Du Fresnoy's work, published the year before, had already filled the corresponding passage with "Ornemens Gothiques . . . monstres . . . mauvais siècles . . . nuit affreuse . . . abysme d'erreurs . . . épaisses ténèbres de l'ignorance."[27] In earlier works on painting and architecture, Roland Fréart de Chambray had told in the same general, sweeping terms the tale of decadence, barbarity, ignorance, degradation, extinction, and sudden renascence.[28]

Fénelon, though a layman like Molière in matters of art, condensed one of the most remarkable indictments of the Gothic, ornamentation and all, in a page of his *Lettre sur les occupations de l'Académie* (1714), which must be quoted in full:

> Il est naturel que les modernes, qui ont beaucoup d'élégance et de tours ingénieux, se flattent de surpasser les anciens, qui n'ont que la simple nature. Mais je demande la permission de faire ici une espèce d'apologue. Les inventeurs de l'architecture qu'on nomme *gothique*, et qui est,

---

[26]Molière, *Oeuvres*, ed. Eugène Despois and Paul Mesnard, 9: 540–42, and Notice; Charles Alphonse Du Fresnoy, *De arte graphica liber* (Paris, 1668), ll. 240–45.

[27]*L'Art de peinture, traduit en françois avec des remarques nécessaires et très-amples*, in *Oeuvres diverses* (1767 ed.), 5: 39–40.

[28]*Idée de la perfection de la peinture* (Paris, 1662), pp. 1–4; *Parallèle de l'architecture antique et de la moderne* (Paris, 1650), p. 108; *Les Quatre livres de l'architecture d'André Palladio, mis en françois* (Paris, 1650), p. 49. In the foreword to the latter, Fréart de Chambray translated the "barbare inventioni" of the Italian version simply as "inventions barbares"; to clarify the obvious, Nicolas Du Bois in his 1715 translation of the *Quatre livres* wrote out "inventions *Gotiques et Barbares*."

dit-on, celle des Arabes, crurent sans doute avoir surpassé les architectes grecs. Un édifice grec n'a aucun ornement qui ne serve qu'à orner l'ouvrage; les pièces nécessaires pour le soutenir ou pour le mettre à couvert, comme les colonnes et la corniche, se tournent seulement en grâce par leurs proportions: tout est simple, tout est mesuré, tout est borné à l'usage; on n'y voit ni hardiesse ni caprice qui impose aux yeux: les proportions sont si justes, que rien ne paraît fort grand, quoique tout le soit; tout est borné à contenter la vraie raison. Au contraire, l'architecture gothique élève sur des piliers très-minces une voûte immense qui monte jusqu'aux nues; on croit que tout va tomber, mais tout dure pendant bien des siècles; tout est plein de fenêtres, de roses et de pointes; la pierre semble découpée comme du carton; tout est à jour, tout est en l'air. N'est-il pas naturel que les premiers architectes gothiques se soient flattés d'avoir surpassé, par leur vain raffinement, la simplicité grecque?[29]

Lucid, smooth, reflecting like a mirror the clarity of Fénelon's insight into his own taste, this page defines and interprets a point of view and does not merely echo it. Fénelon seems to have given it thought throughout his mature life. Some thirty-five years earlier, in the second *Dialogue sur l'éloquence*, he had already contrasted the "colifichets" of the Gothic with the simplicity of Greek art, as again in 1693, in the speech he delivered at his reception into the French Academy.[30]

It is possible to hear similar charges up to the Revolution and beyond. La Bruyère, intervening like Fénelon in the eternal Quarrel, speaks for ancient Greece and Rome: "On a dû faire du style ce qu'on a fait de l'architecture. On a entièrement abandonné l'ordre gothique, que la barbarie avait introduit pour les palais et pour les temples; on a rappelé le dorique, l'ionique et le corinthien."[31] An aesthetician of the eighteenth century restates the theory of moderation in ornamentation: "quel est l'œil assez gothique pour pouvoir supporter cette multitude affreuse de colifichets dont on ornait autrefois les frontispices de nos temples, ou les vestibules de nos vieux chateaux? Ce n'est pas que dans cet assemblage de petites figures architectoniques, il n'y ait beaucoup d'art: il y en a trop."[32] Charles Pinot Duclos, a man of letters who had mostly political and philosophical observations of interest to make on his trip to Italy in 1767, but very few remarks on Italian art, did rise to the occasion at the

[29]Ed. A. Cahen (Paris, 1920), pp. 159-60.

[30]*Oeuvres* (Paris, 1820-30), 21: 76, 128-29.

[31]"Des ouvrages de l'esprit," 15 (this passage appeared in the 5th ed., 1690). Cf. "De quelques usages," 3, where an antiquated term is called "gothique."

[32]Yves-Marie André, *Essai sur le Beau*, new ed. (Paris, 1820), pp. 173-74 (this passage first appeared in 1763).

sight of the modern Saint Peter's cathedral in Rome; the Duomo of Milan, on the other hand, was an "édifice surchargé de figures et d'ornements, dont l'ensemble m'a paru d'assez mauvais goût."[33]

Others, more moderate, will be met later. They cannot be forced into the company of those above, who expressed a one-sided position. One conclusion is possible even now: when those who opposed the Gothic firmly and completely are all accounted for, their ranks look rather thin. It was hard to maintain an absolute stand, as Fénelon showed on one occasion when he perceptibly softened his judgment: "Les ouvrages les plus hardis et les plus façonnés du gothique ne sont pas les meilleurs";[34] there was apparently a better sort of Gothic, not overwrought. One can imagine Fénelon seeing with his own eyes capital exceptions to his generalizations. For here is another important feature of the declarations against the Gothic reviewed thus far: most of them are condemnations in the abstract. Du Fresnoy, Fréart de Chambray, Molière, Rapin, La Bruyère, Thomas Corneille, Fénelon, Louis Racine, Yves-Marie André, all express judgments without once pointing to a monument. As will be observed, that gesture alone, directing the glance upon a Sainte Chapelle or any of a score of cathedrals, will suffice to alter or upset the formula.

The century of humanists, little quoted thus far, will provide one good example in the writings of Blaise de Vigenère, embassy secretary, traveler, prolific author of learned works in various disciplines, and friend of the cultural leaders of his time. Though chiefly interested in Antiquity, he knew his Villehardouin and the *romans* from the Round Table to *Jehan de Paris*. Yet he might say, in general terms: "ces gothiques désolations, gastz et ruines ont laissé leur nom à tout ce qui s'est depuis ensuivy de grossier, goffe, lourd et rural, tant ès arts et sciences, qu'ès mestiers." He was an admirer of Bramante, Michelangelo, Germain Pilon, and others of the Italian and French Renaissance. But he could also wonder at the tower of the Strasbourg cathedral, and feel before the church of Saint Nicaise in Reims that it was "l'une des plus belles et hardies . . . et des mieux conduittes et entendues qui se voye de ça les monts." And he could even assert on a general plane that granting Antiquity its due, "il ne s'ensuit pas pour cela que rien ne se doibve lire, rien ne se doibve veoir, louër ny approuver que les ouvrages des anciens, ou ce qui est moullé-poché là-dessus, . . . et qu'il n'y ait assez de beaux bastiments çà et là par le monde, . . . nonobstant que les règles de

---

[33]*Voyage en Italie, ou considérations sur l'Italie* (Paris, 1791), pp. 62, 321.

[34]*Discours prononcé par M. l'abbé de Fénelon pour sa réception à L'Académie Française*, in *Oeuvres choisies* (Paris, 1894), p. 370.

l'architecture ancienne et la disposition de ses ordres n'y ayent été si exactement observées."[35]

In that century there is as yet no condemnation of Gothic taste as articulate as Fénelon's. Usually "gothique" alone said everything, even without "grossier, goffe, lourd et rural." It was cliché, with roots in Italian usage that made elaborate definition superfluous. It fitted into a new idiom that expressed, more than it analyzed, a humanist experience—or, as historians will have it, an illusion—of rediscovery. Long after the experience had ceased to be novel, this idiom persisted. One gathers the impression, when well into the seventeenth century, that the continued use of "gothique" had now come to be a gesture of cultural orthodoxy or consistency, for some of our authors, and that for others like Fénelon and Louis Racine the term, grown hackneyed, needed to be refreshed, elaborated, and justified. In all they said, the central consideration was proportion, which, in the doctrine derived from Vitruvius through a cumulation of editions, translations, and commentaries by Leone Battista Alberti, Sebastiano Serlio, Andrea Palladio, Giacomo Barozzi da Vignola, and others, had become the basis for the French classical explanation of beauty. "Le beau," Bernini reiterated to the French during his sensational visit in 1665, "le beau de toutes les choses du monde, aussi bien que de l'architecture, consiste dans la proportion."[36] And proportion is fitness of correspondence, as they often defined it. For example: "Pour la beauté, elle se trouve dans la forme et belle correspondence des parties avec leur tout, et dans le rapport qu'elles ont entre elles: de sorte que toutes les pièces du bastiment semblent estre nées ensemble, et composer un beau corps, dont chaque partie luy sert comme d'un membre nécessaire."[37] From this could be derived all else, including ornamentation.

Proportion, as the very configuration of beauty, was a reflection of "raison," which under various names was the ultimate source of all values intellectual, moral, and aesthetic. Authority was seldom more than a secondary factor; the Ancients were to be followed not automatically but, in good classical doctrine, solely in the name of "raison," when it upheld them and in their works set a felicitous

[35]See works on Chalcondylas, Livy, Caesar, and a *Traicté des chiffres*, from 1577 to 1589, quoted in Métrat, *Blaise de Vigenère*, pp. 90-105, which is also the source for biographical data.

[36]*Journal du voyage du Cavalier Bernin en France*, trans. Paul Fréart de Chantelou, ed. L. Lalanne (1885), p. 13.

[37]Fréart de Chambray's French translation of Palladio, *Les Quatre livres de l'architecture* (Paris, 1650), p. 3. Cf. Nicolas Du Bois' 1715 ed. It would be tedious to enumerate all the echoes to this doctrine; e.g., François Blondel, *Cours d'architecture*, pt. 5, pp. 754ff., where proportions are considered as natural as chords in music; Jacques-François Blondel, *Architecture françoise* (1752-56), 1: 22-25.

example. That "raison," which was forever invoked, now looks dull to us; it is taken for some dreary business of rules. Or it seems perplexing in its variability.[38] But in descriptions of the search for truth or for beauty, "raison" in fact was ascribed a constant, single, luminous role, which needs to be restored to it if the critical terminology of those centuries is not to be badly misconstrued.

In the very title of Descartes' *Discours de la méthode pour bien conduire sa raison et chercher la vérité dans les sciences,* "raison" is seen as something which requires to be directed by a *méthode* a.id is therefore not itself that *méthode.* It is a "bon sens," not the common sense of old saws but, like Montaigne's "sens" or "jugement," "cette capacité de trier le vray"[39] that is latent in all men; it is "la puissance de bien juger, et distinguer le vrai d'avec le faux": a "puissance," then, not a procedure or body of rules—the power of affirmation and negation, and of utmost certitude. "Idées claires et distinctes" are not arguments but illuminations, primal insights that take hold. The certitude they awaken is an immediate feeling of complete belief, a "croyance" so powerful as to make doubting impossible. To describe this state Descartes often alludes to the act of vision. "La connaissance intuitive," for example, "est une illustration de l'esprit, par laquelle il voit en la lumière de Dieu les choses qu'il lui plaît lui découvrir par une impression directe de la clarté divine sur notre entendement, qui en cela n'est point considéré comme agent, mais seulement comme recevant les rayons de la divinité."[40] The eye and other senses of the body, to Descartes, are notoriously unreliable; it is worthy of note that nevertheless he retains "le bon sens," and sometimes just "le sens," as a synonym of "la raison," as if satisfied with the implicit analogy to this extent, that insights, very much like sensory experiences, convey specific, direct, instantaneous impressions, impossible not to receive; insight has the quality of a flash, but perceived by the *good* or *right* sense ("le sens qui est *bon*"), all others being untrustworthy.[41]

[38]See R. Michéa, "Les Variations de la raison au XVIIe siècle. Essai sur la valeur du langage employé en histoire littéraire," *Revue Philosophique* 126 (1938): 183-201; René Bray, *La Formation de la doctrine classique en France* (1927).

[39]"De la praesumption," *Essais* (2: 17), ed. Plattard, 2: 85.

[40]In the letter believed to have been addressed to the Marquis of Newcastle in March or April of 1648, in *Oeuvres et lettres,* ed. André Bridou (Paris, 1952), p. 1300. See also in Gilson's monumental edition of the *Discours* (Paris, 1947) his notes on "le bon sens," intuition, innate ideas, and deduction. For Descartes' definition of certitude, see *Réponses au secondes objections,* in *Oeuvres,* ed. Adam-Tannery, 9: 113; also the introductory pages to the *Logique de Port-Royal* (1662) by Antoine Arnauld and Pierre Nicole.

[41]Cf. the parallel and distinction that Descartes draws between "nos sens intérieurs" and "nos sens extérieurs" in *Les Passions de l'âme,* art. 85.

One might say that Descartes' whole philosophical strategy was to extend intuition, against its nature. For intuition is a privileged moment. Moving from one such moment to another, and hence retaining the first intuition as but the recollection of an intuition, the mind no longer possesses it immediately or "clearly and distinctly," that is, no longer with absolute certitude. The need for memory's labor, and the limited quality of its light, created a major dilemma: "Comparez maintenant ces deux connaissances, et voyez s'il y a quelque chose de pareil, en cette perception trouble et douteuse, qui nous coûte beaucoup de travail et dont encore ne jouissons-nous que par moments après que nous l'avons acquise, à une lumière pure, constante, claire, certaine, sans peine, et toujours présente."[42] Yet the Cartesian method was intended to resolve the predicament by prolonging intuition, as it were, into a sustained deduction, a succession of intuitions kept as close or simultaneous as possible "par un mouvement continu et ininterrompu de la pensée."[43] Whether Descartes succeeded is hardly to be debated here. What draws our attention is the predicament as Descartes confronted it, and the role he set for method-deduction, in his endeavor to make reason-intuition enduring. His highest good was not the method (or means) but the enlightenment.

Something analogous is plainly discernible outside of the Cartesian system—and in other ages as well—for the primacy of live, quick sense has been a principle often formulated by man. It was a particularly widespread and persistent tenet of French thought from the humanists to the *philosophes*; these were not half so much awed by the "rules" as the romanticists who were to revolt against them, but they probed in earnest the relationship of method to inspiration; in times of great post-medieval expectations and inquiries, it was a way of inspecting the very nature and working of the mind, newly reoriented and turned upon itself, and of considering the paradox of the mind's power, discovered to be final because innate and yet requiring a sustaining discipline. Not only to Descartes was it a matter of intensifying the power, by means of and despite the labor.

The old idea of poetic furor was about. Montaigne described the "saillies poëtiques qui emportent leur autheur et le ravissent hors de soy," the orator's "mouvements et agitations extraordinaires," the painter's strokes "surpassans sa conception et sa science."[44] Eloquence and poetry, Descartes himself declared, are "des dons de

---

[42]Letter to the Marquis of Newcastle, *Oeuvres et lettres*, p. 1300.

[43]*Regula III* (ca. 1628), French translation by Georges Le Roy, in *Oeuvres et lettres*, p. 44. See also *Regula VII*.

[44]"Divers événemens de mesme conseil," *Essais* (1: 24), 1: 177.

l'esprit, plutôt que des fruits de l'étude," by which the gifted may excel without ever having known the rules of rhetoric and poetics.[45] But the fire of inspiration is as difficult to sustain as the light of intuition, and therein lies a whole classical aesthetic, parallel in its broad strategy to Cartesianism in philosophy; Pierre Nicole of Port-Royal, in his *Traité de la vraie et de la fausse beauté dans les ouvrages d'esprit*, sets it forth very simply: "Si on veut examiner de bien près la nature de l'esprit humain et rechercher avec soin les sources du plaisir, on trouvera que notre esprit a beaucoup de force jointe à une grande faiblesse . . . La force de notre esprit nous fait rebuter d'une trop longue inaction, et la faiblesse ne nous permet pas de l'avoir toujours tendu." Hence the great challenge is to create by art a lasting spell. That is beautiful which shows "de la convenance [fitness] avec sa propre nature, et avec la nôtre," that is, in which nothing will obstruct and all will induce and enhance our belief and response.[46] Concentration and continuity of effect become vastly important; loss or interruption of control on the artist's part and a break in attention, interest, or illusion on his public's part are the negation of art.

Jean-Baptiste Du Bos, an early aesthetician much better known for his comparative critique of poetry and painting, follows a similar psychological approach. In pages on *l'ennui* distantly reminiscent of Pascal, he postulates that one of man's most urgent needs is to have "l'esprit occupé"—seized, invaded, engrossed—and that the purpose of the arts, by which man escapes the torments of "l'inaction de l'âme," is to move and captivate. In artistic creation, what matters the most is "le génie," which is inborn and is like a heaven-given fire; "la régularité et les beautez de l'exécution" are not goals but means. So in appreciation: discussion and analysis can explain the causes of our feelings, but "le sentiment" alone tells us what we feel; it is a kind of *bon sens*, a "sixième sens" within us, which judges swiftly, as "le cœur s'agite de lui-même, et par un mouvement qui précède toute délibération. . . . Tous les hommes, à l'aide du sentiment intérieur qui est en eux, connaissent, sans savoir les règles, si les productions des arts sont de bons ou de mauvais ouvrages, et si le raisonnement qu'ils entendent, conclut bien."[47] Very

[45]*Discours*, p. 7.

[46]The original Latin text, *Dissertatio de vera pulchritudine et adumbrata*, served as preface to Claude Lancelot's *Epigrammatum delectus* (1659); the French translation by Richelet (1698) is quoted from Bruzen de La Martinière's *Nouveau recueil des épigrammatistes français anciens et modernes* (Paris, 1720), 2: 169–220.

[47]*Réflexions critiques sur la poésie et sur la peinture* (1740 ed.), 1, sec. 1, 2; 2, sec. 13 (2e Réflexion), 22, 23 (1st ed. 1719). Cf. Marcel Braunschvig, *L'Abbé Du Bos, rénovateur de la critique au XVIIIe siècle* (1904).

plainly, here, the aesthetic and intellectual experience become analogous at those high moments when the soul is instantaneously "occupée" and has a sense of complete rightness.

Charles Batteux, representative of a very wide realm of opinion in the eighteenth century, defines in *Les Beaux Arts réduits à un même principe* (1747) related zones of discernment, commingling the intellectual, moral, and aesthetic:

> l'intelligence: la faculté de connaître le vrai et le faux, et de les distinguer l'un de l'autre [i.e., *le bon sens*]; et le goût: la facilité de sentir le bon, le mauvais, le médiocre et de les distinguer avec certitude. . . . Notre âme connaît, et ce qu'elle connaît produit en elle un sentiment. La connaissance est une lumière répandue dans notre âme: le sentiment est un mouvement qui l'agite. L'une éclaire: l'autre échauffe. L'une nous fait voir l'objet: l'autre nous y porte, ou nous en détourne . . . on sent plus qu'on ne prouve.

The two operations go together; our "goût," itself instantaneous, is always preceded by "un éclair de lumière."[48]

Those who expressed their views on the nature of beauty and art were legion, and cannot all be passed here in review. They are well represented by those above. But one cannot overlook Racine's rule of rules, in the preface to *Bérénice*: "La principale règle est de plaire et de toucher. Toutes les autres ne sont faites que pour parvenir à cette première"; or Molière's, in *La Critique de l'Ecole des femmes* (sc. 6): "Laissons-nous aller de bonne foi aux choses qui nous prennent par les entrailles." Or Boudhors': "le bon goût est le premier mouvement ou, pour ainsi dire, une espèce d'instinct de la droite raison, qui l'entraîne avec rapidité, et qui la conduit plus sûrement que tous les raisonnements qu'elle pourrait faire."[49]

Boileau particularly would deserve a careful rereading. As he was writing *L'Art poétique* (1674) he was also preparing his translation of Longinus (1674), from whom he learned to define the sublime as "cet extraordinaire et ce merveilleux qui frappe dans le discours, et qui fait qu'un ouvrage enlève, ravit, transporte."[50] He criticized his

---

[48]Pp. 59–61. For an account of aesthetic ideas in the eighteenth century, see W. Folkierski, *Entre le classicisme et le romantisme* (1925); it shows, unfortunately, an astonishing unawareness of possible seventeenth-century sources; also André Fontaine, *Les Doctrines d'art en France; peintres, amateurs, critiques de Poussin à Diderot* (Paris, 1909); and Raymond Naves, *Le Goût de Voltaire* (Paris, 1938).

[49]*La Manière de bien penser dans les ouvrages d'esprit* (1743 ed.), pp. 466–67. Cf. Méré, "De la conversation," *Oeuvres complètes*, ed. Ch.-H. Boudhors (Paris, 1930), 2: 109: "Il y a deux sortes d'études; l'une qui ne cherche que l'art et les règles; l'autre qui n'y songe point du tout, et qui n'a pour but que de rencontrer par instinct et par réflexions, ce qui doit plaire en tous les sujets particuliers."

[50]Boileau's preface to the *Traité du Sublime*, ed. Ch.-H. Boudhors (Paris, 1942), p. 45. Cf. in ch. 5, p. 58, Boileau's translation of Longinus' own definition.

many victims for their lack of felicity and fire, and never, in fact, for disobeying any body of rules. One of his most crushing arguments was his recurrent caricature of the "sot" paralyzing his reader with drowsy, weary boredom. What he could not abide was a vacant mind, and a heavy hand. His "goût" was a "bon sens," and his rationale of art, which can be reconstructed, posited at the same time man's capacity for vital, absorbing, quickened experience, and his incapacity to keep this experience alive indefinitely; if the rules serve an important function, it is to help keep up "cet extraordinaire et ce merveilleux," or more exactly to prevent a break and disenchantment. As Valéry put it: "Les dieux, gracieusement, nous donnent *pour rien* tel premier vers; mais c'est à nous de façonner le second, qui doit consonner avec l'autre, et ne pas être indigne de son aîné surnaturel. Ce n'est pas trop de toutes les ressources de l'expérience et de l'esprit pour le rendre comparable au vers qui fut un don."[51]

This dread of vacuity, and this wish to communicate, or to "occupy" the human being, spreading far and wide, can be discerned in the dynamic thought of Diderot. Boileau—this rapprochement is perhaps not unthinkable—would have found much in the *philosophe's* aesthetic system within his grasp, and could have subscribed readily enough to his views on "vraisemblance," spontaneity and immediacy of response, unity, "le beau" blended with "le vrai" and "le bien," and technique as related to imagination and enthusiasm. He might have found elements of Diderot's materialism and transformism little to his taste, but in his definition of "le beau" as "tout ce qui contient en soi de quoi réveiller dans mon entendement l'idée de rapports," he would have heavily underlined "entendement," "rapports" (though to Diderot these were second-nature abstractions and not first-nature innate ideas), and particularly that "réveiller."[52]

When artists theorized, they echoed the men of letters. The master Nicolas Poussin declared of painting: "sa fin est la délectation." "Beauté," "grâce," "vivacité," "vraisemblance," "jugement," and other elements of the art, he asserted more than once, are "parties . . .

[51]"Au Sujet d'Adonis," *Variété II, Oeuvres,* ed. Jean Hytier (Paris, 1965), 1: 482. For a fresh view of Boileau the critic, see especially Jules Brody, *Boileau and Longinus* (Geneva, 1958), and E. B. O. Borgerhoff, *The Freedom of French Classicism* (Princeton, N.J., 1950), pp. 200-212.

[52]*Traité du beau, Oeuvres complètes,* ed. André Billy (Paris, 1946), p. 1126. On Diderot's aesthetics, see Yvon Belaval, *L'Esthétique sans paradoxe de Diderot* (Paris, 1950); Folkierski, *Entre le classicisme et le romantisme*; Albert Dresdner, *Die Entstehung der Kunstkritik im Zusammenhang der Geschichte des europäischen Kunstlebens* (1915), pp. 235-84. For Diderot's views on genius and imagination, see H. Dieckmann, "Diderot's Conception of Genius," *Journal of the History of Ideas* 2 (1941): 151-82; O. E. Fellows, "The Theme of Genius in Diderot's *Neveu de Rameau*" and M. Gilman, "Imagination and Creation in Diderot," *Diderot Studies II* (Syracuse, N.Y., 1952), pp. 168-99, 200-220.

du peintre et ne se peuvent apprendre." Like the poet's power, by which it seems "qu'il mette devant les yeux avec le son des paroles les choses desquelles il traite," the artist's kind of strength, by which "la chose se conserve en son être," is a "puissance d'induire l'âme des regardants à diverses passions."[53]

To the academician André Félibien, rules and the past experience of the masters have their utility, but "le génie," the primary quality in a painter, cannot be acquired by study; it comes with "la lumière de la raison," and may at times have to go counter to the established rules. In an architect, he prizes "la force de son imagination," a "saillie ou . . . promptitude d'esprit." His idea of "le grand goût" is "un usage des effets de la nature bien choisis, grands, extraor-dinaires et vrai-semblables"—"grands" because we are insensitive to the small, "extraordinaires" because the ordinary "ne touche pas" and "n'attire pas l'attention," "vrai-semblables" because disbelief would create an interference.[54] "Séduire nos yeux," would say the amateur and critic Roger de Piles, author of various works on paint-ing; indeed, "tromper les yeux," for the ultimate purpose of convey-ing a more complete impression of reality. And so on from school to school.[55]

To the builders, Vitruvius had handed down in the first chapter of *De architectura* a sketch of the perfect architect: "eum etiam in-geniosum oportet esse et ad disciplinam [instruction] docilem. Neque enim ingenium [talent] sine disciplina aut disciplina sine ingenio perfectum artificem potest efficere." A sixteenth-century French translator, Jean Martin, interprets "ingeniosum" as "de bon entende-ment" or "bon iugement,"[56] which reminds one of Montaigne's "sens;" in the heyday of French classicism, Claude Perrault translated the passage in this rather free but revealing manner: "il faut qu'il soit ingénieux et laborieux tout ensemble; car l'esprit sans le travail, ny le travail sans l'esprit, ne rendirent jamais aucun ouvrier parfait."[57]

Jean Martin also translated Leone Battista Alberti's *De re aedificatoria*, which afforded a much more explicit theory of the beautiful, based, as so many others later, on the swift, irresistible

---

[53]Letters of Nov. 24, 1647, and Mar. 1, 1665, in *Correspondance*, ed. Ch. Jouanny, 5: 370–75, 461–66.

[54]*Entretiens sur les vies et sur les ouvrages des plus excellents peintres anciens et modernes* (1685 ed.), preface, entretien 1, and passim; *Conférences de l'Académie Royale de peinture et de sculpture* (1706 ed.), pp. 9, 130–31.

[55]On Roger de Piles and those who followed, see Fontaine, *Les Doctrines d'art*, ch. 5 and passim. The whole work is useful, but the charges of academicism leveled against Charles Le Brun seem rather excessive.

[56]*Architecture* (1547), p. 1.

[57]Vitruvius, *Les dix livres d'architecture de Vitruve* (1673), p. 2.

action of "une bonne raison née avec la personne," an "instinct de nature": "car certainement en toutes formes d'édifices il y a quelque chose de naturel, excellent et parfait, qui émeut le courage [soul] incontinent que l'on vient à la voir, et croit qu'en ce point-là consistent la majesté, et la beauté, avec leurs semblables: dont si on ôte une part, ou qu'on la diminue, ou change, soudain tout se corrompt, et en perd la grâce." There is "quelque je ne sais quoi," a "correspondance" of form, position, and number, "un accord, ou une certaine conspiration (s'il faut ainsi parler) des parties en la totalité" by which, as soon as it is perceived, "l'on voit entièrement reluire la face de cette beauté."[58]

Two centuries later, the Jesuit architect Marc-Antoine Laugier is still trying to express the same thing, in terms of "un enchantement dont on n'est pas maître de se défendre," a "transport," a sight stirring the soul.[59] The teacher-architect Jacques-François Blondel is still seeking a definition of "la sublimité de l'Architecture," in terms that echo Boileau's understanding of the sublime according to Longinus:

> il faut songer que l'esprit méthodique, la méditation, le flegme, peuvent produire un bon architecte, et que le génie, l'âme, l'enthousiasme, élèvent seuls l'artiste au sublime; que l'esprit définit, que le sentiment peint, et que celui-ci donne la vie à toutes les productions. En un mot, il serait à désirer qu'un édifice puisse, à son aspect, entraîner, émouvoir, et pour ainsi dire, élever l'âme du spectateur, en le portant à une admiration contemplative, dont il ne pourrait lui-même se rendre compte au premier coup d'œil, quoique suffisamment instruit des connaissances profondes de l'art.[60]

This sampling, though scattered, should suffice for the present purpose. A thorough survey could show that many difficult questions were raised around the concept of *goût-sens-raison*: if *le goût* is innate, can it be granted that any private taste is absolutely valid? What is the relation of *l'usage* to *le goût*: can *le goût* be improved? The answers varied, but what is important in explaining the anti-Gothic position is that in all factions the operation of taste was conceived as a spontaneous psychological act. The theory hardly wavered here, and was generally upheld in practice.[61] No itemized account of

---

[58]*L'Architecture et art de bien bâtir* (1553), fol. 191.

[59]*Essai sur l'architecture* (1753), pp. 2–3.

[60]*Cours d'architecture . . . contenant les leçons données en 1750* (Paris, 1771-77), vol. 1 (1771), ch. 4.

[61]Naves, *Le Goût de Voltaire*, ch. 1, argues that Houdart de La Motte and others at the beginning of the eighteenth century whom he calls "géomètres" substituted method for inspiration, and that Reason in their thinking killed Poetry. This has often

rules broken by medieval architects was drawn up. The primary charge concerned proportion, but this was taken to be essentially a matter of *goût*; those who had failed to strike the right "correspondances" offended an inner sense of fitness. Fénelon and the others used terms that to them expressed not dogma but forceful feeling that compelled acquiescence.

One important characteristic of instantaneous perception as then understood was its wholeness and singleness. Descartes' "idées claires" were absolutely "distinctes," unmixed, unblurred. In aesthetic feeling this becomes an urgent need for oneness, concentration, and density of effect—hence the famous unities. Hence, in architecture, a reaction against any manner based on what seemed, rightly or wrongly, to be but profusion and dispersal of effects. Crousaz, in his *Traité du beau* (1715), explained the weakness of obtrusive ornamentation in these psychological terms:

> l'esprit humain aime ce qui le fixe et ce qui s'empare de son attention, sans qu'il ait besoin de faire d'efforts pour la lui donner. . . ; les colifichets gothiques sont tombés dès que le goût est devenu meilleur; on a pré- féré une simplicité dans les parties, qui laissât voir d'abord [immediately] les proportions qu'elles ont les unes avec les autres, à une infinité de petits ornemens et d'enjolivemens qui amusaient, qui détournaient l'attention du principal, et qui, dans leurs variétés, ne présentoient pas assez à l'esprit ces vérités et ces convenances qu'il aime, soit dans les parties comparées les unes aux autres, soit dans le rapport de tout leur assemblage avec un but commun.[62]

In a similar spirit, Boileau had objected to "le clinquant du Tasse." But it becomes apparent that Crousaz, Fénelon, and the others, who did not cite examples of the frills and curlicues unpleasant to their taste, were thinking especially of the flamboyant and northern Italian styles.

Like overabundant ornamentation, excessive mass went counter to moderation, which was not felt as a repressive force but as a flair for the exquisite point of rightness that lies away from disconcerting ex-

---

been repeated, but the thesis ought to be reexamined. Though usually painstaking, Naves on this subject tends to let the terminology of reason merge unwarrantedly with that of rules and regularity; he does not clearly separate reactions to the artificiality of verse from comments on poetry. The presentation is not convincing. On the possibility of drawing Cartesianism and classicism together, see Brunetière, "Descartes et la littérature classique," *Etudes critiques sur l'histoire de la littérature française*, 3d ser. (Paris, 1887), pp. 1-28, and Gustave Lanson, "L'Influence de la philosophie cartésienne sur la littérature française," *Revue de Métaphysique et de Morale* (1896): 517-50; both these studies have pronounced negative judgments, still prevalent, which seriously require revision.

[62]Amsterdam ed. of 1724, 1: 23, 29.

tremes. "Il y a dans l'art un point de perfection, comme de bonté ou de maturité dans la nature. Celui qui le sent et qui l'aime a le goût parfait."[63] In his *Dissertation sur le mot "Vaste"* (1685), one of the most illuminating essays on the subject, Saint-Evremond draws a distinction between "le grand," a perfection, and "le vaste," an excess and therefore a vice. "Le vaste" is wild, unbounded, frightening, and goes beyond what can be satisfying to a human being: "la vue se dissipe et se perd à regarder de *vastes campagnes*."[64] So, for a Fénelon or a Louis Racine, did the daring, astounding vastness of Gothic cathedrals seem abusive.

The certitude that "il y a dans l'art un point de perfection" resulted in an attitude of complete assurance, in its true nature removed from pedantry or formalism. Escaping the latter, it yet tended at times toward a spirit of absolutism in judgment which, impatient of explanations, baldly rested the case against the Gothic in the cliché *gothique*.

But the cliché did not remain entirely set. With time, attempts were made to rectify it. The dates of Gothic structures are often cited, more or less accurately, and one often senses that as a consequence the term has ceased to be taken literally; it is even denied at times that the Gothic invasions were first responsible for the "decline" of art; signs of earlier "degeneration" are detected in the Roman Empire itself.[65] André Félibien, learned historiographer of the Academy of Painting and secretary of the Academy of Architecture, introduces a first touch of the historical approach: as a stronger monarchy brought greater security to the land, he suggests, kings and great lords began to build their castles less crudely than they had done before for purposes of warfare, and gave greater heed to pleasure;[66] in other words, a development had occurred, and Gothic art had not all been of a mass.

André's son, Jean-François Félibien, setting a pattern which already roughly suggests our Romanesque-Gothic sequence, divides

---

[63]La Bruyère, "Des ouvrages de l'esprit," par. 10.

[64]*Oeuvres en prose*, ed. R. Ternois (Paris, 1966), 3: 380.

[65]Pierre Monnier, *Histoire des arts qui ont rapport au dessein* (Paris, 1678), preface and pp. 32ff.; Du Bois, *Quatre livres*, 2: 192–93. Cf. an unsigned letter-article, "Sur les temples du christianisme," in the Trévoux *Mémoires pour l'histoire des sciences et beaux-arts* 1 (1759): 2045–59, which argues that the Goths did not create Gothic architecture; also the Abbé Drouet de Maupertuis' "Discours sur l'histoire des Goths" in his translation of Jordanis, *Histoire générale des Goths* (Paris, 1703), p. xviii, where he argues that the Goths progressed in time. On rare occasions, one is reminded that the term Gothic does carry a literal meaning, as in Jean Scholastique Pitton, *Annales de la S. Eglise d'Aix* (Paris, 1668), p. xxxvi: "d'une architecture Gottique, . . . par conséquent du temps des Gots."

[66]*Mémoires pour servir à l'histoire des maisons royalles* (Paris, 1681), pp. 7–8.

medieval architecture into two stages, running from the fifth to the eleventh century and then from the eleventh to the fourteenth: "deux sortes de bastiments Gothiques, savoir d'anciens et de modernes. Les plus anciens n'ont rien de recommandable que leur solidité et leur grandeur. Pour les modernes, ils sont d'un goût si opposé . . . qu'on peut dire que ceux qui les ont faits, ont passé dans un aussi grand excès de délicatesse, que les autres avaient fait dans une extrême pesanteur et grossièreté, particulièrement en ce qui regarde les ornements." Now the idea of development is stressed. The period of heaviness and crudeness is itself seen not as one unbroken stretch but as an era rising to peaks of its own, particularly in the days of Dagobert, who first built the abbey of Saint Denis, of Charlemagne, and of the Lombards in Italy. Arab architecture is also brought into the general picture.[67]

This amplified theory of the Gothic became, as it were, official. The Jesuits of Trévoux, the artist, archaeologist, and collector Florent Le Comte, the architects Jacques-François Blondel and Pierre Patte, Père Marc-Antoine Laugier, Louis Avril (known as l'abbé Mai), the historian Pierre-Adam Origny, and the artist and art historian Antoine Nicolas Dézallier d'Argenville all restated it, with variations. The first period might begin now in the fourth, now in the sixth century, and end in the twelfth, or as early as the ninth. The second period might last till the fifteenth or sixteenth century. The Byzantine style is also singled out, and detected in the San Marco of Venice, but as another heavy, unattractive form of art, an old "manière grecque non antique," as the painter Monnier called it, or a mixture of "goût antique" and "goût arabesque," according to Le Comte. In time, a Blondel could come to define even the first Gothic period more favorably, asserting that architects of that time had not been ignorant of proportions but had bent all their efforts toward attaining solidity and durability, and an "air de merveilleux" by means of mass rather than elegance; the "Gothique ancienne," according to him, kept some features of "la belle architecture"—a glimpse of the relationship of Romanesque to Roman. But this first period, almost unanimously labeled heavy and coarse, seems gradually to become the chief target in the case against Gothicism, and to release the second period. In the "Gothique moderne" it becomes easier to see boldness, or delicacy and lightness, not as excesses but as qualities. The theory of Arab origins, now and then proposed, seems for

---

[67]*Recueil historique de la vie et des ouvrages des plus célèbres architectes* (Paris, 1690), preface and pp. 143ff., 187ff. (1st ed., 1687). There is the suggestion of a distinction between Gothic and Romanesque in F.-N.-B. Dubuisson-Aubenay's *Itinéraire de Bretagne en 1636*, probably drawn up around 1650; see the Maître and Berthou ed. (Paris, 1898–1902), 1: xxi, 2: 37–39 and notes.

Blondel a way of explaining or excusing the excesses he does find in the second period, and on the contrary, in Laugier's case, a way of accounting in part for what is wondrous in the same period.[68]

On reading a succession of such definitions one has the impression of watching the strategic retreat of a cliché. *Gothique*, to remain a usable term, has to give ground, and must even come to express a favorable view, by ceasing to mean literally *of or by the barbarous Goths*. This permits Du Bos, though to him the Gothic as ornamental style is but of middling interest, to concede there was a "bon Gothique." And still at the very end of the eighteenth century, this mechanism is evident in the thinking of the historian Pierre-Charles Lévesque, who continued the work of Watelet's *Dictionnaire des arts*, who feels that the Goths themselves, not out of depraved taste but as a result of childlike ignorance, had indeed corrupted painting and sculpture, introducing raw tones, flat colors, stiff and lean forms without animation, but that the very opposite, apparently, happened in architecture: "Ce qu'on appelle l'architecture *gothique* avoit ses grâces; mais elle n'appartenoit pas aux Goths"! Its originators were surely the Saracens.[69]

The simple but capital discovery that there had been a succession of styles in the Middle Ages made it also possible to differentiate and choose. Some could see only a mixture or variety of styles, and not a sequence. Thus, rejecting all notions of progress in time, an anonymous correspondent of the Jesuits of Trévoux found that of two cathedrals built in the same period Notre Dame of Rouen (1202-1220) "est une masse énorme" and Sainte-Etienne of Bourges (1190-1275) "ne pèse point sur la terre"; to his taste Luzarches, architect of Notre Dame of Amiens (1220-1288), "avait plus de légèreté dans l'esprit" than can be seen, not long before, in the planning of Notre Dame of Paris (1163-1235).[70] But generally the tendency in the eighteenth century was to separate the two manners

[68]On all these points see Monnier, *Histoire des arts*, pp. 101, 128, n. 4; the *Dictionnaire de Trévoux*, new ed., 1771 (1st ed., 1704), 4: 562; Florent Le Comte, *Cabinet des singularitez d'architecture . . .* (Paris, 1699-1700), 1, preface; Furetière, *Dictionnaire universel* (1727 ed.), s.v. "Gothique"; Jacques-François Blondel, *Architecture françoise*, 1: 12ff.; Blondel and Patte, *Cours d'architecture*, 6: 206-9; Laugier, *Essai sur l'architecture* (1755), pp. viii-ix; *Encyclopédie*, s.v. "Gothique;" Louis Avril, *Temples, anciens et modernes* (1774), pp. 133ff.; Pierre-Adam Origny, *Dictionnaire des origines, découvertes, inventions et établissements* (1777), 1: 200ff., 2: 246; Dézallier d'Argenville, *Vies des fameux architectes, depuis la renaissance des arts, avec la description de leurs ouvrages* (1787), pp. xxviii-xxxviii. Also Fénelon, *Dialogues sur l'éloquence*, p. 76, for the theory of Arab origins.

[69]Du Bois, *Quatre livres*, 2: 198; Charles-Henri Watelet and Pierre-Charles Lévesque, *Dictionnaire des arts de peinture, sculpture et gravure* (1792), s.v. "Gothique."

[70]*Mémoires pour l'histoire des sciences et beaux-arts* 1 (1759): 2056-58. Cf. Avril, *Temples*, p. 143, who reproduces this passage verbatim.

chronologically, and to praise what we still call the Gothic while remaining severe for an "earlier" Gothic. Le Comte, for instance, feels free to praise "les superbes édifices" that still bear witness to the piety and splendor of French kings and dignitaries of old and, in the course of a century-by-century account, to recognize the "magnificence" of Notre Dame de Chartres and record the work of medieval architects like Robert de Luzarches, Thomas de Cormont, Hugues Libergier, Jean de Chelles, Pierre de Montereau, Eudes de Montreuil, Robert de Coucy, and Jean Ravy. He marvels at the solidity of the old structures.[71] The painter Pierre Monnier, an academician and in many ways a conservative champion of Le Brun's teachings, follows the newer approach in denying that the Goths started the Gothic and in trying to catch a glimpse of factors responsible for its rise. But in 1698 he has not yet learned to split his "Gotique" in two, and the term covers vaguely all that was medieval, from the fifth century on; his long discourse is chronologically blurred, or even incorrect. Yet he too seems to have yielded somewhat to the pull of the later centuries and, although severe for all medieval styles, he can say about Notre Dame de Paris, despite its "mauvaise manière": "Toute la beauté de cette Eglise consiste en une vaste grandeur et un beau plan, en d'extraordinaires roses vitrales, et d'ingénieuses coupes de pierres, et pour faire des membres délicats d'architecture, qui pourtant soutiennent de gros poids"; or about the Duomo of Florence: "la magnifique Eglise de sainte Marie Delfiore."[72] J.-F. Félibien, and some of the others, went even further in paying tribute to the Gothic.

But here we are looking ahead, beyond the boundaries of the hostile camp. These concessions intimate that the feeling of opposition to the term *gothique* itself failed to gain ascendancy, and yielded to pressures of opinion from other areas.

[71]*Cabinet*, preface, and 1: 183ff., 160ff.
[72]*Histoire des arts*, pp. 142-47.

The Mixed Metaphor
in Descartes

FOR DESCARTES, the "certitude" was all: a "croyance" or "persuasion si ferme, qu'elle ne puisse estre ostée." That was the crucial commitment. It was not solely a methodological requisite but a deep, absolute personal requirement. He needed to receive, immediately and irresistibly, a "connoissance intuitive," "une lumiere pure, constante, claire, certaine, sans peine, et tousiours presente," "une illustration de l'esprit . . . en la lumiere de Dieu . . . par une impression directe de la clairté divine sur nostre entendement."[1] Aspiring to this mode of contentment—to angelism, as Maritain would describe it—Descartes, it is often presumed, did powerfully achieve within himself a sense of utmost assurance. He seems to have set aside, in confident, assertive fashion, all critiques of his philosophy. But "que peut un homme?" In the privacy of his mind, the question of "certitude," immanent and irreducible, remained in suspense. There, it turned into a psychological rather than a philosophical predicament: to cleave to certainty, to maintain oneself and to dwell in that state of mind.

Many ways of probing Descartes' experience are possible. Few, perhaps, would be more enlightening than a study of his habits of style. An analysis of his complex sentence or of his shifting use of *donc* and *car*, for example, would be revealing. More directly, here, a

Originally published in *Romanic Review* 41 (1950): 167-78.

[1]Letter of March (or April) 1648 (to the Marquis of Newcastle?), in *Oeuvres*, ed. Charles Adam and Paul Tannery, 5: 136, 137. This edition will henceforth be cited as *AT*, and the Adam and Milhaud edition of Descartes' *Correspondence* as *AM*.

form of Cartesian metaphorical language will lay open, I believe, an intimate region of the philosopher's mind.

In general, Descartes, who was sensitive to poetry, used figurative language soberly but willingly.[2] His metaphors and similes are numerous enough to attract attention. Many of his comparisons are elaborately balanced, and rounded out in Homeric style. Drawing material from a variety of sources, including the arts, warfare, nature, and dreams, they serve mostly to describe analogically Descartes' method, to illustrate an argument, or simply to highlight a passing comment. Although introduced with simplicity and fitness, and occasionally with impressive ingenuity, those images on the whole retain an obvious and conventional character.

But out of this collection, two images emerge, fraught with significance, and bearing directly on "certitude." One portrays the philosopher-traveler: "ceux qui ne marchent que fort lentement, peuvent avancer beaucoup davantage, s'ils suivent tousiours le droit chemin, que ne font ceux qui courent, et qui s'en esloignent;"[3] and the other a philosopher-architect:

> je tâchois partout d'imiter les architectes, qui, pour élever de grands édifices aux lieux où le roc, l'argile, et la terre ferme est couverte de sable et de gravier, creusent premièrement de profondes fosses, et rejettent de là non seulement le gravier, mais tout ce qui se trouve appuyé sur lui, ou qui est mêlé ou confondu ensemble, afin de poser par après leurs fondements sur . . . la terre ferme: . . . de la même façon j'ai premièrement rejeté comme du sable et du gravier tout ce que j'ai reconnu être douteux et incertain.[4]

These images are not sensational flights of the imagination. But it is precisely because they are rather unoriginal, and yet are used incessantly by Descartes, with equal readiness in French and in Latin, like forms of expression indispensable to him, that they assume uncommon significance. These two figures alone occur frequently; they

---

[2]This point still remains to be studied. But see Hartwig Tornau, *Syntaktische und stilistische Studien über Descartes* (Leipzig, 1900), pp. 66–91; Petit de Julleville, *Histoire de la langue et de la littérature françaises* (1897), 4: 521–23; Foucher de Careil, *Oeuvres inédites de Descartes* (Paris, 1859), pp. cvi–cxi; William McC. Stewart, "Descartes and Poetry," *Romanic Review* 29 (1938): 212–42; Marcel De Corte, "La Dialectique poétique de Descartes," *Archives de Philosophie*, cahier II, 1937, 13: 101–61.

[3]*Discours de la méthode, AT*, 6: 2.

[4]*Objectiones septimae in Meditationes de prima philosophia cum Notis authoris*, 1642: cf. *AT*, 7: 536–37. I quote the French translation in Victor Cousin's *Oeuvres de Descartes*, 1824–26, 2: 506. Here, and every time a Latin work of Descartes is quoted from a French translation (whether or not authorized by Descartes), I have checked the French against the original.

require more space than all the other images together. Of the latter, very few appear more than once or twice, or in more than one work. The architect and the traveler haunt Descartes throughout his career, in his juvenilia, in his letters, in the *Règles pour la direction de l'esprit*, *La Recherche de la vérité*, the *Discours*, the *Méditations*, the *Principes de la philosophie*; and the traveler, at the very end, reappears in *Les Passions de l'âme:* In the *Discours* alone, the architect is seen some ten times, digging, destroying, or building, and the traveler fifteen times, groping for or discovering "le droit chemin." But that is not all. These two figures of speech are like poles of Cartesian style around which gravitate myriads of related expressions. Words like *recherche, voie, chemin, route, progrès; voyager, chercher, rencontrer, découvrir, trouver; suivre, conduire; tomber, fuir, s'éloigner, s'écarter; avancer, approcher, passer par degrés, passer plus outre, parvenir, venir à bout*—and words like *fondements; ferme, solide; renverser, ébranler, bâtir, fonder, affermir, appuyer, élever* —betray a constant mental image of the builder-traveler. Scarcely any of these words, taken separately, would normally be considered a metaphorical expression; each, of course, is in current usage. But here they recur together so persistently, again both in Latin and French, that, along with the true figures of speech of which they are unmistakable echoes, they grow into a language with a ring all its own. Small wonder that after many readings of Descartes, scholars of successive generations, unconsciously no doubt, have made it a practice forever to reconstruct the Cartesian edifice, as they put it, and to retrace, each in turn, the journey—the road—the itinerary of Descartes!

Why such habits of style rather than others? Because Descartes, in fact, did travel a great deal? Or because, very early, in the Netherlands, he studied military architecture? But he studied drawing at the same time. He studied music, and looked into many sciences. He had intimate knowledge of military life. His career was full of important experiences none of which is very markedly reflected in his style. Why, out of all these experiences and out of the stock of traditional images, did the mind of Descartes fasten upon the figures of the traveler and the architect?

They both appear to symbolize, in identical fashion, Descartes' method. His traveler is one who follows but one road, the only "droit chemin" ("rectum iter") which step by step will lead to the ultimate goal, "un chemin qui nous conduira" to a knowledge of all things.[5]

---

[5]Cf. *Regulae ad directionem ingenii* (ca. 1628?), ed. Georges Le Roy (Paris, 1932), pp. 12, 13, 14, 15; *Discours, AT,* 6: 2, 3, 63; *La Dioptrique, AT,* 6: 81; *Méditations, AT,* 9: 42 (Latin text, 7: 53).

The initial methodological doubt is "une eau profonde. . . . J'avoue qu'il y auroit du danger, pour ceux qui ne connoissent pas le gué, de s'y hasarder sans conduite, et que plusieurs s'y sont perdus"; at first, "comme si tout à coup i'estois tombé dans une eau tres-profonde, ie suis tellement surpris, que ie ne puis ny asseurer mes pieds dans le fond, ny nager pour me soutenir au dessus."[6] Nevertheless "ie continuëray tousiours dans ce chemin, iusqu'à ce que i'aye rencontré quelque chose de certain." Some "voyageurs, . . . ayant laissé le grand chemin pour prendre la traverse, demeurent égarés entre des espines et des precipices";[7] for example, certain early theologians who reasoned poorly "s'estoyent détournez du droit chemin, ainsi que font les voyageurs quand quelque sentier les a conduits à des lieux pleins d'épines et inaccessibles."[8] Often, some blindly "per ignotas vias deducant ingenia (conduisent leur esprit par des voies inconnues)" and grope aimlessly about; "nihil prius a recta quaerendae veritatis via nos abducit, quam si non ad hunc finem generalem, sed ad aliquos particulares studia dirigamus (rien ne nous éloigne plus du droit chemin pour la recherche de la vérité, que d'orienter nos études, non vers cette fin générale, mais vers des buts particuliers)."[9] To be sure, "mon esprit" also "se plaist de s'égarer. . . . Relachons-luy donc . . . la bride, afin que, venant cy-apres à la retirer doucement et à propos, nous le puissions plus facilement regler et conduire."[10] I shall go on questioning all my beliefs until I have so trained my judgment that it may never be "détourné du droit chemin qui le peut conduire à la connoissance de la verité. Car ie suis assuré que cependant il ne peut y avoir de peril ny d'erreur en cette voye."[11] To move along other routes, however arduously and swiftly, is futile:

> tout de mesme qu'en voyageant, pendant qu'on tourne le dos au lieu où l'on veut aller, on s'en éloigne d'autant plus qu'on marche plus longtemps et plus viste, en sorte que, bien qu'on soit mis par après dans le

---

[6]*La Recherche de la vérité*, *AT*, 10: 512 (I follow G. Cantecor, who dates this work between 1620 and 1628); *Méditations*, *AT*, 9: 18 (Latin text, 7: 24). Using the same image somewhat differently, Descartes explained that, holding back his "Traité de Physique," he proposed "de lui préparer le chemin, et sonder le gué" by first putting out his *Discours* and three appended *Traités*: cf. his letter (to the Abbé de Cerisy?), end of May 1637, *AM*, 1: 356. He would also "sonder" a cardinal on the subject of the earth's motion: letter to Mersenne, December 1640, *AT*, 3: 258.

[7]*La Recherche de la vérité*, *AT*, 10: 497.

[8]*Responsio ad quartas objectiones*, *AT*, 7: 253; French text, 9: 195.

[9]*Regulae* IV and I, pp. 26, 28, 4, 5. French translation by Georges Le Roy.

[10]*Méditations*, *AT*, 9: 23 (Latin text, 7: 29–30).

[11]*Ibid.*, 9: 17 (Latin Text, 7: 22).

droit chemin, on ne peut pas arriver sitost que si on n'avoit point marché auparavant; ainsi, lors qu'on a de mauvais Principes, d'autant qu'on les cultive davantage, et qu'on s'applique avec plus de soin à en tirer diverses consequences. . . . d'autant s'éloigne-t'on davantage de la connoissance de la verité et de la Sagesse.[12]

It is a slow road; "comme un homme qui marche seul et dans les tenebres, ie me resolus d'aller si lentement, et d'user de tant de circonspection en toutes choses, que, si ie n'avançois que fort peu, ie me garderois bien, au moins, de tomber."[13]

These samples, drawn from various French and Latin works, are typical of the whole collection.[14] The "morale provisoire" does warn us that the traveler who hesitates is lost; Descartes, in his actions, would be as resolute as possible,

imitant en cecy les voyasgeurs qui, se trouvant esgarez en quelque forest, ne doivent pas errer en tournoyant, tantost d'un costé, tantost d'un autre, ny encore moins s'arester en une place, mais marcher tousiours le plus droit qu'ils peuvent vers un mesme costé, . . . car, par ce moyen, s'ils ne vont justement où ils desirent, ils arriveront au moins à la fin quelque part, où vraysemblablement ils seront mieux que dans le milieu d'une forest.

Yet the same practical wisdom prompts him to choose, from among several accepted opinions, only the most moderate, "affin de me détourner moins du vray chemin, en cas que ie faillisse, que si, ayant choisi l'un des extremes, ç'eust esté l'autre qu'il eust fallu suivre."[15]

Descartes would travel a true, straight, unerring, safe road.

[12]*Les Principes de la philosophie*, "Lettre de l'autheur à celuy qui a traduit le livre" (1647), *AT*, 9: 8-9.

[13]*Discours*, *AT*, 6: 2, 16-17.

[14]Besides other samples given below, cf. Descartes' *Correspondance*, *AM*, 1: 421; letters to Mersenne (Dec. 24, 1640?), to Princess Elizabeth (Nov. 1643, Aug. 18, 1645, Jan. 12, 1646), to the Marquis of Newcastle(?) (March or April 1648: "vous vous détournez du droit chemin"): *AT*, 3: 266; 4: 46, 272, 357; 5: 136, 137. Cf. *Regulae*, pp. 22, 23, 28, 29, 60, 61, 74, 75, 90, 91; *Recherche*, *AT*, 10: 497; *Discours*, *AT*, 6: 3 (ll. 4-5, 19-20), 4, 8, 9, 10, 14, 19, 28, 59, 63 (ll. 15-17), 71-72; *Méditations*, *AT*, 9: 50 (Latin text, 7: 63), 59; *Responsio ad secundas objectiones*, *AT*, 7: 133 (French text, 9: 105); *Principes*, "Lettre de l'autheur," *AT*, 9: 13-14, 15, 17, 18-19, 20; also, *Principia*, *AT*, 8: 5, 14 (*Principes*, *AT*, 9: 26, 35); *Lettre apologétique aux Magistrats d'Utrecht*, *AT*, 8: 223. Attention has seldom been drawn, and then but cursorily, to the traveler-image in Descartes: cf. Petit de Julleville, *Histoire*, p. 522; Tornau, *Syntaktische*; Henri Gouhier, *Essais sur Descartes* (Paris, 1937), p. 205. For uses of the traveler-image that Descartes could have seen in Seneca and in Francis Bacon, cf. E. Gilson's edition of the *Discours, texte et commentaire* (Paris, 1947) (1st ed. 1925), pp. 84-85; A. Lalande, "Quelques textes de Bacon et de Descartes," *Revue de Métaphysique et de Morale* 19 (1911): 297.

[15]*Discours*, *AT*, 6: 23-25.

And—he often adds with a touch of pride—he would travel it alone. It is the untrodden way of "un homme qui marche seul." On the subject of "les passions de l'âme," "ce que les Anciens en ont enseigné est si peu de chose, . . . que je ne puis avoir aucune espérance d'approcher de la verité, qu'en m'éloignant des chemins qu'ils ont suivis."[16] "Viamque sequor ad eas explicandas tam parum tritam, atque ab usu communi tam remotam," he declares in the preface to the *Meditationes,* "ut non utile putarim ipsam in gallico . . . docere, ne debiliora etiam ingenia credere possent eam sibi esse ingrediendam."[17] There are those who should not take to doubting accepted principles: "s'ils avoient une fois pris la liberté de . . . s'escarter du chemin commun, iamais ils ne pourroient tenir le sentier qu'il faut prendre pour aller plus droit, et demeureroient esgarez toute leur vie."[18] But this version of the traveler-image varies greatly. Good-humoredly poking fun at Ismael Bouillaud, Descartes admits him among those who, trying "des routes nouvelles," have at least the merit of moving off the main highway, "qui ne conduit nulle part et qui ne sert qu'à fatiguer et égarer ceux qui le suivent." In a less indulgent mood, he says well-nigh the opposite: "ceux qui s'égarent en affectant de passer par des chemins extraordinaires, me semblent bien moins excusables que ceux qui ne faillent qu'en compagnie et en suivant les traces de beaucoup d'autres."[19] Now he seems to despise the easy, short, but misleading road of others; then, to stress the simplicity of his own method, he compares it to "planas tantum et faciles vias," to "un chemin plus facile," "plus court."[20]

His references to philosophical method turn as automatically into images of digging and construction. "Toute la connoissance acquise jusques à present," he early learns to say, is like

quelque maison mal bastie, de qui les fondemens ne sont pas assurés. Je ne sçay point de meilleur moyen pour y remedier, que de la jetter toute

[16]*Les Passions de l'âme, AT,* 11: 327-28. Cf. *Responsio authoris ad primas objectiones,* 7: 106 (French text, 9: 84), on Descartes' not following the same road as Aristotle and St. Thomas.

[17]*AT,* 7: 7. "Son dessein étoit de frayer un chemin tout nouveau," says Adrien Baillet (*La Vie de Monsieur Des-Cartes,* 1691: cf. *AT,* 10: 190), reporting on the *Studium bonae mentis* (a lost fragment which, according to *AT,* 10: 176-77, Descartes may have written between 1619 and 1621, or in 1627-1628); this sentence may be an echo or translation of Descartes' words.

[18]*Discours, AT,* 6: 15.

[19]In two letters to Constantin Huygens (March 9, and March or April 1638), *AM,* 2: 167, 171.

[20]Cf. *Recherche, AT,* 10: 498; *Regulae,* pp. 4, 5; letters to Mersenne (Jan. 1638; May 3, 1638; Oct. 11, 1638), *AM,* 2: 74, 251-52, and 3: 84; letter to Elizabeth (Nov. 1643), *AT,* 4: 38, 40; "Synopsis" at head of *Meditationes, AT,* 7: 12 (French text, 9: 9); *Epistola ad P. Dinet* (1642), *AT,* 7: 579.

par terre, et d'en bastir une nouvelle; . . . pendant que nous travaillerons à cette demolition, nous pourrons, par mesme moyen, creuser les fondemens qui doivent servir à nostre dessein, et preparer les meilleures et plus solides matieres, qui sont necessaires pour les remplir.[21]

The sensualists have built on sand "au lieu de creuser plus avant, pour trouver du roc ou de l'argile." Moral treatises of antiquity are comparable "à des palais fort superbes et fort magnifiques, qui n'estoient bastis que sur du sable et sur de la bouë. Ils eslevent fort haut les vertus, . . . mais ils n'enseignent pas assez à les connoistre." Among the moderns, Galileo on the subject of falling bodies "a entièrement bâti en l'air." A theoretician of music "falso fundamento superstruit."[22] This all-important "fondement," Descartes writes to Mersenne, is "ce qui est comme le plus ample et le moins diversifié et qui peut servir de sujet sur lequel on bâtit le reste."[23] And, "suffossis fundamentis, quidquid iis superaedificatum est sponte collabitur"—"la ruine des fondemens entraine necessairement avec soy tout le reste de l'edifice."[24] Indeed, there are minds so impatient and devoid of care that "mesme ayant des fondemens bien solides, ils ne sçauroient rien bastir d'assuré."[25] But—Descartes likes to repeat this— "tout mon dessein ne tendoit qu'à m'assurer, et à reietter la terre mouvante et le sable, pour trouver le roc ou l'argile."[26] The *Meditationes* open with words expressing the same purpose: "Animadverti jam ante aliquot annos quam multa, ineunte aetate, falsa pro veris admiserim, et quam dubia sint quaecunque istis postea superextruxi, ac proinde funditus omnia semel in vita esse evertenda, atque a primis fundamentis denuo inchoandum, si quid aliquando firmum et mansurum cupiam in scientiis stabilire."[27] In my youth, says Descartes, I took special delight in the mathematical disciplines "à cause de la certitude et de l'evidence de leurs raisons; . . . et . . . ie m'estonnois de ce que, leurs fondemens estant si fermes et si solides, on n'avoit rien basti dessus de plus relevé."[28]

---

[21]*Recherche, AT*, 10: 509; cf. also 496: "jetter les premiers fondemens d'une science solide."

[22]*Ibid.*, p. 513; *Discours, AT*, 6: 7-8; letters to Mersenne (Oct. 11, 1638), *AM*, 3: 83, and to William Boswell (?), (1646?), *AT*, 4: 686.

[23]Dec. 18, 1629. *AM*, 1: 96.

[24]*Meditationes, AT*, 7: 18; 9: 14. Rejecting a suggestion that "erutis" would be better than "suffosis," Descartes defends the latter on the grounds that "erutis" has several meanings while "suffosis" only one (letter to Mersenne [Dec. 24, 1640?], *AT*, 3: 268): he does have in mind an image of undermining. Cf. "sapper les fondemens," *Recherche, AT*, 10: 513.

[25]Letter-preface of *Principes, AT*, 9: 19.

[26]*Discours, AT*, 6: 29.

[27]*AT*, 7: 17 (French text, 9: 13).

[28]*Discours, AT*, 6: 7.

The architect, like the traveler, keeps an eye on the "morale provisoire"; part 3 of the *Discours* opens in this vein:

> Et enfin, comme ce n'est pas assez, avant de commencer à rebastir le logis où on demeure, que de l'abattre, et de faire provision de materiaux et d'Architectes, ou s'exercer soymesme à l'Architecture, et outre cela d'avoir soigneusement tracé le dessin; mais qu'il faut aussy s'estre pourvû de quelque autre, où on puisse estre logé commodement pendant le tems qu'on y travaillera; ainsi, . . . ie me formay une morale par provision.

But the architect is especially preoccupied with the foundation for his new abode.[29] Often, in this mood, he does not appear to raise his work above the surface; he seems to remain below, persistently digging for a rock bottom.

Descartes would build on a firm, solid, secure foundation.

And again the image takes on at times another nuance—a tinge of haughty independence—especially where the architect finally raises his work upward. He would erect a completely original edifice; "car je ne veux pas estre de ces petits artisans, qui ne s'employent qu'à raccommoder les vieux ouvrages."[30] Of course, the débris of old beliefs need not all be thrown away, "comme en abattant un vieux logis, on en reserve ordinairement les demolitions, pour servir à en bastir un nouveau."[31] But "mon dessein," as he defines it again, is "de bastir dans un fons qui est tout à moy."[32] The opening paragraph of part 2 of the *Discours* is well known: too many cooks spoil the broth or, in architectural terms, "Ainsi voit on que les bastimens qu'un seul Architecte a entrepris et achevez, ont coustume d'estre plus beaux et mieux ordonnez, que ceux que plusieurs ont tasché de raccommoder, en faisant servir de vieilles murailles qui avoient esté basties à d'autres fins."

A straight road for the traveler—a solid foundation for the architect—for Descartes, a method true and "assurée." Such then is the apparent symbolism; set off occasionally by declarations of self-sufficiency and supremacy, it would seem to proclaim that Descartes had attained "certitude" to his own satisfaction.

---

[29]For other samples, cf. letters to Mersenne (May 10, 1632), *AM*, 1: 225; to Regius (Mar. 1642), *AT*, 3: 537; to Elizabeth (Sept. 1646), *AT*, 4: 486; *Discours, AT*, 6: 9, 31, 32; *Responsiones* to the second, third, fourth *Objectiones, AT*, 7: 144, 151, 172, 247 (French text, 9: 113, 118, 133, 191). Gustave Cohen has noticed the great number of architect-metaphors, but only in the *Discours: Ecrivains français en Hollande dans la première moitié du XVIIe siècle* (Paris, 1920), pp. 381–82.

[30]*Recherche, AT*, 10: 509.

[31]*Discours, AT*, 6: 29.

[32]*Ibid.*, p. 15; also pp. 13–14. Cf. letters to Mersenne (Apr. 15, 1630; Mar. 31, 1638), *AM*, 1: 130, 2: 214; *Epistola ad P. Dinet, AT*, 7: 597.

And yet all seems left in suspense. The metaphorical routine appears indecisive and ambiguous. The architect and the traveler at times appear to be held back, to pause. The latter, for example, would proceed slowly and with circumspection, so as not to fall; would adhere only to the mean "affin de me détourner moins du vray chemin en cas que ie faillisse"; would learn to distinguish "le vray d'avec le faux," so as to walk "avec assurance" (part 1 of the *Discours*). When the voyager in Descartes speaks, often the route he invokes is a road to be sought, or a way not to be forsaken or lost; it is also a road by which he would move out of "les ténèbres" into "la lumière." The architect is concerned. If Galileo's description of the earth's motion is fallacious, he writes to Mersenne in 1633, "tous les fondements de ma philosophie le sont aussi." He watches over those foundations. One might almost say that he stands guard over them rather anxiously when defending his *Meditationes* against the objections of Arnauld, a critic to be reckoned with: when Arnauld, using Descartes's language, warns him that a statement of his "fundamenta convellit," Descartes retorts: "Neque hoc ulla ratione fundamenta mea convellit"; and when Arnauld briefly remarks that other Cartesian notions "corruunt," Descartes snaps back, with considerable agitation and insistence: "nec corruere, nec ullo modo concuti vel infirmari, mihi videtur."[33] Why deny here with such excessive imagination, and so much emphasis, that foundations and structures will quake and cave in? Where Arnauld merely used a phrase, Descartes, one feels, saw and heard the crash.

A more playful critic, the Jesuit Bourdin, in the seventh *Objectiones* to the *Meditationes*, maliciously inflated the traveler-metaphor into a drawn-out allegory. For pages and pages he twits Descartes, playing the role of a willing disciple who endeavors, but in vain, to follow in the footsteps of the great traveler-explorer-guide. He is forever putting one foot forward, and then withdrawing it, finding no solid argument to step on. They go off in every direction, "per avia et invia," at every turn losing their way and trying still another "via." But no road leads anywhere. And for all that, answering the satirist indirectly in a letter to the Jesuit Dinet, obstinate Descartes set his belabored voyager on his two feet and sent him off on his perennial journey again.[34] Far from having missed the jest,

---

[33]*Objectiones quartae* and *Responsio, AT*, 7: 207, 213, 235, 244. Cf. the French translation authorized by Descartes, where his answers seem even more interesting: Arnauld's "convellit" becomes "répugne," yet Descartes's "convellit" remains "renverse"; Arnauld's "corruunt" becomes "se détruit de soy-mesme," to which Descartes still replies with "renverse," "affaibly," "ébranlé" (9: 162, 166, 182, 188).

[34]*Objectiones septimae, AT*, 7: 467ff.; *Epistola ad P. Dinet, ibid.* Bourdin even mocks Descartes' "vadum" ("gué"): p. 531. Already in 1638, the mathematician Fermat

which was all too obvious, he was hurt to the quick, as is plain enough
in this letter and especially in his very lengthy "Notae" of the same
year, written in direct reply to the Objections. Here, he matched Père
Bourdin's mock-voyage with a counter-farce. The tables are turned,
the roles completely reversed. The master, competent and skilled,
knows what he is about, and it is now the heckler who is made to
appear ridiculous; and most significantly, the case is all restated in
the language of the building craft! The blundering explorer is transformed into an expert architect, and the disappointed companion into
an envious, stupid, fatuous mason who presumes to criticize his
master in public, and who would expose his new method as sheer
mania for digging. Page after page he mocks the would-be master-
builder who dreads sandy soil and, in terror lest the earth crack open
or shake under his feet, perpetually burrows down for solid rocky
ground, and is never really ready or able to erect any structure over
foundations that are but empty ditches. This elaborate twenty-five-
page Cartesian joke, all in constructional-architectural parlance, deserves to be better known. It underscores the kinship between Descartes' two symbols: to contrast the traveler's distorted features with
his true likeness, his caricature is held up against the portrait of the
architect. Here also we perceive how this metaphorical language
came ready to Descartes's mind; he spins it out interminably. But the
strange fantasy is not all lightness and fun. Although the point of the
counter-parody is evident, Descartes burdens it with a running commentary, as if to crush this impertinent mason who is but a creation
of his imagination; it is manifest, he argues for example, "aedificium
ita in altum sustulisse, ut nullam ruinam minaretur; et denique, non
ex nihilo, sed ex solidissima materia, non nihil, sed firmum et dura-
turum sacellum, in honorem Dei construxisse." The whole piece is
replete with architectural images expressing hesitation, uncertainty,
destruction and the like; these, of course, are calculated to sound
grotesque and alien to Cartesianism; they are fabrications of an ignorant fool, and irony suggests that the very opposite is true; and
indeed Cartesianism, as a set of declared principles and enterprises
determinedly carried through, would roundly give them the lie; but
they do not do the architect himself too great an injustice; they rather
help one to grasp his special, complex role in the Cartesian strategy,
for they echo, in derision, a style that he is wont to use in earnest.
The jest comes close to turning into a "rire jaune." Conceived as

---

seems inclined to mock the road system; he suggests that his own methods may have
appeared too easy to Descartes, "qui a fait tant de chemin et a pris une voie si pénible
. . . dans sa Géométrie": letter to Mersenne, *Oeuvres de Fermat*, Tannery-Henry
ed. (Paris, 1891–1922), 2: 133. Descartes retorted: *AM*, 2: 264–65.

an act of playful self-disfiguration, it grows to sound like ambiguous self-mimicry.[35]

The body of metaphors seen as a whole tells the story more plainly, and in large. Irresponsible debater though he was, may not Bourdin have been right? If I may judge by your voice and your expression, he said, you who charter the course and offer to lead others, you are not yourself exempt from fear.[36] Indeed, what ails a thinker who, from his twenties up to his fifties, needs must play, at every point of his career, the part of a traveler-architect, and whose thoughts all the while are full of "chemins détournés" and "fondements ébranlés"? Why are images of mud, sand, loose foundations, tottering structures, or of straying, groping, falling and drowning voyagers, so familiar to his mind? Why, all along, does he also need to evoke so often the *firm* foundation and the *straight* road? By the very pressure of its persistence and repetitiousness, his figurative language, like a form of subconscious resistance, betrays—although it would deny—the pressure of an uncertainty that remains to be dealt with. Rationally, he may in good faith have thrust back all possible mental qualms, but a sense of insecurity obstinately abides, in regions where argument does not reach it. Beyond middle age, the philosopher is still rehearsing the two selfsame metaphors, as if by an old private ritual conjuring and warding off incertitude. And young or old, reciting those formulas as by rote, Descartes does it almost always on identical occasions: when questions of method arise—irrepressible questions, which spring up anywhere but especially at the beginning of each of his philosophical works, and at the head of various chapters—at those points, that is, where Descartes launches new enterprises in which his method will be at stake.

"Je m'imagine," says Paul Valéry, "qu'il n'est pas à son aise en certaines matières. Il en raisonne très longuement; il revient sur ses pas; il se défait comme il peut des objections. J'ai l'impression qu'il se sent alors éloigné de son vœu, infidèle à soi-même, et qu'il se croit obligé de penser contre le cœur de son esprit."[37] Symptoms of anxiety, uncertainty, and impatience have on occasion been detected by others such as Léon Brunschvicg, Gilbert Gadoffre, Maxime Le Roy, G. Cantecor; even in the studies of Henri Gouhier, who sees in the author of the *Discours* a "philosophe content . . . de sa philosophie et surtout de la méthode," there are abundant hints of a Cartesian "inquiétude."[38] That uneasiness, I believe, is what

[35]*AT*, 7: 536-61. (Bourdin also used, but very incidentally, the architectural style to criticize Descartes: e.g., *AT*, 7: 530.)

[36]Bourdin, *Objectiones septimae*, p. 472.

[37]*Revue de Morale et de Métaphysique* 44 (1937): 706.

[38]Cf. *Essais sur Descartes*, passim.

the Cartesian metaphors bespeak, more patently perhaps than biographical data on Descartes' wanderlust or his elusiveness. Descartes
may well have learned to brook uncertainty, live with it, and keep it
under control, in a sort of *modus vivendi* allowing his rational being
a wide scope of its own, a sort of "jeu à part," in Montaigne's
language. The traveler and the architect, whom we can picture as
guards enforcing this settlement, do appear with lesser frequency in
the later than in the earlier works: with time they may have acquired
greater experience in quelling uncertainty. But it does not appear that
they ever quashed it.

His very method of rational inquiry, in its "jeu à part," one is
tempted to argue, may not have afforded him a sense of complete
security. He found himself obliged frequently to defend and at times
to restate or alter his position somewhat. That, however, is rather
beside the point, for his philosophy may have failed thoroughly to
counteract his feeling of uncertainty, but did not occasion it. Uncertainty, subconscious and unrational, preceded the full-grown philosophical system. It was already present, on the memorable night of
November 10, 1619, in those dreams which seemed to prophesy his
mission. In a first dream, he saw himself painfully trying to walk; "il
était obligé de se renverser sur le côté gauche pour pouvoir
avancer au lieu où il voulait aller, parce qu'il sentait une grande
faiblesse au côté droit, dont il ne pouvait se soutenir. Etant honteux
de marcher de la sorte, il fit un effort pour se redresser." A fierce wind
made him spin about. Dragging on, almost falling at every step, he
finally tried to make for the church of a collège "ouvert sur son
chemin." Others, he noticed on the way, "étaient droits et fermes
sur leurs pieds: quoiqu'il fût toujours courbé et chancelant sur le
même terrain." Here, on a nightmare road of torture—and of sin,
perhaps—is a paralyzed traveler for whom Descartes, during a lifetime, will seek "le droit chemin." Here also looms a structure, toward
which he strains but which he does not reach. And here, already, is
some of the basic vocabulary of Descartes' future metaphors. In
another dream, Descartes suddenly finds a dictionary and an an-
thology of Latin poetry, which he later will interpret as symbols of
Universal Science and Wisdom; as he opens the latter, he immediately comes upon the first line of an idyll of Ausonius: "Quod vitae
sectabor iter?"[39] ("What road shall I follow in life?"). None! Ausonius
had answered. The poem, not a cheerful one, ends on this note: "all
paths lead to unhappy ends . . . it is good for a man not to be born at

---

[39]*Olympica*, as reported by Baillet, *Monsieur Des-Cartes*: cf. *AT*, 10: 181ff. The original
MS is missing, but the editors argue that Baillet's report is trustworthy (p. 175): "il ne
semble pas avoir rien inventé." Most scholars follow this view.

all or, if born, to die promptly." When we consider that it was a poem of this nature that inhabited the young man's mind and, emerging in a dream, obtruded itself upon exultant visions of the future, the underlying nature and inverted meaning of all the road metaphors that will recur for thirty more years grow clear. Six months before the dreams, Descartes had already written in Latin to his friend Beeckman: "Do not expect me to do more writing. I am making ready to set out on the road tomorrow, and already, in spirit, I am on my way. 'Adhuc incertus sum' " ("I am still uncertain") as Vergil says "quo fata ferant, ubi sistere detur" ("where fate may take me, where it may be granted me to stop").[40]

A complete account of the dreams, impossible here, would also show traces of a preoccupation with sin and religion: the striving toward a church, for example. In his two metaphors, which describe a method not concerned with faith, revelation, or theology, Descartes retained evident strains of religiosity, such as the architect's constant refrain: "Not on sand, but on solid rock." One cannot but be reminded of the wise man in the Gospels whose house "was founded upon a rock" and the foolish man who "built his house upon the sand." Similarly, "le droit chemin," "le bon chemin" that will not lead us astray, in its many variations often reminds one of Scriptural language. Was this religious tone unconsciously borrowed to invest the architect and traveler with greater authority?

They were important mouthpieces, who in every way were in need of authority. Certitude was their pressing message, which they urgently reiterated because there was, in Descartes, an indigenous uncertainty still to be muffled. They resorted to what may be called a language of mixed metaphor. In a technical sense, the two images are not mixed or confused: the traveler does not build or dig on the run, nor evidently does the architect.[41] But each figure viewed separately is itself a mixture of conflicting poses blurred together, a portrait of assurance overlying uncertainty. And the two metaphors viewed jointly appear mixed in the mind of Descartes, if not confused on paper. The architect and the traveler, intent on identical problems,

---

[40]*AM*, 1: 13. The full context of this line of the *Aeneid* which had remained in Descartes' memory shows an interesting construction-voyage mixture: "classemque sub ipsa/Antandro et Phrygiae molimur montibus Idae,/incerti, quo fata ferant, ubi sistere detur." In the *Compendium musicae* of 1618, Descartes had also written: "Iamque *terram video*, festino ad littus" (*AT*, 10: 140). Twenty-five years later, another Vergilian line that Descartes still remembers is: "Quam si dura silex aut stet Marpesia cautes" (*Epistola ad G. Voetium, AT*, 8: 31).

[41]On occasion, the two images appear together in the same development, but rather as consecutive statements of the same point; e.g., *Recherche, AT*, 10: 496; *Discours, AT*, 6: 14; letter to Mersenne (Oct. 11, 1638), *AM*, 3: 77–78.

are interchangeable portraits of the philosopher. Thus, the 1637 *Discours de la méthode pour bien* conduire *sa raison et* chercher *la vérité* in 1636 was planned to be "Le Projet d'une science universelle qui puisse *élever* notre nature à son plus *haut* degré de perfection." And yet, though speaking to the same point, they are not a pair, but figures engaged in contrary activities. The one—always pressing forward—drives on, pulls ahead, explores without end. The other—in order to build upward—digs in, and stays on the spot, upon a rock that is immovable. The cumulative impression they create is that they are essentially unblended, and in conflict. We see unfold a complex mixed image, in which the overall construction of immobility-versus-motion is itself a configuration of tension, and in which each of the mixed parts is an intimation of the same tension—a tension between uncertainty and assurance.

Thus it seems to have been with Descartes. He could reach out for utmost certitude, but withal could not outgrow a native uncertainty. And if one of his stature could not, then "que peut un homme?" Are "certitude" and "incertitude" polar opposites or twin states of the human mind?

The Motion of *Phèdre* from Act III into Act IV: An Alternative Reading

A FLAW, in Racine, is a disenchantment. He has habituated us to expect a unity and continuity of effect perfectly sustained, and if the compelling onward motion of his tragic poetry is obstructed, it is as if a spell had been broken. But it may happen that the obstruction has arisen from our way of reading the verse, and is not lodged in the verse itself.

A new "imperfection" in *Phèdre*, which Professor Keller has provocatively called to our attention in a recent issue of this journal,[1] deserves close reconsideration. A dislocation seems to set in between scene 2 of Act IV, where Thésée vents his fury on Hippolyte, and the end of Act III, where father and son have previously confronted one another momentarily in the presence of Phèdre. In Act IV, the youth approaches the incensed Thésée and inquires:

> Puis-je vous demander quel funeste nuage,
> Seigneur, a pu troubler votre auguste visage?
> N'osez-vous confier ce secret à ma foi? (1041–43)

Is this not, we are asked, a strange note? Racine has admirably prepared this scene; reluctant to put on the stage a father too rashly prone to credit false reports about his son, as in the Greek tragedy,

Originally published in *Romanic Review* 50 (1959): 161–69.
[1]"Error and Invention in Racine: *Phèdre*, IV, 2," *Romanic Review* 50 (1959): 99–106.

he created at the end of Act III a situation in which Thésée, ahead of any accusations by Œnone, developed in his own mind some sense of suspicion about Hippolyte. The latter then has witnessed, in the earlier encounter, the effects of a "funeste nuage" on his father's "auguste visage." Although Thésée has suffered a new shock, between Act III and scene 2 of Act IV, Hippolyte still has no knowledge of what transpired during that interval; he cannot but believe that the sinister "nuage" he saw gathering in Act III is still oppressing the king. Why then does he seem to formulate his question as if he had not earlier observed Thésée's dismay and as if Thésée were not aware that he had observed it? Would Hippolyte, the pure young man, be dissembling? At one point (p. 103), Professor Keller seems ready to go so far as to say that Hippolyte's query is not an "honest question," but he does not dwell on this issue. More persistently and fundamentally, he would underscore it as a "mistake." It does not make sense.

But how could it have made sense to the poet? At an early stage in the composition of the play, Professor Keller argues, Racine decided to retain from Euripides the material in scene 2 of Act IV, indispensable for the conclusion; then, after brilliantly laying new foundations for it in Act III, he apparently failed to adjust the borrowed material to the new. But, we may ask, if he did not hear any creaking in the transition, what did he hear?

In the tense final scenes of Act III—the only occasion on which all three major characters are brought together—they meet gropingly in an atmosphere of incomprehension, suspicion, and foreboding. They observe one another apprehensively, and make a series of fatal errors. Already in scene 3, the chain of reactions has started. "Thésée est arrivé," Phèdre hears, "Thésée est en ces lieux." She dreads to confront "son fils avec lui," to face "le témoin de ma flamme adultère" watching "de quel front j'ose aborder son père." Œnone is for taking desperate measures of deceit. Phèdre at first would not "opprimer et noircir l'innocence," but presently Thésée makes his appearance, accompanied by Hippolyte, who has already joined him. Whereas Œnone's glance immediately is leveled upon the king—"on vient; je vois Thésée"—to make sure that he has not yet learned anything, the king's distraught wife has eyes only for the youth on whom her fate rests—"Ah! je vois Hippolyte"—while the latter scrutinizes her own look, with anxiety and horror, to see what she will determine to say to the king. Everything in him recoils at overwhelming his father with what he will later reveal, only to Aricie, as a "mystère odieux." But Phèdre's solitary and unrequited passion has turned the unapproachable Hippolyte into a "monstre effroyable à mes yeux" and an "ennemi" and, fatefully, she misreads his innermost feeling—"Dans ses yeux insolents je vois ma perte écrite." In what has been aptly described as a crucial "malentendu sur un regard,"[2] she chooses, thinking herself at bay, to let Œnone do her worst.

The rest follows swiftly. Phèdre withdraws, turning the joy of homecoming into consternation for Thésée. She cuts him off— "Arrêtez, Thésée"—with brief cryptic utterances, for Œnone to develop later—"Vous êtes offensé," "Je ne dois désormais songer qu'à me cacher"—and disappears within (scene 4). These words, spoken also under the glare of Hippolyte's searching look, in a way are meant for him as well, like the veiled beginning of a confession he could expect Thésée to hear presently. In his turn, Hippolyte necessarily misunderstands her purpose, and is appalled (scene 5). His immediate reaction is to flee, not to witness the catastrophe in his father's house and—surely, this is evident—not to be involved. Ambiguously, in his turn, he reminds Thésée: "Je ne la cherchais pas." "C'est vous," he brings home to him, not without irony, it was you who led Phèdre, with Aricie, to Troezen, and conferred upon me the charge of watching over them here. It is as if he were clearing himself, in advance of a confession by Phèdre, and sensed dimly the possibility of his being implicated. Begging leave to disappear, forthwith, in order to slay monsters and be worthy of his father, he ends with the disquieting wish that a "beau trépas," if not a triumph, "Prouve à tout l'avenir que j'étais votre fils."[3] Stunned by blow after blow, Thésée now reacts, in the thirty-five lines that come next (953-87). Hippolyte has declared evasively: "Phèdre peut seule expliquer ce mystère." Thésée would probe further:

> Parlez. Phèdre se plaint que je suis outragé.
> Qui m'a trahi? Pourquoi ne suis-je pas vengé?
> La Grèce, à qui mon bras fut tant de fois utile,
> A-t-elle au criminel accordé quelque asile?
> Vous ne répondez point.   (979-83)

But he still receives no reply.

It is chiefly with Thésée's full-length speech, which develops his state of mind in all its complexity, that Professor Keller cannot reconcile Hippolyte's "Puis-je vous demander . . . ?" in Act IV. The difficulty, I would suggest, arises partly from a question of fact: how

---

[2]Jean Pommier, *Aspects de Racine* (Paris, 1954), p. 196. It is to be noted that Racine found a powerful suggestion for this exchange in Hippolytus' threats to the Nurse in Euripides' play, ll. 661-63.

[3]Quotations follow the Mesnard edition, for the reader's convenience. But here "l'avenir" replaces "l'univers," in accordance with more recent scholarly editions, which are followed also for the punctuation of l. 1642, quoted later.

much of his father's speech did Hippolyte actually hear? Professor Keller, it is clear, acts on the assumption that Thésée speaks all of the thirty-five lines *to* Hippolyte. On that basis, of course, it would become wondrous strange that Hippolyte should belatedly venture his question in Act IV after having heard the king bewail the "horreur" and "terreur" of his situation in Act III. But such a reading seems untenable, and not only because it creates this incongruity.

The whole first part of the passage, opening with "Que vois-je? Quelle horreur dans ces lieux répandue," is an expression of paralyzed, speechless grief and bewilderment at "l'horreur que j'inspire," at the "frémissements" with which Thésée is greeted upon his return, after he has escaped mortal dangers "dans des cavernes sombres"—would, he laments, that he were still in the cavernous prison. Nothing in those twenty-seven lines shows any direct address to Hippolyte. He speaks in the third person of "ma famille éperdue," and his only interpellation—"O, ciel"—is to the heavens, on whom he calls to witness this woeful homecoming. Psychologically, it is more deeply true that all these words should express the inner agitation of his astonished heart. He has been cruelly, swiftly, repeatedly stricken. He does not understand, and stands dismayed, before his son and in front of the palace quarters into which the queen has just disappeared. He cannot burst into loquacious recriminations with Hippolyte, but needs to recover from the rapid succession of shocks and this sudden feeling of solitude.

Then, rousing himself to seek out the cause, he abruptly turns on Hippolyte, in the lines quoted above, asking for that explanation of Phèdre's hints which Hippolyte has been refusing to yield. There is a brusque change of tone, from grief to insistent inquiry, indignation, and authority ("Parlez"). This is the first point at which Hippolyte is in fact addressed directly, and the first at which the live dialogue is resumed in its urgent course, with Thésée driving his son back, after a poignant pause, to what he senses is the crucial secret.

Again, after Thésée concludes his queries with "Vous ne répondez pas," it would seem inconceivable that Hippolyte should overhear the rest:

> Mon fils, mon propre fils
> Est-il d'intelligence avec mes ennemis?
> Entrons. C'est trop garder un doute qui m'accable.
> Connaissons à la fois le crime et le coupable.
> Que Phèdre explique enfin le trouble où je la voi   (983–87)

"Entrons," like "connaissons," of course has nothing to do with Hippolyte, who is not being invited to trail Thésée. More seriously, it seems out of the question that Hippolyte should hear his father ask

whether "mon fils" has conspired with the enemy (especially after he
has indeed been "d'intelligence" with Aricie), that he should then
not react to such a suspicion, and that Thésée—the monarch, and
the tormented father—should brook such a devastatingly blank, disre-
spectful, and cruel indifference. Could Racine possibly have pictured
his Thésée countenancing a silent admission of guilt by his son, and
withdrawing in the face of it? The king, rather, keeps his suspicion
to himself, and goes within to clear it up. When Hippolyte remains
alone and Racine finally can let him express himself freely (scene 6),
his first utterance is:

> Où tendait ce discours qui m'a glacé d'effroi?
> Phèdre, toujours en proie à sa fureur extrême,
> Veut-elle s'accuser et se perdre elle-même?   (988-90)

Still there is no reaction to the king's suspicion. This terrifying "discours" was not Thésée's, for if Hippolyte had heard it through, he
would know well enough "où tendait ce discours," which was explicit. As is clear in context, and as Professor Keller recognizes, the
"effroi" was inspired by Phèdre's seeming threat to confess.

On such a reading, therefore, all Hippolyte has heard his father
say is "Quel est l'étrange accueil qu'on fait à votre père, / Mon
fils?" (921-22), "Vous, mon fils, me quitter?" (927), and the four and
a half lines opening with "Parlez." Of the direct exchange that he
has had with Thésée, the beginning and the end bear on the hidden
meaning of Phèdre's words. It is the basic question of which he is
aware and which, with natural and credible persistence, he has had
to leave unanswered between his father and himself. His words in
Act IV, then, lose much of their alleged callousness; they do not jar
with unheard lamentations and suspicions of Thésée.

But still, lamentations and suspicions aside, has Hippolyte not seen
a storm gathering in Act III? Does not a postponed query about the
"funeste nuage," in Act IV, strike a discord? Much depends on how
we understand the youth's involvement in the storm. Unquestionably,
with deep filial emotion, he is affected by the king's plight. But, in
the very midst of it all, he has woes of his own.

These woes are most acute. Repeatedly, his impulse is to flee.[4] He
will meet his death when finally making off, unwillingly, under
Thésée's imprecations—"Fuis, traître [. . .] . Fuis [. . .] . Fuis, dis-je
[. . .]." (1053-63)—whereas, ironically, his whole drive was to flee *to*
Thésée. This is forcefully brought out in the very first scene of the
play, which imparts a sense of great disquiet, with the constant

---

[4]Cf. Raymond Picard, Pléiade edition of Racine's *Oeuvres complètes* (Paris, 1951), 1:
1168 (n. 2 to p. 767).

use of "partir" and "fuir." Right off, Hippolyte shows "le doute mortel dont je suis agité"; "je pars," he says, in order to seek my absent father. However, as he talks under the pressure of Théramène's questioning, he confesses that his departure is a flight—"Je fuis, je l'avoûrai, cette jeune Aricie." He will not admit that he loves her, for a set of reasons that, revealingly, lead up to Thésée as the obstacle: he protests that he could not love that very daughter of vanquished enemies to whom the king has rigorously denied all right to marriage and progeny. It is clear that he does, but dares not, love Aricie. As Théramène, brushing aside his denials, concludes:

> Il n'en faut point douter: vous aimez, vous brûlez;
> Vous périssez d'un mal que vous dissimulez.
> La charmante Aricie a-t-elle su vous plaire? (135-37)

and as Hippolyte, without further denial, replies: "Théramène, je pars, et vais chercher mon père" (138), we realize that his quest for his father is linked with his flight from the proscribed princess. He has not been consciously dissembling but in his "doute mortel" his will is not whole or his purpose clearcut. He would believe that he flees from the princess out of respect for his father's will, but his father's orders left him in charge of this captive, and to run off is in itself a disobedience. He would believe that he flees from the princess in order to escape from her, but he could do so without necessarily setting out on a search for his father, who has long been missing and thoroughly searched for by Théramène. He would believe that this new search is commanded by his "devoir," yet admits to himself that it is a flight, that "Hippolyte en partant fuit une . . . ennemie" (49). We feel that, as he strains toward his father, it is with the confused hope to confess, and to remove the obstacle to a love not now permitted—but held up to him by Théramène as not reprehensible.

For this is exactly what he strives to do when Thésée suddenly returns. No sooner has the son joined the father than his preoccupation becomes, storm or no storm, to confront the king with the "doute mortel" in his own mind. Is it an injustice to the unhappy Hippolyte, consumed with love, to suggest that although the threatening clash between Thésée and Phèdre pains him for reasons of filial sympathy, it is, to him, especially ominous as a threat to his private hopes?

> Dieux! que dira le Roi? Quel funeste poison
> L'amour a répandu sur toute sa maison!
> Moi-même, plein d'un feu que sa haine réprouve,
> Quel il m'a vu jadis, et quel il me retrouve!
> De noirs pressentiments viennent m'épouvanter. (91-95)

That is his own "nuage." The tension moreover obstructs, postpones the confrontation he urgently needs to have with his father. As he sees him go in the direction followed by the queen, he does not hear the king's silent thoughts but can surmise he will not be satisfied until he receives an explanation from Phèdre. Whatever the queen does, there is no time to lose. To Hippolyte, the first thing that he must do, while his father, inside, may be drawing close to the shattering truth, is to devise

> par quelle heureuse adresse
> Je pourrai de mon père émouvoir la tendresse,
> Et lui dire un amour qu'il peut vouloir troubler,
> Mais que tout son pouvoir ne saurait ébranler.   (997–1000)

This is not comic, though it could be turned into comedy, like the clicking of any mechanism; it is a self-centeredness of young passion, in a tragedy where all are solitary. Racine is at his best here, and goes deep, portraying an obsession and temptation crossed, complicated, but not repressed by a family calamity. Hippolyte has barely had time to bring Thésée into the palace when, in the midst of the storm developing over his father's head, he speaks not only of Phèdre, as we saw, but also brings in an extraneous reminder that it was by Thésée's orders, after all, that he was thrown together with Aricie. Why this here? Is it not to begin preparing the way for a confession about Aricie? In the same speech, he returns to a possibility foreshadowed in his protestations of Act I, where he explained to Théramène his contempt for the debasing effects of love: they would make me the more contemptible, he said then, because no heroic exploits have given me the right to indulge in amorous weaknesses, as in my father's case. Now, in his father's presence, he proposes in fact to go forth in search of exploits, to emulate the king. The "heureuse adresse" by which he hopes to move Thésée, at the close of Act III, is one which he has already obscurely contemplated.

How he would have devised it is not given to us to know, and it is dramatically far better that it should be so, for one of the developments that heighten the poignancy of Act IV is that Hippolyte, promptly seeking out his father again, with an "heureuse adresse" now impatiently all worked out, swiftly experiences the futility of his preparations, at his very first words. Little time has elapsed, just enough to allow Oenone to launch her plot during the intermission, and to make an end of it in the preliminary scene of Act IV. Has she heard or seen him come? She is suddenly in a great rush to return to the queen, and Hippolyte may well have caught sight of her.[5] At any

---

[5]We know from Subligny that originally Thésée recited at this point a monologue of outcries and lamentations, later suppressed by Racine. But it would not seriously alter

rate, he has returned straight to these quarters, knowing for what purpose the king is there. Eager to broach the subject that preoccupies him, he finds Thésée in a state of rage. Again, there is an exchange of looks. As Thésée for a moment watches him in wrathful silence, Hippolyte scans Thésée's "visage," and breaks in with his question, before the "nuage" bursts: his father's stare is not the same; it is more intense, free from speculation, and directed fully on him.[6] No talk of Aricie is possible; Thésée's fury must first be met. Has Phèdre, or Oenone, told Thésée of the queen's passion, and if so, does he hold Hippolyte in some way implicated or tainted? It may still be that no one has dared to say it outright—how can Hippolyte be sure? But then what is the meaning of Thésée's look? Hippolyte needs to know, but is loath to name the unspeakable misfortune or be perhaps the one to open the king's eyes to it. Thésée must be the first to refer to it. Hippolyte's brief question is sensitively adjusted to this conflict between his wish and his reluctance to probe. Openly, he can admit only to an awareness of something "funeste" visible on the king's face. But his inquiring words indirectly and discreetly bespeak at the same time a deeper awareness of things painful to mention. "Puis-je vous demander . . . ?" expresses not only "May I ask . . . ?" but *"Can* I . . . ?" "Pouvoir," used a second time in the sentence, sustains this shading of meaning; "a pu troubler" carries an overtone of the inner thought: "what cloud may have discomposed his countenance?" and in direct address conveys: "what baleful cloud, Sire, can have discomposed (has had the power to discompose) your countenance?" More strongly still, "N'osez-vous confier ce secret" intimates the unmentionable. Hippolyte can go no further. With "à ma foi," his query ends on a note of respectful but close solidarity which, movingly, rings true, only to be drowned out by Thésée's instantaneous reply. Thésée is incensed by his "N'osez-vous . . . ?"—to him the height of insolent hypocrisy—and it is to this that he retorts as he finally lashes out at Hippolyte: "Perfide, oses-tu bien te montrer devant moi?" (1044). And again: "Tu m'oses présenter une tête ennemie" (1049), "Ne viens point braver ici ma haine" (1053).

A "mistake"? Would that lesser dramatic poets had more often blundered in this fashion! Hippolyte's three lines blend into what precedes, and what follows. They harmonize with the poetry of the whole in other ways, and especially through "nuage," which is not a phrase or rhyme of the moment. The "funeste nuage" that Hippolyte

this supposition, as the monologue could be a pause during which Hippolyte hesitated before advancing toward his father.

[6]Professor Keller raises this point (p. 101), but only to dismiss it, on the basis of the assumption, criticized above, that Hippolyte heard all of Thésée's speech.

distressingly perceives over Thésée's royal head turns into a "nuage odieux" (1431) that will prove to be the undoing of the youth himself; it overcasts the whole tragedy, lowering at the end over Phèdre, as she sees all recede into the growing darkness of death:

> Déjà je ne vois plus qu'à travers un nuage
> Et le ciel, et l'époux que ma présence outrage.   (1641–42)

Professor Keller wonders how a "mistake," so glaring to him, could have escaped Racine's notice, and explains that the poet must have retained Hippolyte's three lines as part of the scene borrowed from Euripides. But would a Racine be satisfied with an unexamined transfer of this kind? The Greek Hippolytus rushes out, on hearing Theseus' outcries, and indeed asks him for an explanation, as Hippolyte will do, but not, it seems to me, "with words closely resembling those in Racine," as Professor Keller argues (p. 102). Euripides has Hippolytus urge his father much more freely to speak; although Hippolytus may already be doing so with some ambiguity, the problem is very different, and the tone not the same at all, as he is inquiring at this point about Phaedra's death; he wonders not at his father's stormy countenance but at his silence, a stress that Gabriel Gilbert, for one, imitated pointedly in his *Hypolite*: "Ce silence m'estonne [. . .]." It is a curious point that the one detail that may have struck Racine in this passage of his French predecessor is the added suggestion of a "nuage": "Loin de mon pere, ô Ciel! destourne la tempeste," reinforced by this further suggestion (for Phèdre's dying words as well) in one of Gilbert's best lines, spoken at the end of his tragedy by Thésée: "La splendeur de mes jours se couvre d'un nuage."[7] A "careless borrowing" (p. 103) from Euripides would have prevented Hippolyte's question from expressing felicitously, as I think it does, the predicament at hand. Far from being purely vestigial and obstructive in Racine, it grows out of the motion of the whole play and his version of the legend, and so necessarily that one must go back to Act I, scene 1, for its source.

If the question was uncalled for and superfluous, why not a final test? Shall we try to correct the passage by eliminating the excrescence? It would be then that a true dislocation would be seen to set in. Thésée would be pouncing immediately on Hippolyte—a burly conceit of melodrama, next to Racine's. It would be felt how necessary it was that Hippolyte should first seek him out, and strain to draw him out, in fulfilment of the taut psychological and tragic buildup.

---

[7]*Hypolite, ou Le Garçon insensible* (Paris, 1647), pp. 86–87, 126.

The Central Image
in *Phèdre*

THE MEANING of Phèdre's tragedy is densely compressed into her
very last words, uttered at the moment of death:

> Et la mort, à mes yeux dérobant la clarté,
> Rend au jour, qu'ils souillaient, toute sa pureté.

A brightness is restored to all its purity, and it seems crucial to the
poet that in dying so, Phèdre suffer her agony and death, unlike
most of his other characters, on the stage and in full view of all.
Phèdre is not dying in order to save Hippolyte's reputation: confession, without death, would have sufficed. She does not come before
us to lament Hippolyte's death. When she first hears the news from
Thésée, she has already taken the poison. After her husband's long,
vehement lament, she answers with a calmness that she has never
known before, and which contrasts sharply with the longing that
Seneca's Phaedra expresses for Hippolytus, over his mangled corpse;
Racine's Phèdre merely absolves Hippolyte of blame, but does not
mourn his death, does not cry out against the irreparable calamity.
Her suffering, she says elsewhere, "mon mal vient de plus loin."
Long before Hippolyte's death, and before the opening of the play,
she had already resolved to die.

When the end, long expected, finally comes, it is an illumination,
and a purification. And death, she says, depriving my eyes of light,

Not previously published.

restores all its purity to the light of day, which they were soiling. The poet calls special attention to her eyes by an inversion ("à mes yeux dérobant la clarté"); by two pauses ("rend au jour, qu'ils souillaient, toute sa pureté"), he sets off and emphasizes "qu'ils souillaient"; unmistakably, he is telling us that it is her act of vision that has had a soiling effect, and that when her eyes no longer can see, the pollution is over.

The whole play tends in the direction of this statement. A rhythm of situations, a progression of revelation impels us toward that last scene: both Hippolyte and Phèdre make their successive confessions first to a confidant, then to the loved one, and finally to Thésée, the master and obstacle. This symmetry of structure is reinforced by sequences of verbal echoes and correspondences. For example:

> Chargés d'un feu secret, vos yeux s'appesantissent.
> Il n'en faut point douter: vous aimez, vous brûlez;
> Vous périssez d'un mal que vous dissimulez. (134-36)

Out of context, this might seem to apply perfectly to Phèdre. And it would. She is often described in such terms. Yet here, these words are addressed to Hippolyte, and they fit as well. The nature of love, masculine or feminine, innocent or criminal, is fundamentally one. It has never been sufficiently shown, even by Gabriel Cahen, how persistently reiterative Racine's manner can grow. His vocabulary is inconceivably restricted, limited, tight—but by design; over and over again, throughout a play, unabashed he dwells on the same configurations of words, even at the expense of the rhyme, achieving powerful effects of unity and focus. In this fashion, a steady flow of repeated symbols is finally gathered into Phèdre's last two lines. It is the language of vision, of light and of darkness, and—along with those—of fire, heat, and extinction. This is not a metaphorical language of startling novelty. It is elemental, and as old as mythology, poetry, religion, and human thought. Racine had glimpses of it in the plays of Sophocles, Euripides, and Seneca. But it could have reached him also by innumerable other channels, ancient and medieval. Yet it remains a fresh, vital network of images; expanding over the whole tragedy, it contains and unfolds its meaning. The forest, the monster, and visions of hiding also constantly recur. They harmonize with the central imagery, deepening it with varying shades and connotations of darkness.

The very first time that Phèdre is revealed to us, "une femme mourante et qui cherche à mourir" (44), Théramène says to Hippolyte:

> Phèdre, atteinte d'un mal qu'elle s'obstine à taire,
> Lasse enfin d'elle-même et du *jour* qui l'éclaire. (45-46)

Weary of the light of day: this could as yet pass unnoticed here, as a cliché. But soon after, in scene 2, Œnone again describes Phèdre's malady:

> Son chagrin inquiet l'arrache de son lit.
> Elle veut *voir le jour*. (148-49)

Phèdre at the same time seeks and shuns "le jour," which now begins to attract attention, from the start growing ambiguous and generating a tension to be resolved only in Phèdre's last words.

After others have introduced her in those terms, Phèdre herself appears. Her strength is dwindling. And yet she has rushed out to see the light of day. Literally, in the physical sense, her eyes are dazzled: "Mes yeux sont éblouis du *jour* que je revoi" (155). But figuratively as well. One obvious but powerful meaning of "le jour," which she has come out to seek, is the fullness of life. Her intention was to bid this alluring light farewell: "Soleil, je te viens voir pour la dernière fois" (172). But at this prospect of abandoning life, she falls into a reverie, dreaming, like the Phaedra of Euripides, of the relinquished possibilities of life:

> Dieux! que ne suis-je assise à l'ombre des forêts!
> Quand pourrai-je, au travers d'une noble poussière,
> Suivre de l'oeil un char fuyant dans la carrière? (176-78)

Hippolyte the horseman and the hunter, though unmentioned, with his presence fills this whole vision, which now has drawn Phèdre far out and into the forest, where the light grows dim: "au travers d'une noble poussière," "à l'ombre des forêts." Forest shades may suggest a coolness and freshness that the feverish crave. But not only that. Throughout the play, Hippolyte is identified with the forest, as in Euripides and Seneca. It is also a sort of hinterland, primitive and wild, removed from the inhibiting civilization of palace and town. It is also a place of hiding. In Seneca's play, Racine had found this suggestion blaringly spelled out by Phaedra: "whither, my soul? Why this mad love of forest glades? I recognize my wretched mother's fatal curse; her love and mine know how to sin in forest depths" (112-15). Racine, vaguely but more impressively, merely suggests this at first; then in the fourth act, when Phèdre realizes that Hippolyte and Aricie have loved one another, with furious envy she cries: "Dans le fond des forêts allaient-ils se cacher?" (1236)—an unfounded suspicion, but revealing. In the case of others as in her own, she has come to visualize love as something that, while irresistible, could only be furtive, hidden, darksome. Not forest shades, but forest shadows; an obscurity that deepens into blackness—"une flamme si noire," as Phèdre herself will say. We begin to gather, as her impulsive return to the light ends in the shadows, what it is that her visual act would perpetrate.

But the dazzling brightness, an unbearable sensation, also conveys her sense of guilt. She grows faint, would stop, would go no further. She undoes the futile, guilty ornaments with which she has ordered Œnone to embellish her, and will not be seen by anyone. "Vous vouliez," says Œnone,

> Vous vouliez vous montrer et revoir la lumière.
> Vous la voyez, Madame; et prête à vous cacher,
> Vous haïssez le jour que vous veniez chercher?   (166-68)

This hiding from the light, as conscious intention, is a resolve to die. But dying, as yet, has nothing to do with purification, or the chances for purification:

> Je voulais en mourant prendre soin de ma gloire,
> Et dérober au jour une flamme si noire.   (309-10)

Phèdre repeats this many times. Her ancestor, the Sun "noble et brillant," is a symbol of purity. But as she rushes out toward this ancestral source of her being, it is not with any hope of being saved, but to banish herself from the presence of the Sun: "je te viens voir pour la dernière fois." Her original purpose is to hide, conceal her shame, and save her reputation. At times, she feels that she is the victim of what we would call heredity, on her mother's side, and at times the victim of fate—which is the same, as hers is an inward fatality, that drives her from within. A victim, she is yet horrified at herself, has tried in vain to stifle her passion, and is now ready to hide in the only way left to her. Still in Act IV, she cries out: "Où me cacher? Fuyons dans la nuit infernale" (1277).

Unconsciously, the same sense of guilt turns her feeling of longing in the direction of secret forests. But under the strain of repression, this longing will out, as is symbolized by her compulsion to rush into the open; she would make of it a gesture of farewell to the light of day, but it was initially, and still is secretly, an outgoing urge—"Un désordre éternel règne dans son esprit" (147)—and is conveyed in all its complications by the conflict, interaction, and confusion of light with darkness.

The outgoing urge, indeed, does not remain unconscious. Startled out of her forest reverie, Phèdre exclaims: "Où laissé-je égarer mes voeux et mon esprit?" (180). She is aware and ashamed, she admits that her "fureurs au dehors ont osé se répandre" (741). We receive the impression, for a long time, that hers is a struggle between the impulse to reveal and satisfy her passion, and the decision to hide it forever. If this were the sole theme, her tragedy—if tragedy at all—would consist in her having failed to hide or to satisfy her passion, which, again, is not at all the deepest meaning of her last two lines. For there, "le jour et la nuit infernale" will have come to stand for something altogether different.

That meaning emerges in her confession to Œnone, where two changes of emphasis are introduced. First, "le jour" and "la lumière," in this description of passion, turn into fire—the "feux redoutables" of Venus, "une ardeur dans mes veines cachée" and, thereafter, "brûler," "embraser," "sécher," "feu," and "ardeur"; all the expressions of heat and fever will constantly appear, intermingled until the end with expressions of light and brightness, and reinforced by "fureur," one of the most frequent words in the play.

The second change consists in focusing attention on the eyes that were dazzled by the light. The whole confession is composed as if it were a series of recollected acts of vision that went far back to that time in Athens when, as Aphrodite reports in Euripides' play, "Phaedra saw him and her heart was filled with the longings of love."

> Je le vis, je rougis, je pâlis à sa vue;
> Un trouble s'éleva dans mon âme éperdue;
> Mes yeux ne voyaient plus.   (273–75)

Her look fastened upon an Hippolyte without existence. "Mes yeux ne voyaient plus": it was not an act of seeing, but of imagining and wishing; "O Eros," says Euripides again, "O Eros, who distills desire upon the eyes" (525). In that state, she says, "Je sentis tout mon corps et transir et brûler" (276). At first she hoped to placate relentless Venus with gifts, sacrifices, and incense, but to no avail:

> Quand ma bouche implorait le nom de la Déesse,
> J'adorais Hippolyte; et le voyant sans cesse,
> Même au pied des autels que je faisais fumer,
> J'offrais tout à ce dieu que je n'osais nommer.

Her look, always fixed with madness upon her image of Hippolyte, transfigured him into a divinity of love, one who would receive her fervent offering—"j'offrais tout à ce dieu"—then she strove to avoid Hippolyte, but also to no avail:

> Je l'évitais partout. O comble de misère!
> Mes yeux le retrouvaient dans les traits de son père.   (289–90)

In her confession to Thésée, at the end, she will repeat:

> C'est moi qui sur ce fils chaste et respectueux
> Osai jeter un oeil profane, incestueux.   (1623-24)

The eye was incestuous. It was also the victim of a mad illusion. In her declaration to Hippolyte, in Act II, speaking of the rumored death of Thésée, Phèdre says, in the bewildering, torturing presence of Hippolyte:

> Que dis-je? Il n'est point mort, puisqu'il respire en vous,
> Toujours devant mes yeux je crois voir mon époux.
> Je le vois, je lui parle; et mon coeur. . . . Je m'égare,
> Seigneur, ma folle ardeur malgré moi se déclare.   (627-30)

As Hippolyte wonders how, "Tout mort qu'il est, Thésée est présent à vos yeux," this painful incomprehension provokes her to go on:

> Oui, Prince, je languis, je brûle pour Thésée.
> Je l'aime   (634-35)

—not as the faithless philanderer, but as he was when first he sailed to Crete,

> Mais fidèle, mais fier, et même un peu farouche,
> Charmant, jeune, traînant tous les coeurs après soi,
> Tel qu'on dépeint nos dieux, ou tel que je vous voi.
> Il avait votre port, vos yeux, votre langage.   (638-41)

The resemblance between father and son tempted, then, a Phèdre whose love for Thésée had died. By the transpositions of her eye "profane, incestueux," seeking the son in the father and the lost husband in the son, she deceived Thésée as she disfigured Hippolyte.

This "comble de misère," as she continues to tell Oenone, drove her to resist, and to make her passion impossible by persecuting and exiling Hippolyte and provoking his hatred. Again to no avail:

> J'ai revu l'ennemi que j'avais éloigné:
> Ma blessure trop vive aussitôt a saigné.
> Ce n'est plus une ardeur dans mes veines cachée:
> C'est Vénus toute entière à sa proie attachée.   (303-6)

The visual act is illustrated and reinforced by another image. The famous line "C'est Vénus toute entière à sa proie attachée" is ambiguous enough to allow the word "proie" to apply simultaneously to Phèdre and to Hippolyte. It can and does suggest that Venus has now completely taken possession of her victim Phèdre. But "proie," as prey or quarry, can be associated ironically with Hippolyte: the hunter hunted down. The image follows this line of development: as I saw Hippolyte, a reopened wound released a passion that would no longer be contained but would fasten desperately upon its prey.

In the next capital scene, Phèdre's confession to Hippolyte (Act II, scene 5), the same impression is powerfully revived. Her passion dare not declare itself, yet her language pulls in that direction. Referring to her past persecution of Hippolyte, "Vous m'avez vue," she says, "attachée à vous nuire," an obvious echo of "à sa proie attachée," expressing attraction by the very terms of pursuit and hostility. Similarly, the line "A votre inimitié j'ai pris soin de m'offrir" (599) is a description of hostility, but by means of an image suggesting the giving or surrendering of oneself.

But the most moving and revealing lines here are certainly in her reverie on the labyrinth of Crete. The whole scene has followed the same movement as her confession to Œnone. She had a conscious reason for coming forth to meet Hippolyte—here, to discuss matters of state, after the rumored death of Thésée. But in his presence—"J'oublie, en le voyant, ce que je viens lui dire"—her eyes, we might say, are dazzled again; she grows weak again; and again, unconsciously, her longing translates itself into a dream of darkness and concealment. Why, she says, were you not there instead of Thésée to be led by my sister Ariane through the labyrinth?

> Mais non, dans ce dessein je l'aurais devancée.
> . . . .
> C'est moi, Prince, c'est moi dont l'utile secours
> Vous eût du Labyrinthe enseigné les détours,

like a

> Compagne du péril qu'il vous fallait chercher,
> . . . .
> Et Phèdre au Labyrinthe avec vous descendue
> Se serait avec vous retrouvée, ou perdue.   (653-62)

Her eyes, in truth, "ne voyaient plus" but created a fervent, unreal likeness of him, an impossible, impure Hippolyte who might have utterly surrendered to her. The real Hippolyte, though identified with the wild forest, is also often identified with light and brightness: "Le jour n'est pas plus pur que le fond de mon coeur" (1112). Phèdre, conscious and remorseful, herself clearly establishes this identity, in her reproaches to Œnone in the fourth act:

> Au jour que je fuyais c'est toi qui m'as rendue.
>
> . . . .
>
> J'évitais Hippolyte, et tu me l'as fait voir.   (1310-12)

But, a prey to her passion, she disfigures Hippolyte. Pity Phèdre profoundly as we must, we cannot escape the feeling that Racine, analyzing it ruthlessly, sees in her visual act not only impurity longing for purity, but a compulsion on its part to defeat and corrupt a shining purity that irritates and shames it—Phèdre leading Hippolyte to the beast or monster in the labyrinth.

One of the most telling commentaries on this image is Hippolyte's response to it. Phèdre naturally expected him to consider her an object of horror: "Si tes yeux un moment pouvaient me regarder" (692). But this is his immediate reaction: "Je ne puis sans horreur me regarder moi-même" (718). He has been horrified by a glimpse of the unthinkable, unmentionable image of himself that she bears in her eyes, and which, he will later say, "je voulais me cacher à moi-même" (1346).

Her look, which more and more is painted as a wishful act of possession, helps to explain her habit of calling Hippolyte her "ennemi." It is she who, for her persecutions of Hippolyte, could more properly be called his relentless enemy. Yet from the start, to her, he was "mon superbe ennemi." This is partly because in reality he did seem "fier" and "farouche," an untamed creature of the forest, a "coeur inaccessible," a prey worth subduing. That, indeed, was the very way in which Aricie herself was attracted to Hippolyte. But Phèdre not only calls him "superbe" or haughty, she sees him also as "insensible," "inhumain," "ingrat," "inexorable"; while condemning herself before Hippolyte, she yet calls him "cruel"; when all collapses, upon Thésée's return, she says of Hippolyte, who knows her secret: "Je le vois comme un monstre effroyable à mes yeux" (884)—she who herself has turned a monstrous look on him. When she cannot but perceive the difference between the image in her eye and the indifferent Hippolyte standing before her, it is as if this Hippolyte, on whom she had no claims he could be aware of, by another transposition had become a cruel, monstrous, hated denier of all that she so fervently and completely offered. These flashes of resentment are entirely outside the pale of her moral consciousness. For then it comes to pass that she loses all awareness of incest or adultery and reacts as if something that was due her had been withheld—"l'insupportable injure," she says, "d'un refus cruel" (1229). Her jealousy, especially a "douleur non encore éprouvée," brings this out. On the point of telling the truth to Thésée to save Hippolyte, she learns that he and Aricie love each other. Hippolyte, then, was capable of love, she cries, and this "ingrat inexorable," with his "coeur toujours fermé" and his "yeux cruels," armed himself only against me!

> Je suis le seul objet qu'il ne saurait souffrir;
> Et je me chargerais du soin de le défendre?   (1212-13)

She even forgets that she has done everything to inspire him with hatred. Illogically, amorally, she reacts to a wrong which, in her passion, has vivid reality, and punishes Hippolyte as if he had committed it.

The great scene of jealousy (Act IV, scene 6) is full of the language of vision, light, fire, and "fureur," particularly where Phèdre asks: "Dans le fond des forets allaient-ils se cacher?" (1236). Suddenly, this suspicion disintegrates:

> Hélas! ils se voyaient avec pleine licence.
> Le ciel de leurs soupirs approuvait l'innocence;
> Ils suivaient sans remords leur penchant amoureux;
> Tous les jours se levaient clairs et sereins pour eux.
> Et moi, triste rebut de la nature entière,
> Je me cachais au jour, je fuyais la lumière.   (1237-42)

There is here the perception of a love that can be pure. Ironically, it is as unfounded as her former suspicion since Hippolyte and Aricie had never known the happiness of such contentment, free, intimate, unrestrained and unhidden. But she learns, deeply and with unerring realism, about herself. She long remains in a paroxysm of jealousy, and regrets that what her criminal eyes had envisioned never came to pass. That surely, is the meaning of these famous lines:

> Hélas! du crime affreux dont la honte me suit
> Jamais mon triste coeur n'a recueilli le fruit.   (1291-92)

She walks off the stage with no intention of saving Hippolyte. Three times, later, she will try in vain to write a note of confession to Thésée. But she has learned enough to reach a fuller understanding shortly.

This occurs in the final scene. If she comes to die on the stage, it is because her death needs to be understood: we must gather its meaning as we watch her discover it, at the moment of death. She is calm. She does not come to lament the death of Hippolyte; she does not even assume full responsibility for the misfortune, laying part of the blame, as well she may, on the gods, and on Oenone. Then, after this, a preliminary explanation, the last half of her speech is a description of what is happening to her as she expires:

> J'ai voulu, devant vous exposant mes remords,
> Par un chemin plus lent descendre chez les morts.   (1635–36)

Why this *slow* descent into Hades? We cannot but remember that shortly before, in Act IV, when she cried "Fuyons dans la nuit infernale," even this escape suddenly appeared to her terrifyingly impossible, as her father Minos would be there to judge his horrible daughter. This play is full of reminders of "ce triste séjour," "des morts la demeure profonde," "les rivages sombres," "les sombres bords," "les bords qu'on passe sans retour." "Mon âme," Œnone predicts, "chez les morts descendra la première." With all these echoes we remain aware, in the mythological context, that Hippolyte, so soon after his death, is also descending "chez les morts." Seneca had called Racine's attention to this; his Phaedra, about to kill herself over Hippolytus' corpse, proclaimed: "through Styx, through rivers of fire will I madly follow thee. . . It was not ours to be joined in life, but surely it is ours to be joined in death" (*Hipp.* 1180, 1183–84). Racine does the opposite; a last time, his Phèdre consciously avoids Hippolyte. But the poison is taking effect:

> J'ai pris, j'ai fait couler dans mes brûlantes veines
> Un poison que Médée apporta dans Athènes.   (1637–38)

The rhythm marks the steady progress of the poison. The "brûlantes veines," with "flamme funeste" and "feu" in earlier lines of the speech, is the last reminder of that fire, which the poison extinguishes:

> Déjà jusqu'à mon coeur le venin parvenu
> Dans ce coeur expirant jette un froid inconnu.   (1639–40)

Coldness sets in. And Phèdre speaks of the heart that longed for Hippolyte as if it were no longer hers: "mon coeur," she says, and then "ce coeur expirant." After coldness, darkness:

> Déjà je ne vois plus qu'à travers un nuage
> Et le ciel et l'époux que ma présence outrage.   (1641–42)

Her ancestors in the heavens and her husband on earth, from whose presence she had sought to hide, now disappear from sight. And the light that she used to see vanishes.

> Et la mort, à mes yeux dérobant la clarté,
> Rend au jour, qu'ils souillaient, toute sa pureté.

We can now find in this couplet all the meanings that the words have gathered along the way: withdrawing me from the light of day— or life—which I sought with impurity, and closing my eyes, which soiled this light as they received it and transformed it into something dark, death, which seemed to me out of desperation the only hiding place where I could conceal forever this "flamme si noire," now on the contrary reopens my soul to a vision of this light, now ineffably pure. For this is surely what Racine meant. When Phèdre says "la mort rend au jour toute sa pureté," she does not say "ma mort" but "la mort," not "the death of me" but "my experience of dying." There is a parallel between "dérober" and "rendre"; by stressing that the light is snatched from her bodily eyes, she means that it is to her new sight that the new light is restored. The light was soiled within her by the action of her eyes, and by altering her vision death or dying makes it possible for her to see "le jour" grown visible "dans toute sa pureté." That purity had always been there, uncontaminated. It is the reflection of that purity in her soul, then, that is, and needed to be, purified. And Racine, by a succession of inversions within the two lines, contrives that the last word uttered by Phèdre, just as she expires, should be "pureté."

But there is in all this the grimness of tragic irony. Thésée's response to his wife's dying words is abysmally uncomprehending; he recalls only the blackness:

> D'une action si noire
> Que ne peut avec elle expirer la mémoire!   (1645-46)

To Phèdre, dying brings purity, and it is dying alone that can bring it. The final new "jour" is a light that can appear only after the fire in her "brûlantes veines" has grown cold and the light of life quite shut out of eyes that can no longer covet, no longer deceive the heart with hallucinations of consummated desire. The freezing, obliterating effect of the poison produces a light that is all pure, but with a deathly purity and paleness, without earthly glow. Purity, with life, had been impossible for Phèdre.

But now impurity, with life, is no longer anything that Phèdre can regret. And not because the satisfaction of purity lies solely in its cleansing effect. "Pureté" is not only moral purity. The purity of "le jour" also refers to its clearness, the absence of anything that could obscure it, as one says today "un ciel pur." "La mort rend au jour toute sa pureté": Phèdre's dying, by closing eyes that avidly feasted on illusions, opens her sight to an unobstructed, unclouded "jour." And it is an immense satisfaction and repose to see thus clearly. Phèdre certainly had suffered because her love was sinful; but, not able to resist it, she had only sought to hide it. Now she has learned that her wrong was more complicated and deeper, for she had lived on images of life that had no substance. The tranquillizing effect of the new light, eliminating the sin, eradicates the illusion, which is still more fundamental in Racine's theater.

Although Francis Fergusson, in the *Idea of a Theater*, does not fully appreciate this, Racine's idea of tragedy renews closely that of Sophocles in *Oedipus Tyrannus*, where Fergusson finds, using a formula of Kenneth Burke, the tragic rhythm of Purpose, Passion, Perception. Like Oedipus, and like other characters of Racine, Phèdre sets out with a purpose that is wrong and insufficient, though righteous—she wants to hide her shame. Passion, breaking out, disrupts this purpose, and reveals its inadequacy. And out of the passion, or suffering, emerges a new purpose, and a perception that both illuminates and destroys. Though she wanted to die for one purpose—a purpose thoroughly defeated, as her shame craves to reveal itself—she discovers in dying that something else, and better, takes place—a purification, which abolishes what she meant death to hide.

The dread of descending into Hades is gone. She feared that she would appear there such as she had been. But now, as she sinks into the nether world and "la mort rend au jour toute sa pureté," she knows that she will no longer see Hippolyte as before.

Whether "le jour" means the light of day, Hippolyte, love, life, purity, or truth—and it means all that—the outcome is always the same. On all levels, after the escape into the forest and the descent into the labyrinth, there is a descent into Hades, which we witness as it reverses the flight from light *to* darkness into a rediscovery of light *out of* darkness.

Therein especially one recognizes the very metaphor of tragedy, which Racine may have encountered in many sources but which is profoundly Sophoclean. In *Oedipus* and in *Phèdre*, pollution and purification, illusion and self-knowledge, death and life are given an expression of their paradoxical relationships in the simple image of eyes that see but do not acquire vision without suffering.

L'Art poétique:
"Longtemps plaire, et jamais ne lasser"

FOR BOILEAU, the only possibilities open to the poet are signal success or utter failure. There is no in-between, no graded scale or measurable percentage of poetic accomplishment:

> Il n'est point de degrés du médiocre au pire.
> Qui dit froid écrivain dit détestable auteur.[1]

A poem is either a joy, or a scandal, and no bickering over details of literary doctrine will settle the matter, or can ever be much to the point.

It is the poet-satirist that animates the critic in Boileau. To portray him as a drill master, an advocate of the three R's—Rules, Regimentation, Regularity—would be grossly to disfigure him; as we have been shown often enough by now, he is not a bureaucrat or technocrat of literature. If his style waxes imperative, to the point of sounding dogmatic to us at times, this comes from the certitude of a strong personal faith in his experience of beauty and art, but not out of any concern with official regulations. It is revealing that he can never be discovered to inveigh against his numerous victims for infractions of

Originally published in *Studies in Seventeenth-Century French Literature Presented to Morris Bishop*, ed. J.-J. Demorest (Ithaca, N.Y., 1962), pp. 231–46.

[1]*L'Art poétique*, 4: 32–33. All quotations follow the Charles-H. Boudhors edition of Boileau's *Oeuvres complètes*, 7 vols. (Paris, 1934–43).

formal, technical rules.[2] But it would be equally misleading to represent him, more flatteringly, as a high theorist intent on unravelling the nature of poetry by a searching process of analysis, and equipped to pursue such a philosophical inquiry, up to the last answerable question. He had no disposition for such a task. His aptitude for understanding was that of a poet, and his account of poetry itself was chiefly a poetic figuration of the subject, even or especially in the long, elaborate *Art poétique*.

It reads like a representation or enactment of what happens between an author and his reader. It is not a portrait of the poet alone, held statically under focus. Boileau would have been at a loss to comprehend poetry as expression sufficient to itself, or as the poet's private concern. He sees it as quite manifestly and essentially a phenomenon of direct and felicitous communication. He requires, as he puts it in one of his most beautiful lines, that the poet, within us, leave of his work a long remembrance—that all he utters "de son ouvrage en nous laisse un long souvenir" (3: 158). Repeatedly he addresses to the poet a question or challenge by which he binds the artist to his reader as to an indispensable recipient and companion in "l'acte des Muses." Would you be cherished, he asks at the outset, "Voulez-vous du public mériter les amours" (1: 69)? Would you, he asks again, endear the opulent creations of your imagination to your readers?— "Voulez-vous faire aimer vos riches fictions" (4: 86)? Would you offer such tragedies as will cast a lasting spell on all of Paris?

> Voulez-vous sur la scène étaler des ouvrages,
> Où tout Paris en foule apporte ses suffrages,
> Et qui toujours plus beaux, plus ils sont regardés,
> Soient au bout de vingt ans encor redemandés?   (3: 11–14)

"Voulez-vous," he urges, "longtemps plaire ["long attract and captivate"], et jamais ne lasser ["never breed lassitude"]" (3: 245)?

These are the two requirements, which are but one, and which he illustrates with a multitude of descriptions, scenes, skits, and thumbnail sketches, all dwelling on the one picture of delight and lassitude, predominantly a picture of motion along a course. Among the smaller genres, for example, the eclogue, which gathers its engaging though humble lore and its quality of style from the rustic scene, has its own path to find, clear of both platitude and pomposity, and "Entre ces deux excès la route est difficile," requiring "et la force et la grâce" of a Theocritus or a Virgil (2: 1-37). The ode, "Elevant jusqu'au

---

[2]As we are aptly reminded by E. B. O. Borgerhoff, *The Freedom of French Classicism* (Princeton, N.J., 1950), p. 212.

Ciel son vol ambitieux," knows no constraint: "Son style impétueux souvent marche au hasard," artfully showing "un beau désordre"— this is no expedition for those timorous rhymesters whose "esprit flegmatique / Garde dans ses fureurs un ordre didactique" (2: 58-81). Along the road of tragedy, one of the major genres, where Boileau expects that "la passion émue (aroused)/Aille chercher le cœur," he requires that the exposition without strain open and clear the way at once ("applanisse l'entrée"), and that all along the poet move swiftly from marvel to marvel: "Il faut . . . /Qu'il coure dans ses vers de merveille en merveille" (3: 151-56). For "Ainsi la tragédie agit, marche, et s'explique" ("unfolds") (3: 159). Epic poetry, in its vast account of a long enterprise, sustains its narration with more grandeur still. The poet, without keeping to an "ordre méthodique," but without straying over lengthy byways ("Il ne s'égare point en de trop longs détours"), moves on and drives forward: "tout marche et se suit." Each verse, each word, speeds on to the final outcome— "court à l'événement" (3: 309, 306).

This metaphorical language becomes indispensable to Boileau, at almost every turn of L'Art poétique. Even the lowly "vaudeville," that malicious offspring of satire, turns into a jolly talebearer, busily on the move; led on by the melody to which it is sung ("conduit par le chant"), this poem scurries from mouth to mouth, and grows larger as it goes—"Passe de bouche en bouche, et s'accroît en marchant" (2: 181-84). We see one poem after another "marcher," "passer," "courir," or even fly upon its course, now in a swift, overpowering onrush and now like "un ruisseau, qui sur la molle arène/Dans un pré plein de fleurs lentement se promène" (1: 166-67).

Whatever the course, or the apparent ease of the traveler, "la route est difficile." It is something of a miracle road on which journeying and arriving are synchronized into one act. The perfection to be reached is "la raison"—but "raison" as Boileau understood it: not ratiocination but, in Descartes's language, a "puissance," a swift, in-tuitive power of "l'esprit." Instantaneous, like sensation, it bears another familiar name: "le bon sens," the good sense, the sense that is right and infallible. Transferred to the aesthetic realm, for Boileau raison-bon sens remains a species of sensitive energy, a prompt and live sense of rightness. That is the desired goal, yet it is also the neces-sary guide. In making its discoveries "raison" exercises upon itself its own critical power of judgment and, therefore, of control. Not that Boileau can ever arrive at a systematic statement of these opera-tions of "raison." With an ambiguity that is perhaps unavoidable and even necessary in these matters, he offered this striking mixed meta-phor:

Tout doit tendre au bon sens: mais pour y parvenir
Le chemin est glissant et pénible à tenir.
Pour peu qu'on s'en écarte, aussitôt l'on se noie.
La raison, pour marcher, n'a souvent qu'une voie.   (1: 45–48)

There is but one road. It leads to "le bon sens"; all must tend toward that goal. Yet this "bons sens" is at the same time the "raison" that goes forward, along the very road of which it is the fixed end. This concurrence of discovery and searching is suggested by the ambiguity of the word "sens" itself, which can mean direction as well as insight: most authors, says Boileau, eager to be original and "emportés d'une fougue insensée,/Toujours loin du droit sens vont chercher leur pensée" (1: 39–42), which suggests both that they miss the right sense and that they stray from the right direction.[3]

The road not only represents an uncommon course, on which discovering and searching are telescoped; it also merges the reader's course with that of the poet. Pictures of felicitously flowing, speeding, or soaring motions are pictures of the reader's as well as of the poet's sustained and elated act of discovery. The poet and the reader are endowed with the same *raison-bon sens*, an essential attribute of all human beings. Boileau, it is true, never states this Cartesian assumption in so many words, and is even accused at times of setting up his own taste as a norm of "raison"; but an assumption of universality would still be implicit in his very self-assurance. If there is an infallible human "bon sens" in both, the reader and the poet cannot but be similarly affected by the finished poem.

And yet, despite the vaunted universality of "raison," Boileau is forever being scandalized by the number of frigid and insipid "sots" that he finds in Paris and beyond. Are they devoid of "raison" and inhuman? Or is it that our native "raison" in them remains dormant, or obstructed? However that may be, they are the bane of Boileau's existence, for the apathy, boredom, and lassitude that they breed. The ineptitude and lethargy of their soul lie heavy on a reader's spirit, and oppress him beyond endurance; it is on such fiascos of poetry that Boileau, a satirist at heart, dwells with special relish and verve.

He opens *L'Art poétique* by sketching at once images of futile and frustrated motion, which will illuminate what he means later by *raison-bon sens*. In vain does an author propose to reach the peak of

---

[3]For a more detailed analysis of these terms and, in general, for the most comprehensive and searching discussion of Boileau's literary doctrine, see Jules Brody, *Boileau and Longinus* (Geneva, 1958). For a capital survey of French classical doctrine in its various stages and tendencies, see Borgerhoff, *French Classicism*.

Mount Parnassus if he is not a born poet. "Dans son génie étroit" ("within his narrow endowments"), he remains a captive, "il est toujours captif." Winged Pegasus restively balks at carrying such a rider. He is condemned to immobility, or to aimless, pointless agitation, like those who burning with a reckless zeal sally forth on "la carrière épineuse" and fruitlessly, upon verses, labor and waste away; or like that would-be epic poet (Saint-Amant) who impudently goes and sings the triumphant Exodus of the Hebrews and, chasing across the desert after Moses, in his rush drowns himself in the sea, along with Pharaoh —"court avec Pharaon se noyer dans les mers"; or like that windbag (Scudéry) who, should he come upon a palace, needs must take me through the whole estate and show me around the whole edifice—to reach the end, I skip twenty leaves of the book, and even then "je me sauve à peine au travers du jardin."

Paralysis, sluggishness, or debility are common afflictions of a motionless spirit, whose "vers plats et grossiers" always hug the ground "et rampent tristement" (2: 19-20). In epic poetry, if the author does not, like Virgil, readily and steadily take hold of us with a force "qui surprend, frappe, saisit, attache," then "le vers tombe en langueur,/ La poésie est morte, ou rampe sans vigueur" (3: 160-92)—his dragging verse is without savor, without warmth, without life. Frigidity especially, with the hardness of ice, congeals all energies, as in those verses of Motin, a weary poet chilled to the bone, who leaves us numbed with cold—"ces vers où Motin se morfond et nous glace" (4: 40). The bombast of "les grands mots," those big, bloated words, induces another variety of stiffness, which makes an author stumble and grotesquely take a hard fall, as in the case of Ronsard, "ce poète trébuché de si haut" (1: 124-29); the most vivid example, more acceptable to modern readers partial to Ronsard, is a caricature, sketched outside L'Art poétique, of Jean Chapelain's pretentious, gawky verses, hoisted upon a pair of pompous big words as on a pair of stilts: "ces vers et sans force et sans grâces,/Montés sur deux grands mots, comme sur deux échasses" (Satire IV, 97-98).

Frozen or stilted verse will not transport us far. But neither will mere agitation. Drowning (or shipwreck at times), seen from a comic angle as a disaster which swiftly brings to naught, with ludicrous finality, a reckless expenditure of energy, is an image which the satirist Boileau particularly fancies. The drowning poet has failed lamentably to steer his course unerringly among "excès"—"excès," it is to be noted, are not just faults of overabundance but, more generally and fundamentally, vices of deviation from "le droit sens."[4] For the live and the quick, there is often but one road to vital discovery

---

[4]Cf. Brody, Boileau and Longinus, p. 66.

and, "Pour peu qu'on s'en écarte, aussitôt l'on se noie." But there are ever so many other ways of straying and coming to a bad end. One author, who dreads the prospect of just creeping along on the ground, goes to the other extreme and gets himself lost in the clouds— "il se perd dans la nue" (1: 68), or drowns, as it were, in the sky. Another, like Scudéry, becomes hopelessly submerged in his own subject. Some, priding themselves on their breakneck speed, remind Boileau of "un torrent débordé qui d'un cours orageux/Roule plein de gravier sur un terrain fangeux" (1: 167–68). Rashly the uncultivated poet, who on random occasions has been kindled by a bright natural flame, would undertake a resounding full-length epic poem:

> Sa Muse déréglée, en ses vers vagabonds
> Ne s'élève jamais que par sauts et par bonds.   (3: 317–18)

L'Art poétique abounds in such vignettes. In lively succession every "excès" is graphically represented, making us perpetually conscious of an incongruous contrast between this vain agitation, or inertia, and the motion that irresistibly carries one away and constantly reminding us that immobility and bewilderment, failures in poetic communication, leave the reader himself inert or bewildered. His plight is abundantly, richly illustrated. For example, the intolerable boredom generated by Scudéry's survey of the palace exterior and interior is farcically pictured by the motion of two forces pulling in different directions: a slow, interminable drag, to which the entrapped reader's desperate, automatic reaction is sudden and swift escape. Similarly, when a vexed rhymester, hard pressed for inspiration, throws down the flute and oboe natural to bucolic poetry and, with boorish zest, in the midst of his eclogue blows on a blaring trumpet,

> De peur de l'écouter, Pan fuit dans les roseaux,
> Et les Nymphes d'effroi se cachent sous les eaux.   (2: 15–16)

Comic pictures of the poet's victims in flight or in panic flash across the scene.

The problem for the victim is to break away in time, for there are lethal verses that deaden a reader's spirit before he can make good his escape, as in the works of those authors, "nés pour nous ennuyer," who drone on and on (1: 71–74), or in the cold rhetorical disputations that chill a tragedy, where all should be "passion" (3: 21–24). Sleep overtakes the reader. Perhaps that is another way out. As he takes the plunge, dropping irresistibly into oblivious slumber, all the meaningless babble and commotion suddenly comes to a dead stop for him, as for the author himself in drowning. The torpor of slumber, however, must be inoculated, there must be some measure of contact between author and victim. The dreariest picture of all is the spectacle of dead books left utterly to themselves—total inertness, within and without—vacuity which creates a spreading vacuum all around itself. There is no public left. The reader is conspicuous by his absence and complete obliteration. There is only an imperceptible stir going on in a bookseller's dark back room, where those books, stored up in piles, "Combattent tristement les vers et la poussière" (3: 331-32). In a way they are themselves steeped in absolute slumber, as they quietly rot away in obscurity, growing mouldy around the edges.

This imagery of motion, sustained or arrested, is the basic language of *L'Art poétique*, reinforced by other images pertaining especially to sound and taste, and most notably to light and darkness. For example:

> Il est certains esprits, dont les sombres pensées
> Sont d'un nuage épais toujours embarrassées.
> Le jour de la raison ne le saurait percer.   (1: 147-49)

The captivity of a mind caught in its own clutter of thoughts is represented here by the thickness and darkness of a cloud, where the broad daylight of "raison" will not break through. Quickening illumination here would itself be a form of animation. Everything tells the story of movement and immobility. One of Boileau's most characteristic habits of style is the continual use of "aller" and other verbs of motion as auxiliary verbs. This is not a mere formality of usage. It becomes necessary that aroused passion "*aille* chercher," that it *go* and seek out the heart; Saint-Amant does not just sing the Exodus but "*s'en va . . .* chanter—*goes off* and sings," and does not just drown but "*court . . .* se noyer—*runs* and drowns himself" (1: 23-27); Ronsard does not merely hum his Gothic idylls but "*vient* encor fredonner— still *comes* humming along" (2: 21-22); hasty epic poets *go* and shout all their power away in their first lines (3: 270-72); constantly "aller," "venir," "courir" seem to absorb the action of other verbs, as if it were the latter that had come to serve an auxiliary function, to particularize numerous instances of motion intensively sustained or grotesquely abortive.

There is, to be sure, nothing so common in literature as the image of motion, of which various components could have reached Boileau from countless sources. But the composite is distinctively his own. For example, a very likely source, in Boileau's library, may have been Descartes, in whose works the image of the philosopher as a traveller, now pressing forward and now groping, is one of the dominant stylistic traits;[5] but it does not have this touch of satire, this dash of comedy and farce, and lays no stress on the merger of the reader's course with the author's. Boileau's own works—his *Satires* and *Epîtres* in particular—were an important training ground for *L'Art poétique* in this respect; there he had already set authors and readers on their straight or erratic courses. In none of these much briefer poems, however, had Boileau achieved the elaboration and saturation of imagery that became possible in the sizable *Art poétique*—except perhaps in the ninth *Satire*, a poem of 322 lines which offers in dense concentration pictures of the road, of "marcher" and "courir," of forceful energy and rash ardor, of tripping, falling, crawling, and drowning, of readers asleep and of books slumbering under thick layers of dust, of frozen mind and of petrified inspiration, of flying and of molten wings.

That in embryo was *L'Art poétique*. All too often we read and interpret the latter purely as a didactic work. Undeniably, it is strewn with instructions to the would-be poet. But one of these, not sufficiently publicized, is the urgent rule to forget about rules, when necessary: the admonition to the poet that he clear his "esprit tremblant" of "scruples" and "doutes ridicules" and learn (still in the language of the road),

> par quel transport heureux,
> Quelquefois dans sa course un esprit vigoureux
> Trop resserré par l'art, sort des règles prescrites,
> Et de l'art même apprend à franchir leurs limites.   (4: 77–80)

Joining example to precept, Boileau here disregards, in the last line, the capital rule of the caesura, as he does elsewhere, and teaches on the spot a lesson in the free creation of rhythm attuned to the subject. His so-called Rules are misnamed. They do not constitute a body of decrees but, interspersed among images of the poet and reader on the move and couched at times in the very language of that imagery, they complement and reinforce with psychological remarks the metaphorical statement of a poetic strategy.

They are drawn up according to a rather persistent pattern of formulation, which Horace no doubt suggested but did not develop with so much emphasis. The Roman poet, for example, does not confine himself to prohibiting the showing of horrible events on the stage; he suggests, as an explanation, that such repellent spectacles create disbelief. So does Boileau: Never show, he says, anything unbelievable

---

[5]See, by the present author, "The Mixed Metaphor in Descartes," *Romanic Review* 41 (1950): 167–78, reprinted in this volume.

on the stage. That is the famous rule of *vraisemblance*, stated in the imperative. It is followed immediately, in the expository mood of the indicative, by a brief psychological elucidation or justification: an absurd marvel, he says, is for me "sans appas"; "L'esprit n'est point ému de ce qu'il ne croit pas" (3: 50). Time and again, with a shift from the imperative to the indicative, Boileau translates a rule into an observation on psychological action, stimulation, and effect. In the imperative: discard unnecessary details. In the indicative: what is superfluously uttered is "fade et rebutant," and the mind, being cloyed, throws it up instantly—"L'esprit rassasié le rejette à l'instant" (1: 62). In recommending purity and clarity of language, he explains that if comprehension comes slowly and laboriously, "Mon esprit aussitôt commence à se détendre," and "prompt à se détacher,/Ne suit point un auteur qu'il faut toujours chercher" (1: 145–46). In requiring that the end, in a tragedy, without labor bring "le trouble toujours croissant" to a resolution, he explains that "L'esprit ne se sent point plus vivement frappé" as when a final revelation gives everything a changed and unforeseen meaning (3: 55–60).

Boileau goes on and on in this fashion. We have grown accustomed to isolating and underscoring the imperative and hortatory in his rules, but to him a rule is essentially a commentary on what happens in "l'esprit." A term which comes to dominate these "rule" passages, "esprit," used more often there than "raison," is not always easily distinguishable from the latter, but can be understood in a more general or fluctuating sense to designate the natural endowment of spirit and mind, which includes not only "raison" but other mental powers. "Esprit" is that inner world which Boileau visualizes as constantly threatened with chaos, inertness, or complete vacuity. The life of the mind, for him, hangs on its intense wakefulness, attentiveness, and concentration. This is an obsession, with him, and that is why the great epic poem, as we saw, is the one which "surprend, frappe, saisit, attache," or why even in the eclogue, for example, its sweetness must caress, stimulate, and rouse us—"Il faut que sa douceur flatte, chatouille, éveille" (2: 9).

If these be rules, they certainly are not for all and sundry to follow. Boileau may well enjoin upon the tragic poet to warm and rouse the heart and to leave "l'esprit ému" and "frappé." "Le secret," he can only say, is at once (*d'abord*) "de plaire et de toucher." With astonishing strokes unceasingly the poet must waken us—"Que de traits surprenants sans cesse il nous réveille" (3: 155). That is indeed more of a secret and a challenge than a working rule, like the recommendation that a comic poet have "un esprit profond," to penetrate the secret hearts of men (3: 361–62).

The rule of rules that every image and every proposition in *L'Art poétique* asserts or implies is that a poem communicate a live, overwhelmingly convincing experience of reality. "Coeur" and "esprit," which Boileau also does not systematically distinguish, are both to be gripped, astounded, enthralled. The Sublime, as Boileau understood it in his reading of Longinus, is "cet extraordinaire et ce merveilleux qui frappe dans le discours" and brings it about that a work "enlève, ravit, transporte"—a sequence which depicts with rising intensity a sudden motion of carrying away. Intellect and emotion are associated; the pleasure of beauty is a pleasure of cognition, or recognition of things as they really are. Let us not expect Boileau to demonstrate; he dramatizes and metaphorizes all this. But he does state more formally, in a 1701 survey of his lifework: "L'esprit de l'homme est naturellement plein d'un nombre infini d'idées confuses du vrai, que souvent il n'entrevoit qu'à demi; et rien ne lui est plus agréable que lorsqu'on lui offre quelqu'une de ces idées bien éclaircie, et mise dans un beau jour."[6] "Rien ne lui est plus agréable." Boileau had also previously stated in the ninth *Epître*, written shortly after *L'Art poétique*: "Rien n'est beau que le vrai. Le vrai seul est aimable" (43). "Le vrai," he claimed for his own works, "partout se montre aux yeux et va saisir le coeur" (54); "mon coeur toujours conduisant mon esprit,/Ne dit rien aux lecteurs, qu'à soi-même il n'ait dit" (57–58). "Le faux" in poetry, to him, breeds lassitude and revulsion precisely because, in direct contrast to "le vrai," it disintegrates this cognitive-emotive grasp; it is "toujours fade, ennuyeux, languissant,/ Mais la nature est vraie, et d'abord [at once] on la sent" (85–86). As will be elaborated in 1701: "Puis donc qu'une pensée n'est belle qu'en ce qu'elle est vraie; et que l'effet infaillible du vrai, quand il est bien énoncé, c'est de frapper les hommes; il s'ensuit que ce qui ne frappe point les hommes, n'est ni beau, ni vrai, ou qu'il est mal énoncé."[7] Obviously, by "nature" and "le vrai" Boileau does not mean a literal rendition of reality, which can be true but platitudinous and soporific. He means a seductive presentation of reality that makes it irresistibly present before us. Beauty is an aesthetic experience of the true.

But Boileau would not have it remain a momentary experience. He must have given thought many a time to a description of the mind included by one of his Jansenist friends, Pierre Nicole, in his *Dissertatio de vera pulchritudine et adumbrata*:

Naturam humanae mentis si penitus introspicere velis, et interiores in ea delectationum fontes rimari, robur quoddam in ipsa deprehendes, quadam infirmitate conjunctum, unde magna varietas et inaequalitas oriatur. Robore enim fit ut perpetuam remissionem grevetur; infirmitate contra,

[6]In the 1701 preface to the *Satires*, ed. Boudhors, p. 4.

[7]*Ibid.*, pp. 5–6.

ut perpetuam contentionem pati nequeat. Hinc est quod ipsi nihil diu placet, nihil sui undique simile.[8]

For Boileau as for Nicole, the mind is such that it delights in the exercise of its power, but a power which by its very nature cannot be lastingly excited and exercised. The wonder of great poetry, for Boileau, is that it defies this law and transcends this routine, intermittent, fitful life of the mind. Analogously to Descartes, whose great and probably impossibly ambitious strategy was to connect a series of distinct and necessarily isolated intuitions into a continuous, unbroken line of deduction which might be like one extended, prolonged intuition, Boileau required above all the delight of continuity, wholeness, and oneness in poetic experience. If there are any rules as such in *L'Art poétique,* and if some turn to scattered matters of technique, versification, or formal structure, their purpose is always to keep the continuity and the oneness undisturbed and unjeopardized by the shock of displeasure, disbelief, incomprehension, or any other disruption. The secret, then, is not only "de plaire et de toucher"; the rhyme to "toucher" is "attacher." Find magical ways, says Boileau, of holding on to me, "Inventez des ressorts qui puissent m'attacher" (3: 26). Not only is the reader to be drawn in but he is to be "ému" and "frappé" throughout, and the poet must, in his verses, run "de merveille en merveille." In translating Longinus, Boileau inserted characteristic words of his own on the subject of the sublime in the *Iliad,* "qui marche partout d'un pas égal, sans que jamais il s'arrête ni se repose"[9]—a steady advance with never a break or a rest.

The fundamental image, around which all pictures of animation and inertia gravitate, is the ambiguous but (to Boileau) not impossible image of a road on which "raison" intently progresses toward a goal which is "raison" itself. It is on this road that "longtemps plaire, et jamais ne lasser" is crucial. "Longtemps" does not only refer to the distant future, when time and again a poem will be "encore rede-

---

[8]The *Dissertatio* was published in *Epigrammatum delectus ex omnibus tum veteribus, tum recentioribus poetis accurate decerptus* (Paris, 1659). The pages are unnumbered; the quotation is to be found at the head of the section entitled "Interior quaedam et magis arcana verborum cum natura consensio." A French translation by L.S.G.L.A.C. (Germain de Lafaille) was published by the same press in 1689; it would seem superior to the one by Richelet published in *Nouveau recueil des épigrammatistes français anciens et modernes,* ed. Bruzen de La Martinière (Amsterdam, 1720), 2: 169–220. In the Lafaille translation (p. 20), this passage reads as follows: "Si l'on doit examiner de près la nature de l'esprit humain, et considérer ses inclinations et ses plaisirs dans leur source, on trouvera qu'il a en soi une certaine force jointe à une certaine faiblesse qui le rend inégal, et sujet à varier. Sa force ne peut souffrir un relâchement continuel, et sa faiblesse ne peut soutenir une continuelle contention. C'est pour ce sujet qu'il ne saurait s'accommoder toujours d'une même chose."

[9]See Brody, *Boileau and Longinus,* p. 58.

mandé," although this is a capital test. The prior meaning of "long-temps," and of "jamais," has to do with the sustained continuity of a work within the duration and extent of its own course. Paul Valéry, one of the twentieth-century minds who best understood French classicism, put it in terms that Boileau would have appreciated:

> Les dieux, gracieusement, nous donnent *pour rien* tel premier vers; mais c'est à nous de façonner le second, qui doit consonner avec l'autre, et ne pas être indigne de son aîné surnaturel. Ce n'est pas trop de toutes les ressources de l'expérience et de l'esprit pour le rendre comparable au vers qui fut un don.[10]

[10]"Au sujet d'Adonis," *Variété* (Paris, 1937), 2: 81.

The Eye of the Beholder: Reflections on Classical Order

THE LIGHT COMES, in the story of Creation, after the night; at the beginning darkness was upon the face of the deep. So, to man the beholder, it must always have appeared: the light as genesis, as awakening of life. In the perpetual round of night and day, each unendingly precedes and follows and there is no fixed before or after, except in the eye of the beholder. At times it may seem to him so ordered that the night is to come after, at the last, as in the tragedy of an Oedipus, a Phèdre at the end descending among the dead—"la mort à mes yeux dérobant la clarté." From the earliest of times the wonder and mystery of the cycle may have been to man a compelling sign of the impossibility of an eternal day. Yet in much of ancient lore, darkness is but initial lifeless void and the day comes after, rousing, stirring life again; night is an effacing of the vanishing scene, the day a return, a renewal.

This image comes to be like a basic pattern for men of the Renaissance and their successors. To them a dark age, an age of *ténèbres*, is followed, as it was preceded, by luminous times—the primeval image, well suited to their new perspective. Or rather, the new view drawn from, or fitted into, the primal pattern. But perhaps we have been too exclusively concerned with this perspective as an historical panorama of the human spirit; with much learning we have marked

Not previously published. This was to be part of an introduction to a survey of Renaissance and classical aesthetics.

the range of centuries that the tableau had been designed to encompass, and also debated whether a renascence had truly taken place or had been but wishfully visioned. We discuss the literal meaning, and the merits, of an historical outlook. This it was, of course, but with extensions into other levels of meaning generally unprobed. For the human spirit seen in the large, even over a millennium, had its ways of resembling rather closely the private soul. By old habits of analogy, of comparing great things to small, the general is made to impersonate the individual and, here, on the grand scale of centuries the spirit must sleep, vanish, die perhaps, and wake to life again, quite like the consciousness of a man in the space of a day. This is not solely a chart of the cultural ups and downs of mankind in time, but it entails as well an interior sketch or anatomy of the mind, an image of its inward condition without the pale of an historical context.

The purpose here, specifically, is a rereading of what goes under the awesome name of the French classical doctrine, still a considerable specter haunting literary and art history. It has been useful and liberating toward this end to relearn in a way the language of Renaissance and seventeenth-century France—this whole stretch, one experiences very early, is the most direct route to any of its points—and in particular the language concerned with the meaning of beauty and art, and its relation to the nature of the mind; that is to say, to read the aesthetic speculations of those generations in their own idiom, and as they understood it, without scrambling it with later -isms or -ologies of which they had no notion.

It is for example an elementary but sobering fact, worth a moment's reflection, that "la doctrine classique" has been so named for a long time, but never by the authors and artists to whom it is ascribed or by their contemporaries; "classique" is something of a post-"classical," and not infrequently anti-"classical," slogan. Whatever did they then call themselves? It has been possible to be and to know that one was, let us say, a romanticist, a symbolist, an expressionist, and so on. By now every avant-garde in fact has taken to announcing its denomination right off. There was in the days called "classiques" a bevy of -iques and -istes, to be sure, in matters of philosophy and faith, with names derived from past or current issues; one might be, for example, an Aristotelian or a Platonist, a Stoic or a Skeptic, a Thomist, an Augustinian, or a Jansenist; one might have become a Cartesian. There were labels galore for schools of thought, but what new names for new schools of art? One might be a partisan of the ancients or a modern, or as gracefully as possible straddle the fence. This indeed was a continuing point of contention around which groups formed and opposed each other. We are in the habit of localizing the famous Quarrel narrowly in our imagination within the radius of a high-visibility incident, the head-on collision of Boileau and Charles Perrault; but the Quarrel had been rehearsed for generations, and Du Bellay's *Deffence et illustration de la langue françoise* over a century before had been every bit as explosive, and louder perhaps, in expressing an ardent note of national sentiment: let us emulate the ancients in order to surpass them, but while we are at it let us in this outshine and confound proud Italy. Yet in "ancien" and "moderne," twin terms gathered into the dominating image of "renaissance," or in "humaniste," the answer to our question about self-denomination remains elusive. The ancients and the moderns alike might have answered it articulately enough to their mind by citing select masters and works, by describing their characterizing style, quality, and effect, but without stamping on them a sectarian mark of the craft, although this sort of branding was common enough in other vocations. Why this difference? Some "why," or possibly more than one, may show through the "how"; the task will be to see how, first, the artistic vocation was conceived. For the discussion dwelt on vocation, rather than sect.

Ask Boileau then what he holds against any of his favorite targets; he will dramatize it in unforgettable lines, but will have no way of saying: "He is not classical." Nor will he say: "he has broken *les règles*." He will never criticize, or for that matter praise, by the book of rules, author of *L'Art poétique* though he is. The "rules" are too much with us, certainly more than with Boileau and most of his contemporaries. They are the doctrinaires that we, largely, have made of them. "Rules" of a kind there were, now recognized and now haggled over, bypassed, or hoodwinked, as often happens to rules, precepts, and maxims of the *métier*. The real problem is that we harbor these "rules" in the mind like an ancient grudge, confused heirs that we are to the Romantic declaration of independence from "classicism." For the young new school in the early nineteenth century it had become a polemical necessity and opportunity to mount such a revolt from a tradition which by then, in its die-hard representatives, had waned into obsolescence; for their posterity this cause, no longer the combat of the day, has remained an inherited issue. Seventeenth-century France still looms large, in one version of our own historical panorama, as a fortress of repression and authority; under its dominion it seems the native hue of inspiration is sicklied o'er with the pale cast of Reason, another uncongenial name for Order, Rules, and the whole tyranny of it all: the divine right of kings and the *lettre de cachet* mistaken for a doctrine of art. And if Versailles rather than the Bastille dominates the view, with Order under the guise of Decorum, then all seems repressed and muffled as in enveloping urbanity.

At the same time, when the "rules" are not too much with us, the view opens up freely and the age looms large with stirrings of things to come, with queries, preoccupations, and discoveries to be pursued to this day. In art we know full well the abundant power of creativity that flourished then and, rather noticeably, failed to be stifled by the "rules." Recent and current schools of new criticism in competition have been actively reinterpreting this art for our times. We sense in it more acutely now the rumblings, the tensions, the agitation in the depths, and the strains in the smooth surface itself. It would have grown increasingly awkward to manage all this under the old caption of "classicism," and thus the "baroque" has been discovered. Penetratingly analyzed in Heinrich Wölfflin's *Principles of Art History*, then grafted onto literature and even, after much hesitation and parleying, onto French "classical" works, this concept has been explaining them to us and all the while conditioning our responses, and undoubtedly manifesting latent uncertainties in many minds concerning the conventional meaning of "classical." It has not, however, charmed away the old "order"; it has not displaced or dispelled the old terminology and concept, which hang on. The "baroque" in any of its ramifying varieties is something we can be induced to consider, to debate at least, as a quality of the created works, but when it comes to the aesthetic in terms of which these presumably were created or appraised in their own times, the "rules" take over, an "order" inimical to the vitality and freedom of the spirit sets in again. The result is a hazy dichotomy, as if *Phèdre* for instance were one thing, the then prevailing idea of art quite another, and each were seen, somehow, apart; as if the "rules" had achieved some autonomous existence and reality without reference to particular works, as the very abstraction of constraining "order," to be resented on its own; or as if we had simply come to this: a Racine, yes, a Boileau, never.

It has not always been left just there. Baudelaire, Valéry, and Gide have probed for a more deeply grounded significance of order in "classical" art. But the tradition stands generally undisturbed. A clear-sighted reopening of the question by the late Professor E. B. O. Borgerhoff, *The Freedom of French Classicism* (1950), coming from overseas, went unreviewed in France and was for a good while, it would seem, unknown. Historians of aesthetics abide by Croce's dictum: "Boileau, slave to rigid *raison*," and in one of the explorations of art most widely read today, Malraux's *Le Musée imaginaire*, glimpses of an "esthétique impérative," of its "royauté," set us back at once, with new phrases, under the shadow of the olden fortress. That irrepressible jack-in-the-box bugaboo of a "doctrine classique" may yet prove too persistent to lay low, and it is undoubtedly as presumptuous to argue with a legend as to go against the grain, but it may be worth trying once more.

What is order to the mind, or spirit, or soul, whatever its name in any language? When imagined as oppression and frustration, it is abhorred. But in the main we do not disprize order, in art or science as in life; rather, we cleave to it. Much sooner than any order grown irksome, intimations of non-order or chaos that at times break in on us will offend the mind. But what is the mind itself, that it should value order so? What was it to the generations of three and four centuries ago? It has always been hard to apprehend in itself, and the constant temptation and compulsion of man has been to objectify, body forth the soul to his view. Even spirit imagined as breath, in the primal sense of *spiritus*, evokes the touch of some airy element brushing by, however lightly. Sometimes one quick glance, a wink, one stroke or two, and a sketch is drawn: "a mind like a sieve," "like a steel trap," "like a file cabinet," or in the latest idiom, "like a computer." At times a mind looks more like a labyrinth, a cave, a prison, or a hell of its own. Or an oasis. Or a vast realm with large dimensions of profundity, scope, and loftiness. Metaphorical representations abound, and we shall soon have a mind weightless as a rocket spaceship.

Most commonly, man tends to see in the mind likenesses and analogies to his own self in the flesh. He personifies the mind; he anthropomorphizes it, if that is not too paradoxical a thing to say about a mind that is human. Thus, like a man, often the mind hungers and thirsts; when nurtured, it absorbs and digests, it drinks deep, and it savors delights of its own; and there are insatiable, omnivorous minds. There are likewise healthy minds and sick, anemic, or contaminated minds, seminal minds and sterile slave minds and free, plebeian, aristocratic, pontifical, and sovereign minds. Who first saw the mind construct or demolish, weave or unravel, forge or batter, cultivate or devastate? Every condition, function, activity, and capacity of a human being has probably served to describe the human mind, with a few borrowed from other species: for it can ruminate, it can also fly off, wing away, and soar. All the senses of the body, the mind at one time or another has acquired metaphorically. Within the period canvassed here, for example, the mind's faculty for fine, delicate discrimination was for the first time likened to and called a sense of taste or *goût*. Sight, however, was a predominant sense.

Criticism, in a Thousand Hard Lessons

THE CHARM of Montaigne—I have this on the authority of every college youth who has read works on the French Renaissance but not the *Essais* of Montaigne; also on the higher authority of university professors—the charm of Montaigne lies in his conversational style. Good stuffing for the manuals, but I wonder what it means. Last night, a motley crowd gathered in my parlor, and there held forth on many subjects; it was a festival of conversation, an obstinate ceremonial, observed, as any set of rites, with great patience and monotony: a bewildering variety of topics, with many devious turns, like a small park in the center of a town, where everyone knows, through force of habit, the rocks, the flowers, the mounds behind every bend of the path. Yet everyone, ever so often, crosses from end to end—as hurriedly as possible. Their aim is to have talked at last, not to be talking. And that passes for conversation.

There are others who follow a more vivacious impulse, and overflow abundantly beyond the limits of any code. Their nature, their life, is wild gossip, racy chatter that feeds on the patient silence of others, while they disgorge anecdotes as rapidly as they possibly can: it's good for a whole evening. And that too passes for conversation.

Our sophomores and university professors will be quick in finding a wordier distinction. Montaigne is a spontaneous conversationalist,

Not previously published.

who yields to every suggestion of his mind and leads us from idea to idea; his rich intellect knows no plan; he reveals his lively train of thoughts, and should he begin a discourse on imagination, soon you find him turning around the problem of divine miracles; suddenly, he slips away and draws you into a long talk on sexual difficulties and their remedy, not to mention some scatological observations. What is next? Some pungent remarks on free will; and for an ending, a page or two on the method of his *Essais*! Who would tolerate such an interlocutor! In our drawing room, when a friend rambles through a serious debate, constantly off the track, we roughly pull him back; he fairly exasperates us. But not Montaigne. How then does he, for one, ramble on with felicity?

Well, Montaigne is cultured, they say. He possesses all of antiquity. And he has a world of experience. His art of conversation lies in his fondness for the concrete; his digressions are so many citations by which he materializes his ideas. A plausible fancy, I agree. I know an excellent Greek scholar who has familiarized himself with Homer to such an extent that he can cite one or two Homeric passages for every remark he makes; another has a profound knowledge of the Greek tragedians and can do as well with them; a Latin scholar can do the same with Virgil; others can quote Plutarch, or Lucretius, or Plato, or St. Augustine; each has his specialty. Others know a modern author, and lean heavily on his books. And everyone can remember, once in a while, a tale conveyed by word of mouth. But I never heard, in anyone's conversation, such numerous, facile and accurate impromptus of memory as Montaigne displays in one essay. Every statement winds in and out of epigraphs, allusions, quotations, references, where it is hard to find an error, although all the specialties are incorporated. Small wonder, Montaigne's *Essais* being a composite of elements that he constantly added to his first edition, working at leisure in a private tower. He claims, for his second output, six hundred additions to his first version.

What conversationalist will rest his laurels on a conversation of twenty years? Will you return, a year from today, adding a spicy morsel to your present discussion, and will I exclaim: "Indeed! What a fine talker you are! How alert! How you can think immediately of every appropriate illustration!"? Montaigne, they say, derives a powerful advantage from this; but is he conversing?

Yes and no, they answer. Of course, even in those days of humanism, when a learned man had a swollen memory crowded with ancient verse and prose, none could have ornamented a short talk with so many fitting and extemporaneous recollections. So much the less today. When we stop to analyze how Montaigne expanded his essays over two decades or more, it becomes impossible to fancy that you or I, or Montaigne himself, could ever converse in quite that manner. But nevertheless, his art produces that effect. His way of writing is not our way of talking; he may even digress extravagantly, enough to make an interlocutor squirm in his armchair, but, on paper, the magic works: we think that we are following a conversation—a supreme and delightful conversation.

Magic! Supreme, delightful! So that's where we were heading for! I could feel it coming on, I expected it. Pray, what is a delightful conversation? Now don't say, it is precisely a conversation with a certain charm like that of Montaigne. I don't squander charity on weaklings who beg the question. Come, now—what is a delightful conversation? Often enough, I have been delighted by talks with very interesting characters; once, a solid fellow soberly depicted for me the great happiness in the life of Reason, and I experienced a vast delight on hearing him; at another occasion, a charming soul, a youthful soul in bloom, luxuriously endowed, spoke ardently to me of the prodigal life, of passions and vivid impulses, and what he said was also a great delight; another, simple and kind, spoke very feelingly of our slums, and his goodness, candidly expressed, was a rich delight. Which of these delights pertains to Montaigne? Or is it some other? A combination of several? Or don't you know specifically?

Come now, again—what is a supreme conversation? Or shall we say once more, that there is more than one kind of conversation? Tell us, I say, the particular supremacy of Montaigne. And what is magic, Montaigne's magic? Or do you seize upon this word to prove by its use that there can be no definition, and to admit you cannot define?

There are other words. Variety—but Shakespeare has variety; alertness—but Aristotle is very alert; familiarity—but every good comedian is exceedingly familiar; frankness—but Lucretius is also perfectly frank; intimacy—but Lamb, as they say, is "delightfully" intimate; lucid intelligence—and Descartes, then? flexibility—how about Socrates? These words bind Montaigne loosely to a general history of the human mind. Find something for me that will describe the individuality of Montaigne's style; his resemblance to others is not hard to catch at a glance.

Well and good, we shall find you some words, they say, that will draw the very marrow from his *Essais*. What you want is simply a greater number of words, for profundity's sake. We shall find you words galore, until you cry: enough!

Quite enough, as it is. Words will never dissect; I rather think they will always be like greasy rubber stamps, smeared with too much ink, and applied to the surface, where they leave a foreign stain.

Dissect? Is that what you want us to do—dissect? With what, then? —With the meaning of words. Pascal tells us, when we utter a word, mentally to substitute for the word its complete meaning. If you should ever follow this golden rule, dissection itself will come and pull you by the ear, until you must follow, and yield to it.

Such is the strength of analysis. It springs from clarity, arousing a more intense brightness that sets off the shadow from the man. Distinctions such as yours thrive in the fog, where the man is a shadow of a man, and where every shadow bears a striking resemblance to the others.

Analyze, then. Don't tell me what an author does, he can speak for himself. Show me how he does it, that's your part. If he's original, show wherein. Don't tell me your impressions: chances are they will not interest me—analyze the author, and question your impressions; show me why he has had such an effect on you, and it will teach me, perhaps, about the impressions he can make on all.

See how the French, our modern humanists, instruct their teachers-to-be. All year, they analyze the works of authors. At the end, as part of their examination, they are asked to scrutinize unfamiliar excerpts from these same authors, often selected as exceptional, not as characteristic passages; thus, a student knowing that Calvin wrote in a sober and dry style would be confronted with one of those rare pages where the theologian, turned polemicist, wrote in an altogether different vein, ironic and picturesque; if the student has a sense of style, he will know the change, though his memory cry out and swear that Calvin is sober and dry. And the student will show the irony, and of what brand he finds it.

Such analyses require a thorough search, and style, I grant, is only one aspect. But style is what I am after, at present; nor can it harm to dwell on the subject of its criticism, which is always a matter of uninspired nonsense. Style is the man, we say; and we study the man as seen through his heredity, his environment, and his grocery bills, never getting around to his style, which is part of the man, indeed—at least as much as the onions and garlic he eats.

There is a general antipathy for the study of another's style. Not that we prefer to study and develop our own—we certainly don't; if we wanted to, we should soon learn how much we need to rub and polish our rugged sentences against the durable compositions of the masters. But we find our reasons in an honorable stock in trade. We are dutiful heirs to many strange notions. Thus, following a long line of schools and critics, we imagine that a thing of beauty is so fragile it cannot stand under analysis. If you so much as look at it, beware! It will vanish. Close your eyes, then you will see it so much better; it will rise before you, intact, as a virgin who dares appear before you only in a dream, as the vision of Alastor. Don't touch it, even if the maiden is but a poem in black and white. But I, for one, when I shut my eyes in reverence, like the faithful parishioner, I soon fall into a heavy slumber, and, very plainly, I snore. A thing of beauty must dazzle my open eyes. Then it holds me, and as I gaze upon it, I slowly unravel its fine lines. Whereupon I discover the rich layers that a transparent surface had filtered through; I find the subtle under-currents, and when I contemplate the whole mass again, it holds me through a deeper power. It grows upon me, sinks within me, and through its multiple grip gains a stronger claim for remaining, as the poet says, a joy forever.

Others fear that in plunging so far we may lose our way, following our instinct, and reaching at the end but our prejudice. Yet a traveler would be much wiser, in a similar predicament: thrown into the heart of a forest, he could tell it was a forest, but nothing more; to know its wealth and what forest it was, his first impulse would be to search; though he might blunder, still he has a better chance of widening his surroundings than if he lies upon the moss. So the stu-dent of art ought not maintain a supine attitude toward one of his most complicated problems. How much more hazardous than analysis our first impressions can be! In wandering about and analyzing, we may correct them; and if they are right, we give them the life and blood of conviction. It befits a layman to read for the punch and the kick in it; we too must start at that point; but if we think our task is to interpret art, we must reread that work, slowly. If we merely swoon, uttering a few incomprehensible words, we were made to build bridges or plant potatoes, not to teach and explain art. We were not even made to teach grammar, for we don't know the value of words.

Others are skeptics, and glad of it. They have learned that a defini-tion of style is so ticklish a matter that very few have agreed upon it in the past. That is a great relief to them—how shall they study some-thing they cannot definitely describe? Observe how readily they as-sume that a difference of opinion ruins all opinions. No matter what I say, I must be wrong if someone thumbs his nose at me. In their lazy minds, how comfortably all opinions are dispatched for lack of suffrage! They themselves will not stir to examine a single opinion to see if it will stand in spite of pamphleteers, who usually argue about something else.

The past guarantees an easy time of it in the present. Thrice happy, in our field and others, those who have acquired the certainty that they are as dull as the dullards of the past! Everything already has been botched up; they need not meddle with it.

There is a final group, faithful guardians of all the confusions: I mean the university professors, the professors of literature. If a pro-fessor of biology showed only what he knows about painting, he would be asked to leave and seek out some academy; but when a professor of literature philanders with outmoded systems of psychology and nibbles at history, we flock to his course, confident that he is explaining his authors through and through. It reminds me of a visiting professor who came here to teach Hispanic literature and spent his time waltzing and fox-trotting with the girls of the department: his revelries had about as much to do with his mission as present academic custom with the teaching of other literatures. We dance around a pleasant topic, we do an easy jig, perform some crazy Charleston, and there's an end to our business. Not that we are out of breath—God knows our wind is powerful, and the trick is not so hard—but we go no further because we have been trained for academic vaudeville, and we know no other act. The greatest farce of all is that we think our comedy is a solemn piece.

Why do we consider literature a field in itself? It has its own riches, aesthetic riches. We would not easily grant that it holds a purely historical, philosophical, or psychological interest. Ever so often, the content of literature is oldish, stale, unoriginal. To borrow, to readapt, is no sin in art, so long as we find a new and fresh expression for what we repeat. Voltaire is not a colossal thinker, yet we return ever and anon to his writings. Is it because of his influence on others? But why this influence, if he finds nothing very new in itself? Is it not because of the vitality he adds to what he transmits? His claim to our attention, then, is based on his artistic qualities, his ideas being available in sources far more profound. Yet, being drawn to him, we study everything but his art and his style. We aim at the author; we don't exactly miss him, but instead of hitting at the heart of his work, we scratch his little toe, or clip his ear.

We imagine that the problem of meaning and value dispels the problem of technique: meaning, we say, even when our authors try to write against it, is always the power behind expression. Indeed, there's a valid objection, but to something else, such as the aesthete's fancy, not to the criticism of style. For any critic who is not determined to win fame by the strangeness of his notions will maintain that expression is the expression of something; his main problem is, precisely, how intimately expression captures and renders its object. Those who with all their might besiege and attack the object alone, especially when it is easily recognizable, have not begun to study literature, although they have been teaching it for many years.

Then, analyze. You critics and professors, you have a perfect right to read as Tom, Dick, and Harry; you have a perfect right to close a book and dash off snappy or vague words—but keep your impressions for your admiring relatives and your good friends; don't feed our public, all too anemic, with watered blood. Young critic, be a real teacher, analyze. Beauty is not so low that it need not be understood. Analyze. If you are a critic, analyze; that is your role.

Book Reviews

André Burger. *Lexique de la langue de Villon*. Geneva: Droz, 1957.

MANY COMMENTARIES have elucidated Villon's language, but these are not as yet all available in one manageable instrument of interpretation. The best editors of Villon have been rather cursory and unimaginative about the difficulties with which the poet's language, still medieval and strewn with obscurities peculiar to the poet, besets the general reader. Longnon-Foulet offer an incomplete and somewhat capricious glossary, including some obvious details and omitting others that would require clarification; at the end of his two volumes of notes, Thuasne hardly closes the gap. In this respect, few difficult poets have been presented in so nonchalant a fashion.

An exhaustive lexicon is now supplied by Professor Burger. Compiled, by the author and his students, in the course of several years devoted to the study of Villon's language, it bears the stamp of workmanship and thoroughness. A minimum of items with questionable explanations might be listed;[1] such accidents attend the best of lexicographical ventures. But every detail of the poet's vocabulary is accounted for; definitions or translations into modern French are, in the vast majority of cases, precise and dependable. No text that can safely be ascribed to Villon is excluded, except the ballads of the *Jargon*; on this score, a lone note of protest may be registered: the patterns and details of language in these often neglected pieces should not be excluded from Villon's canon; cross reference to them suggests interesting new analogues and extensions of meaning.

Originally published in *Romanic Review* 49 (1958): 191-94.

[1]Some have already been mentioned by Felix Lecoy in *Romania* 77 (1957): 415-17, and need not be repeated.

The lexicon rests on a textual base reconsidered and strengthened by Professor Burger. In introductory "Notes critiques," he follows Foulet, who argued the superiority of MS C, but puts the latter to fuller use, with more rigorous consistency, while still challenging its reliability in a few remaining cases. Reviving old problems, and bringing new questions to the fore, he contributes emendations of the Thuasne and Longnon-Foulet editions that will need to be studied seriously. While some may eliminate but minor obstructions, others will significantly affect the flow of Villon's poetry. For example, where we are accustomed to reading, according to Longnon,

> Que c'est nature femenine
> Qui tout vivement veult amer,

MS C reads: "Qui tout unyement veult amer." "Vivement" electrifies the line, but with a feeling that must have often surprised readers at this point. "Unyement" ("également, sans distinction"), not lyrical but derisive, sustains the tone of the context, which dwells ironically on the mysteries of promiscuity, and at bottom rings much more true. One might also mention, among many other examples, "Le Débat du cuer et du corps de Villon," a poem which has not yet been made to yield all the light it could shed on the composition of the *Testament*. Its meaning depends largely on the sense of the last part, and it is here that Professor Burger's proposed emendations present a text far more coherent than Longnon's.

The glossary, noteworthy for its comprehensive coverage of vocabulary and its carefully revised textual foundation, is also valuable as a word count. For each item, all occurrences are noted with faithful accuracy, as a trial of many samples consistently shows. This kind of statistics, which scholars have been applying to others, notably Corneille and Racine of late, can grow to be a handy instrument in the study of a poet's habits of language and style. In Villon's case, it makes very visible, as it were, an absence or sobriety of color: only "blanc" and "noir" show any appreciable frequency; "coulourez et blesmes" (1 occurrence), "blons" (1), "cler" (1), "dorez" (1), "morillon" (1), "vermeille" or "vermillon" (2), "vert" (3), and "rouge" (3—"rougir," 1) seem to be the only remaining touches of color; it is difficult to find, in addition to adjectives or verbal forms like "noircir," names of things used to stress impressions of color, as in "mouche en lait"; in "neiges d'antan," for example, the intention lies elsewhere. The glossary helps to document and analyze with precision what stands out, by contrast, as an abundance of action and motion imagery, and brings home the expansiveness and variety of the vocabulary Villon draws from sources such as gastronomy, anatomy, clothing, mock-chivalry, legal procedure, religious doctrine.

But the word count as it stands could mislead the inexperienced reader of Villon. A word used a given number of times would not necessarily have the same value in all cases, not solely because of the normally expected variability of connotation, but particularly because of Villon's inveterately allusive manner, which perpetually suggests a double or triple meaning. Professor Burger often reminds us of this possibility, but not in all likely places. In "amant martir/Du nombre des amoureux sains" (*Lais*, vv. 47–48), to take one case, "sains" is listed under the heading of "saint," which was certainly the first, surface meaning, related to "Par elle meurs"; yet there is surely a play on words here, intended to convey ironically—as a mockery of the courtly love style of Charles d'Orléans—the idea of "amoureux sains" (safe and sound, and very much alive). The reader must be constantly awake to such possibilities of irony; a running commentary, more refined still than Thuasne's, and not a lexicographical compilation, could alone underscore all of them.

The limitations of word counting are especially apparent in the case of "povre," a key to Villon's poetry. Its numerous uses are exhaustively listed, but under two rigid headings: "poor" as opposed to "rich," and "poor" as "inspiring pity." For one thing, the tonality of a given verse does not always allow "povre" to fall distinctly into the one category rather than the other; both meanings can be present at once, even as in ordinary parlance. But, above all, this reduction of the word to two elementary meanings obscures the multiplicity of shades of feeling, including humility and self-depreciation, that it expresses, and that Italo Siciliano has ably analyzed.

A listing of cases is extremely useful in bringing out qualities of vocabulary like frequency and bulk, but not such features as the place or pressure of a word within the structure or flow of the work. One is reminded at a glance that "boire" is a sizable entry in Villon's lexicon; but the entry does not reveal that the *Testament* both opens ("Que toutes mes hontes j'eus beues") and closes ("Ung traict but de vin morillon") with a draught—a point to be borne in mind in discussions of the composition of the poem. On the other hand, the concentration of all like cases into compact entries does illustrate Villon's way of recasting and imitating his own modes of expression. The image of going on foot and on horseback, appearing in one of his most moving stanzas (*Testament*, vv. 173-74):

> Il ne s'en est a pié allé
> N'a cheval,

produces, in a different mood (vv. 1144-45):

> A pié ne va comme une caille
> Mais sur roncin gras et reffait.

The "s'en est allé" is freely and felicitously repeated, with reference to "le temps de ma jeunesse" as above, in "Allé s'en est, et je demeure" (v. 177) and "Mes jours s'en sont allez errant" (v. 217). One legatee is "tres bon marchant" (*Lais*, v. 179) and another "Homme de bien et bon marchant" (*Testament*, v. 1111), in both cases by antiphrasis and with unpleasant innuendoes. "Lequel vault mieulx?" Villon asks merrily in "Les Contrediz de Franc Gontier" about city and rural life—as between the "paillart" Villon and the "paillarde" Margot, he asks grimly again: "Lequel vault mieulx?" And so "Bourdes n'ont icy temps ne lieu" (v. 1646), "Icy n'y a ne ris ne jeu" (v. 1736), "Hommes, icy n'a point de mocquerie" ("L'Epitaphe Villon," v. 34).

Many are the uses to which Professor Burger's contribution can be put, in studies of Villon both linguistic and stylistic. To be more useful still, it might have included a glossary of proper nouns, even at the cost of stretching the meaning of *lexique*; at every step, the names of the poet's numerous and often obscure legatees require prompt and clear identification, and for this the reader still has to use as an adjunct the third volume of Thuasne.

An index of rimes would also have been an appropriate and welcome appendix. Villon's art of riming is of capital importance, in the use he makes of words; it contributes to the fun, the play of irony, and the lyricism as well as to the musicality of his verse. In Boileau fashion, one might say, names of persons round out many of his lines, and clinch them at the rime. Like their sense, often the sound of words and names draws the poet into a network of sustained correspondences. A major example is the "Ballade des dames du temps jadis." Shortly before it, Villon had written "Et meure Paris ou Helaine" (v. 313) and it is as if, in working in the ballad, he was struck by the possibility of echoing and prolonging the harmony of -*is* and -*aine*, in the same order; -*aine* remains the dominant, as in the keynote *Helaine*, blending with -*is* and introducing the other secondary rime in -*an*, which yields the refrain on the "neiges d'antan." One is reminded of Baudelaire's "Harmonie du soir," where in advance of the poem the title strikes, approximately, the rime scheme of the whole and announces its essential tonality. But -*aine* also stands out as something of a habit with Villon. He returns to it in various *laisses*, but what attracts attention is that he uses it especially in the ballad form, which particularly requires sustained riming: outside of the ballad mentioned, it is found, in widely varying contexts of tone, in the "Ballade pour Nostre Dame" (in the rime -*ienne*), "Les Contrediz de Franc Gontier," the "Ballade des femmes de Paris" (with -*iennes*), the "Ballade de bon conseil," and the "Ballade contre les ennemis de la France" (with "Helaine" again). Such facts, and numerous others that would emerge from a complete account of Villon's riming ways, could be the starting point of fruitful technical studies of his verse.

But even lacking these refinements, the instrument that Professor Burger has put at our disposal will be invaluable. No Villon shelf now can do without it.

Lawrence E. Harvey. *The Aesthetics of the Renaissance Love Sonnet—An Essay on the Art of the Sonnet in the Poetry of Louise Labé.* Geneva: Droz, 1962.

A STUDY of poetry that will actually bear on poetry is an uncommon contribution. We have developed many other approaches, which take poetic and other literary creations as bases from which to explore outlying and remote realms, up to the very outersphere, where cataclysmal clashes of cosmologies nowadays are detected at every turn of the centuries, or at every turn

Originally published in *Modern Language Notes* 78 (1963): 538-44.

of the page. As we confront a poem we are swept up in a swirl of centrifugal energy that sends us off at once to explicate everything around and beyond the work, but not the created work itself. With all this accrued background, we then would besiege and capture the essence of the poem, but we do not know what essence is to be surrounded; we enwrap it in explanations of its exterior, not knowing to what the latter is circumferential. We have got answers, but no focal problem. It is a boon now and then to come upon a study that will bear on poetry as art, and, recognizing that a poem is a fusion of form and content that reorganizes and re-creates human experiences, will begin by inquiring not merely *what* occurs in the poem—a summary would not convey it—but *how* it happens, how within the poem it is organized into being. The buildup of interrelationships, resonances, and jolts that bring masses and details together in a particular manner gives the whole its specific, coordinated accent and meaning. To search this out requires an investigation initially, if not exclusively, aesthetic or formal. This is the nature of Professor Harvey's undertaking.

With an abstinence that will upset those who expect the usual first chapter of biographical discourse in a professional piece of work, he refrains from including any rehash of the facts concerning Louise Labé's life already established by Dorothy O'Connor, and reckons with wise economy that little might be added that would further clarify her poems. He knows what is now to be known around the subject, and indubitably has applied this knowledge to the elucidation of certain points, but it is refreshing, and sobering, to note that he can manage elaborate and searching explications without spelling out gratuitous parallels between poetic fiction and biography.

In page after page, uncluttered with such superfluities, he consistently pursues his primary objective: with an approach "basically structural," "to examine the aesthetics of the sonnet" as exemplified in Louise Labé's work. As we proceed from sonnet to sonnet, each in due course explicated in terms of its own form, but each appropriately situated within a group of related sonnets, and all finally incorporated into the whole series of twenty-four, complex variety is resolved into meaningful unity. The collection progressively, compellingly achieves coherence.

One brief development along the way may lure the reader into a light dispute with the author. This concerns a confrontation of techniques which distinguishes the use of repetition, accumulation, compression of tension, and related constructions from the use of comparison and contrast. The former are patently distinguishable from the latter, but is it quite clear that the former alone induce "intensification," as would appear from the argument? Without producing crescendos or other progressive pressures, comparison and contrast could immediately in their own way intensify, as Professor Harvey himself has illustrated in other contexts, and as his very discussion of examples in these pages would betray; these techniques can serve to "heighten" feelings, or make them "more acute" (p. 70). Intensification, I suggest, has been stricken out and then unavoidably here has had to be written over again in other terms. This blur however is but the ransom of an earnest desire of the author to bear diversity in mind; he keeps on differentiating, before and while unifying. The difference between contrast-comparison and intensification, indistinct as it turns out to be, is meant to carry further an otherwise clear distinction between sonnets predominantly lyrical—in which juxtaposition in effect is more prevalent—and sonnets that evolve dramatically—with a more noticeable use of cumulative and contracting techniques. This differentiation, kept tentative enough to admit some degree of interpenetration between the lyric and the dramatic modes within a sonnet, basically is sound and interesting.

In the full-length development, which stays on its course, the obstruction is but momentary. Professor Harvey, sensitive to form, fashions for the presentation of his material an effective plan of his own. First, after a brief statement of purpose, comes the most elaborate explication in the book, devoted to sonnet XXIV; it illustrates in detail a method that then will be put into effect more compactly in subsequent analyses; by turning at once to the final sonnet, it puts us at the outset in the vicinity of the terminus to be reached. We are on our way, and promptly. In chapter 2, the author orients us by organizing the twenty-four sonnets, typologically, into groups. In the first, sonnets re-creating "an experience of the power of passion" build up either a cumulative structure, a pattern of obstacles overcome, or a comparison of a particular conquest to some absolute conquest. In the second, sonnets either evolve a series of alternation inducing a "tension between stability and change," and remaining therefore inherently unstable and poignantly frustrating, or set up a "single instance of opposition," as between sorrow and hope, to enact "the ambivalence of love." In the third group, on "the joy of love," which is generally a "utopia" or wishful vision, fictionally realized or defended, there are likewise two subdivisions, as in the fourth, which conveys the utmost "suffering of love" as an absolute of present time, or relates it by contrast to past happiness. Both these groups generally portray states rather than tensions. But a state cannot always be easily or naturally marked off from a tension, and Professor Harvey does not unrealistically keep them apart. He moves from one into the other. He does not rigidly consider, let us say, the "suffering of love" only at the appointed time and refrain from discussing it, for example, under the heading of "ambivalence of love," where it cannot but appear. He weaves it all together, crossing his own boundaries. Each heading chiefly serves the purpose of considering a special area, related to others, but placed under some significant focus. There are eight subdivisions in all, and each is exemplified by a sonnet singled out for analysis; each new, diversified explication is the substance of its section, and all eight in succession animate the systematic classification.

It needs to be stressed that Professor Harvey does not catalogue subject matter, in the conventional manner, but surveys the types of structure giving expression to the subject matter. Structure is the sign whereby he catches meaning. To tell us literally that sonnet VIII, for example, is about the longing and torments of love would be adequately accurate but would leave little more than a blank in our imagination, or the dead weight of generalized labels. But by showing how touches of life and death, laughter and tears, flaming and chilling, wilting and blossoming, and other contraries intermingle in a rapid alternation which itself alternates, as it were, passing now from swift affirmative-to-negative shifts on to similar changes in inverted order, now back to the original arrangement, and so on further, and setting in an overall reversal as well between the two major parts of the poem divided by "Ainsi Amour inconstamment me meine"—with the octave beginning and ending on a happy note, and the concluding development opening and closing with laments—by following the dynamics of the poem and not just thinly or verbosely identifying its theme, Professor Harvey brings out the very action of the passionate, frustrated agitation set in motion by the poetess. But it is almost as futile to summarize the explication as the poem. The reader will see this analysis and others for himself. No single one sets up a pat formula for the others. It is an essential endeavor of the method to rediscover afresh the particular shape and motion with which each form comes alive.

The structural, or the relational, which has to do with disposition and configuration, from one angle is seen by Professor Harvey as "internal form," or "the arrangement within the author's fictional world of characters, events, ideas or feelings, time, and space" (p. 11). He is interested for example in the pressures of absence, and the pull of the past and the hypothetical future on the current moment. From another angle, there is "external form," "the syntax of the words," the arrangement of "phrases, sentences, and larger groupings." To cite but one example, Professor Harvey astutely calls attention to hypotaxis and parataxis, commonly overlooked as high-sounding grammatical technicalities; they concern the use or omission of subordinative links between syntactical elements; a change from one construction to the other may significantly characterize the entire structure. Internal and external form, of course, do not operate apart but are coordinated, not necessarily as parallels but sometimes in counterpoint.

One cardinal question of "external form" concerns the given, conventional structure of the sonnet—the function of quatrains, tercets, octave, and sestet within the whole body of fourteen lines. Professor Harvey, necessarily, concentrates on this network of relationships in chapters 3 and 4, on "The Sonnet and Literary Tradition" and "Violation of the Tradition." Louise Labé, we find, is versatile; as often as not she is unfaithful to the fixed form, to very good effect. Only thirteen of her sonnets show the expected break after line 8. In the eleven that violate the 8-6 division, the structure changes to 7-7, 8-1-5, 9-5, 10-4, 11-3, and even 13-1, as in sonnet XIII—"Oh si j'estois en ce beau sein ravie"—where punctuation at line 8 is no veritable break in the flow, which moves cumulatively on to the end and climax in "Bien je mourrois, plus que vivante, heureuse." Likewise, owing in part to changed relationships between the two major parts, the regular pattern for quatrains and tercets is often broken up. Of special interest is the fact that only four of the twenty-four sonnets abide by the Italian tradition as to the sestet, while all the rest adopt the rhyme *c-c*—quite congenial, one might add, to a Du Bellay or a Ronsard—followed by *d-e-e-d* or *d-e-d-e*, with most of these dropping the division in tercets. One of Louise Labé's most distinctive marks turns out to be a very noticeable predilection for this kind of flexible sestet, in which *c-c* can a few times form a tercet with the next line, or stand out as a distich, or continue the octave or second quatrain. Some of these shifts and redistributions had already been studied through chapters 1 and 2, for nothing in structural analysis can long be put off, and in a sonnet least of all the organization of verses, but all of it here is rounded up for further probing and synthesis. One remains convinced that the frequent irregularities, and the overflowing of *enjambements* that may also be noted, are not symptoms of inexperience but the refinements of searching art. The "aesthetic values" of the sonnet, Professor Harvey concludes about the genre in general, are "made possible by tensional forms used in counterpoint to the traditional form existing as an expectation in the mind of the reader" (p. 37); it should be revealing to look for this counterpoint in the art of other sonneteers.

Chapters 3 and 4 sustain the chain of explications, concentrating on specimens not fully analyzed before. Many new explications are further distributed along chapter 5, which introduces "special configurations," among which "condensation and containment," "pseudo-logic," "analogy and understatement," and "tragedy" (which indeed has its configuration), to insist on the individuality of techniques within the types previously set up. There are more explications in chapter 6, on the broader new differentiation now proposed between "the dramatic and the lyric," and more still in the conclusion. What is smooth and effective about the total plan is that we end up by having absorbed twenty-four explications, not massed together amorphously in one part of the book but well spaced, and progressively distributed under successive significant headings, each appropriately illustrating some points and radiating out to other points previously or subsequently emphasized. The writing may tend to the abstract, unavoidably so at certain junctures. The composition of the book carries us right along an interestingly laid out course.

What would a study bearing on imagery have yielded? Much less, without any doubt. One may safely assume it would not have changed Professor Harvey's findings, although it seems excessive on his part to set the question aside on the grounds that Louise Labé's style carries almost no imagery (p. 9). It manifestly does not luxuriate in similes, but brings in certain metaphorical strains, of which in effect he later notes a few. In Louise Labé perhaps, as in certain poets of Racine's family, the scarcity of rich similes may well be in any case an absence not by failure of inclusion but by artistic choice; possibly a positive trait of style, it might have been studied with profit.

What in addition would have been yielded by a study of the musicality of verse? Professor Harvey, who unravels prosody with skill where it has to do with the assembling of versified lines, is inclined to leave the analysis of versification itself by the side. I would rather be inclined to reintroduce it. If once we but acknowledge that poetry is meant to be voiced, then rhythms and distributions of sound surely are of the essence. We *hear* a consonance, relatedness, and coherence. Is it heard in Louise Labé? It might not be too harsh to suggest some doubts. One receives an impression of unevenness. In some sonnets, at length or in stretches, there seems to come no musical flow, no fitness of rhythm. Her ear for example is not sensitive, in sonnet XV, to the untoward heaviness and awkwardness of two lines depicting frolicsome gambols:

Les Nynfes ja en mile jeus s'esbatent
Au cler de Lune, et dansans l'herbe abatent.

There are on the other hand melodious impulses, though not sustained, not equal to flights of song heard from the Pléiade, and but on occasion really rising to incantation, to speak the language of Henri Bremond. Some happy experiments or hunches of the poetess discover meaningful rhythms. Would the alexandrine, instead of the decasyllabic verse she chose, have been a suppler and more constant instrument for metrical development? The unevenness, which I believe is there to be heard, is not discussed by Professor Harvey, who rebuilds these poems with infectious enthusiasm, but does not judge them as to their relative quality.

A surprise, which delights this reader for one, as it will some others no doubt, is Professor Harvey's omission of the word "baroque" from his parlance, and from his thoughts. This acts as a balm. Though he turns to topics and techniques commonly labeled baroque, with a freedom hard to match today he does not surrender to the slogan. This transposes one to another climate of critical work, not because of the mere absence of a word; the emended vocabulary goes concomitantly with a sanity of method. Instead of starting out with a commitment to a preestablished theory of some baroque spirit of the times and then making an individual fit this *Zeitgeist*, Professor Harvey begins by apprehending the particular work of art in its complex individuality, and then ventures on to generalizations that will absorb it. In his conclusion still, he can wind up without benefit of the baroque. Having found the temporal and the timeless, a sense of flux and the longing for immutability, and closed and open forms in Louise Labé's work, he is mindful of her environment and suggests how the poems, while speaking for the poetess, reflect a human situation at the time of the Renaissance, and the condition of the universal human being as well. Not a haggling word on baroquism—this takes courage, against the mores of our republic of letters. Disputants may now, if they so wish, argue whether Louise Labé was not after all "baroquisante," "baroquisée," or just perhaps a trifle "classico-baroquifiée," if not "baroquacalifiquée." Already it has been disputed whether she was a "cortegiana onesta" or a "courtisane publique." Who will tell us whether *la belle Cordière* was not ever so little a "barocoquette"?

Professor Harvey works otherwise, from inside out, confronting and probing the poem itself. Although lending an ear to the sound-structure of the sonnets would have contributed more fully to the rounding out of the explications, these as they stand present a penetrating analysis of the aesthetics of Louise Labé's love sonnets, and of the sonnet in general. More generally still, it should be fruitful to apply this approach to any writings that are concerned with the reorganization and expression of human experience.

Donald M. Frame. *Montaigne: A Biography*. New York: Harcourt, Brace and World, 1965.

MONTAIGNE was his own first, probing biographer. In the glow and turmoil of the Renaissance, in sixteenth-century France, what had come to him with the most penetrating urgency and conviction of rediscovery, out of the wisdom of antiquity, was the Socratic, Apollonian injunction: "Know thyself." Self-portrayal became for him, and was to remain lastingly, a crucial undertaking. "Others always go elsewhere," he wrote; "as for me, I roll about in myself." In the welter of change, instability, and unknowing, self-gathering turned into self-formation. Molding the figure in the multifarious *Essais* "upon myself, I have had to fashion and compose myself so often to bring myself out, that the model itself has to some extent grown firm and taken shape." For this purpose, in a book which is the first to bear such a title, he progressively unfolds a new literary form: incessantly he "essays" or samples, tries out, tests, and experiences his hold on that realm of the self which alone, but copiously and most proximately, lies open to him, and within which he ultimately uncovers as well "the entire form" of the human condition at large.

It is this capital event in the early literature of the modern world, this search from within, that Professor Frame brings forcefully under focus. We are already indebted to him for an outstanding translation of Montaigne's works, quoted here; it is the best in English, felicitously congenial to the original, in substance, spirit, and accent. Rethinking as directly from the inner source as possible all the writings of a great kindred spirit of his choice, he has all the while also searched out and sifted whatever is known about the *Essais* and their author from without, making as he went important contributions of his own to this vast body of historical and interpretive commentary. His present biography is the seasoned, live outgrowth of long acquaintance with Montaigne, and a synthesis of many searches.

Various imponderables have gathered around and grown into Montaigne's self-portrait. About his departed, irreplaceable friend La Boétie: what pressure did he exert, alive and dead, both against and toward Montaigne's self-discovery? About his origins: on his outlook and experience, what from afar may have been the full impact of the Marrano, Spanish-Jewish strain in his mother's ancestry, which included more than one Villanueva burned at the stake by the Inquisition? About the public function of this humanist bent on privately exploring and ruling within: did he after all come to play a capital mediator's role in the difficult ascension of Henry the Great to the throne, and thus by his action no less than his writings leave an indelible but unmeasurable mark on the France, and the world, to come? Professor Frame, reopening these and other questions ultimately unanswerable, judiciously brings out their distant, plausible potential.

Out of the limitless outlying areas of background, origins, and afterlife through the centuries, Professor Frame selectively and solidly reconstructs the world upon which the *Essais* broke. The center which persistently draws

Originally published in the Baltimore *Sun*, November 28, 1965.

to itself the clarifications of biography and history is the book itself. There is a progression of stages in the external developments drawing France into devastating civil wars, in the personal developments leading Montaigne to assurance and fulfilment, and in the successive editions or strata of the book itself, a "record of the essays of my life." This record, presenting innumerable soundings, is not concerned with the straight chronological account, which remains for the biographer from without to rebuild. Professor Frame, with a masterly command of the material, retells the complex story; consecutive groups of chapters relate the personal and public setting to each of the consecutive levels in the evolving book of essays, according to a simple, compelling plan already tried out in his *Montaigne's Discovery of Man* (1955). An enlargement of the original self-portrait unfolds, ample, rigorously faithful, searching. Though a generous interpreter of previous investigators, Professor Frame on his own fastens primarily on Montaigne himself. A residue of earlier twentieth-century writing was the simplistic image of a Montaigne who had been first a Stoic, then a Skeptic, and finally an Epicurean—the "evolution" of Montaigne, as it was popularly taught in a nutshell, hardened into a geology, as it were, of his *Essais*. In Professor Frame's book, now the very best general study of Montaigne that we have in English, and undoubtedly ahead of any biography in French, at last we are liberated from the rigidities of that formula. We read the far more real and engrossing story of that which, in and out of his readings in all the schools he essayed, became more and more centrally Montaigne's occupation: self-study, the gathering drive of his then-novel inquiry.

He did not go garnering the exterior formulations and structures of ideologies. In his views on specific issues, which may be itemized, he may sound now progressive, as in his celebrated essay on education, and indeed revolutionary, as he establishes man's free judgment in the "magisterial seat," or now contradictorily conservative, as he resists insurgents and reformers. The grim, bloody commotions of the latter he basically derided, however, for the same reasons as he did the agitations of the legions of learned professionals, vacant within but always astir afield, busily categorizing the unknowable unknown *ad infinitum* and presumptuously ordering all disorders but their own. "I presented myself to myself, as theme and subject." Long before our contemporaries, he did thus discover, left to his own devices, the absurd in life, or rather, as Professor Frame cogently reminds us, our absurdity—the absurdity of man, who, not so much full "of evil as of inanity," embraces the universe, and remains "the investigator without knowledge, the magistrate without jurisdiction," and, after all, "the fool of the farce." But self-study is neither self-debasement nor self-sublimation, but possession, acceptance of what authentically, as we would say today, we are. In the "condition" peculiar to man, Montaigne perceives a dignity inherent in this cognizance of the very absurdity. Unlike one of his first great readers, Pascal, who went on from this paradox to humble man, Montaigne had brought his own dialectic to bid man confidently to apprehend, affirm, and realize his given and only being, body and soul, to the full. "It is an absolute perfection and virtually divine to know how to enjoy our being rightfully"—*loiallement*, in whole good faith.

Paul Frankl. *The Gothic. Literary Sources and Interpretations through Eight Centuries*. Princeton, N.J.: Princeton University Press, 1960.

EVER SINCE the romanticists reported that they had "rediscovered" the Gothic, this architectural style has been a major topic for historians of taste, not in the realm of the fine arts alone but in other provinces as well, and notably in the literary field. The fortunes of the Gothic have come to be a crucial or rather, by now, a settled issue, dramatically resolved like a main plot of *Geistesgeschichte*, observing strict unity of action. A whole scheme of aesthetic currents across the centuries is dialectically organized according to positive and negative charges of interest in the Gothic. Much of this talk unfortunately remains rather glib, superficial, sparsely documented, although it would adopt the resonance of historical thinking and parlance. Writers of literary history in fact are among those most trustfully addicted to this "method." In surveys ideologically adventurous but factually tenuous and misty, they have told and confidently retold a facile story of Gothic architecture accursed and acclaimed, and fancied that this corroborated their account of developments in their own field.

The very fact that the late Professor Paul Frankl, distinguished authority on the Gothic, endeavored to gather material on this subject for some twenty years should serve notice that this chapter in the history of taste is far from closed. Massive as this study is, indeed, it cannot be considered definitive or even, in some parts, thorough and probing, though it is a complex, imposing work, more comprehensive still than the title might indicate.

In content and manner, it tends to grow into an encyclopedic account of the subject. The "sources and interpretations" that the author compiled are not by any means exclusively or preponderantly "literary" in a belletristic sense; more loosely or inclusively, the "literature" here assembled is a body of commentaries on Gothic art ranging from technical analyses to tributes in prose and verse. Centuries, generations, movements, and authorities are codified. The literature is cross-referenced; influences and associations are noted. Many writers wander into the text, and at times are so closely crowded as to afford but a cursory glimpse of each. Some, such as Willis, William Whewell, and Edward J. Willson, in this compilation receive less attention than they deserve. Over the entire book there hangs the feeling that it was a slow, strenuous accumulation of many years of scholarship. Some of the essays, ignoring recent contributions, appear to have been drawn up years ago. The argument on Viollet-le-Duc, for example, does not take into account the more significant new studies of his achievement. There is no appreciation of medieval town planning. Neither Patrick Geddes nor Lewis Mumford is mentioned, although their work belongs in this history. The author shows no sign of having taken notice of Samuel Kliger's *The Goths in England—A Study in Seventeenth and Eighteenth Century Thought* (1952), an interesting study of political factors that gave the term "Gothic" a favorable ring in those times.

Written in collaboration with Phoebe Stanton. Originally published in *Modern Language Notes* 77 (1962): 541-47.

There is nevertheless a generous display of material drawn particularly from German sources of the last century and a half, and commentary on these often difficult works. For the English reader, this will be a very strong compensatory point.

A deep, irrepressible personal note, in the very midst of a work of this encyclopedic nature, was inevitable, in the case of a Paul Frankl who himself had sought so strenuously to define the meaning of the Gothic style. A compiler of commentaries, he also remains an outspoken theorist on his own, stoutly in dispute or competition with those whose views he compiles, and not signally patient with some whose definitions of Gothic have not coincided with his own. A weakness of the book—unless this be appreciated as its basic unity—is that it yields to the temptation of turning into an historical introduction leading up to the Frankl concept of Gothic. Even some of the early writers, more or less directly, are judged to be on the wrong or right road, according to the final outcome of the investigation that lies far ahead. Harshly, the school headed by Pugin, Ruskin, and George Gilbert Scott for its moralizing aesthetics is charged with Pharisaism and consigned to a "cul-de-sac," without reference to the substantial literature which relates these theorists to the growth of ideas and forms pointing the way to modern architecture. Although noticeably slanted or self-oriented at numerous points, it is chiefly toward the end that this study pulls resolutely in the direction of Professor Frankl's own view, when he is called upon to survey the history and philosophy of art that was elaborated by his contemporaries and to which he was himself a potent contributor. This whole section of the work, which recounts the genesis and development of concepts of polarity underlying twentieth-century thought, is masterful, and conveys something of the excitement that accompanied vigorous theoretical debates. Against this setting, Professor Frankl's personal interpretation—which lays stress on the *diagonal* and *divisive* effect of Gothic *partiality* and *interdependence* confronted with the *frontal* and *additive* effect of Romanesque *totality*—is finally at home in its own climate. Though one did not anticipate as much, or just this, one is moved to find here the concluding statement of a great expert, at the end of a lifetime of study. Literary scholars interested in formal analysis will draw from these pages, though they deal with a different medium, an absorbing lesson in the search for the structure and meaning of a style.

In defense of a point of view, this treatise yet aims to work itself out as a cumulative record of other attitudes past and contemporary, as promised by the title, and basically it is as a contribution of this character—a history of responses to the Gothic—that it will be approached and evaluated. It would be grotesque pedantry to expect a survey of eight centuries to pick up every stray utterance on the Gothic, and ingratitude not to underscore that, for certain areas, the author puts together an impressive array of primary sources. His excursions into the nineteenth century, and into German aesthetic thought, with its ramifications in other literatures, are extensive. Although, relatively speaking, interpretations of Gothic architecture are rather scarce in the Middle Ages proper, this period also furnished Professor Frankl with material for some of his most solid, penetrating developments, as on the lingering vestiges of Vitruvian principles, the *lux continua* of Suger, the commentaries of Gervase of Canterbury and Villard de Honnecourt, the secrets of the masons' lodges, the experts' reports on reconstruction at Chartres, Milan, and Gerona.

In following up the reputation of the Gothic, through the Middle Ages and from romanticism on at any rate, Professor Frankl did not simply recapitulate the obvious but endeavored to expand, correlate, and integrate what was generally but loosely familiar, adding new facts and insights into the relationships of successive waves of feeling for the Gothic to the unfolding historical scene, the evolving concepts of style, and the developing methodologies of scholarship. There was no need or possibility to alter or reverse the traditional account, but he broadened and deepened it, despite his injustice to some writers in his disfavor.

It would not be unfair to say that his history breaks down considerably, adding very rarely to the little that has been publicized thus far, when it deals with the area that lies between the Middle Ages and romanticism. Among the personalities of that long and complex period, there is this time but a fitful representation of the Germans. Without explanation, no discussion of England before 1600 is attempted, while Italy and France—although the latter ever so slightly—are considered in the sixteenth century, and scarcely more is offered, after that date, than can be gleaned from the publications of Kenneth Clark, Reinhard Haferkorn, and B. Sprague Allen. As for the Mediterranean countries, virtually nothing from Hispanic sources— a customary gap in the literature on the subject. The treatment of Italy and France, with that of England after 1600, helps to give these pages a semblance of body and substance. But to the round of Italians, few are added whose testimony has not been labored and overworked before. On the French, there is little evidence that the author's research extended far beyond the findings of the Abbé Jules Corblet, whose flimsy, cavalier essay of over a hundred years ago unfortunately still remains the foundation for most statements on this particular question. No history of the term Gothic is tightly put together. Slips and blunders go unchecked—as when octosyllabic verses of *Il Penseroso* turn into a passage of *Paradise Lost*, or when the great Benedictine pioneer in medieval studies Jean Mabillon is seriously misrepresented as having said nothing about the Gothic. Unaccountable gaps confront the reader. In England, for example, Hawksmoor and Vansbrugh, whose work has been the subject of recent commentary, are omitted. In France, it is a surprise that the special importance of the Gothic to Soufflot, in the development of his own architectural forms, is not brought out, and more of a disappointment still that there is no mention at all of Claude Perrault, a distinguished and independent architect in the heyday of French classicism—he is the forgotten man in histories of the taste for Gothic, and yet the Gothic figured prominently in his controversy with François Blondel, a most interesting episode in the famous Quarrel of Ancients and Moderns.

To dispute a welter of other points one after another would only end up as patchwork. A fresh book or round of monographs would need to be written, on the period from the Renaissance to the eighteenth century, for it is not merely a matter of touching up with corrections. Methods are at issue here. One primary principle is to let facts be. Professor Frankl falls to quibbling and haggling with what is set down in black and white. When, for example, he has to face the fact that in the seventeenth century the influential Jean-François Félibien discussed Gothic architecture with interest and appreciation, he cannot but whittle this down somewhat; not in a position to account for it in terms of the stipulated *Geist* of the age, he now insinuates a bit of casual Freudian guesswork, suggesting that Félibien's "more friendly attitude toward Gothic may be interpreted as mild opposition to his father" (p. 343)—to this same André Félibien who, as it happens, has just been described a few lines above as showing "a certain respectful indulgence" for the Gothic! By turning the father-son complex around, in another instance, one can as readily rationalize downward an attitude that fails to square with the *Zeitgeist*: one can hint that in the case of Philibert de l'Orme, the son of a *maître maçon* of the old school, "perhaps" his "positive" attitude toward Gothic architecture "must be accounted for by filial piety" (p. 297). This sort of wrangling with facts, not limited to these examples, sounds for all the world like last-ditch skirmishing.

And skirmishing for what? For the conventional view. Professor Frankl encounters others, besides Félibien and de l'Orme, who must be reckoned admirers of the Gothic, but it does not occur to him to question seriously whether their taste—not confined to any underground movement—may be symptomatic of a widespread attitude. We are left rather hazily to infer that somehow their declarations are accidents, against the spirit of the times. Is not Aeneas Silvius (Pope Pius II) a man of the Italian Renaissance? Professor Frankl records the enthusiasm that this humanist geographer expressed for Gothic structures in the German cities he described. Striking texts are put before us, yet they do not move Professor Frankl to inquire what numerous other describers of cities may have had to say; he remains unaware, for example, of Flavio Biondo in the fifteenth century, or Leandro Alberti in the sixteenth. He does not seek out an ample supply of fresh evidence, because he is satisfied with the preconceived notion that he is dealing, still, with "The Period of Reaction against Gothic," come what exceptions and contradictions may.

One does not first set up the image of a *Weltanschauung*, and then let examples fit in as they will. It is for that image to fit the given facts. But there is another elemental problem, evidently not troublesome to many historians of taste: what constitutes evidence? The testimony of selected "representatives" of an age? How are these to be selected, without a wide acquaintance with the age? What, in effect, will confer the quality of "representative" to a witness? His prominence in our eyes, or in the estimation of his contemporaries? Molière, admired today and in his century for his great comedies, penned or rather translated a diatribe against the Gothic— shall we in all seriousness confidently assume that, by his sheer genius, on the matter of Gothic architecture he was the spokesman or translator of seventeenth-century France? Even if, in sixteenth-century Italy, we turn to the very Vasari, is it clear that we find him proclaiming a public view? Rather, may he be protesting, crusading? Ultimately, we will not know whether, or whom, the "representatives" represent, until we sound out those presumed to be represented. The literate public of many voices, spreading through the provinces and the professions, must be heard out, lest one be left with the overpublicized whoops and hoots of a school or a coterie with vested interests in an aesthetic program. The multifarious writings not only of artists but of travelers and of scholars digging into the past, and a host of other publications in which authors irresistibly take occasion to depict and commemorate landmarks of countries and localities, all may well count, all is to the purpose in a faithful portrait of the live and much-ignored public. If Professor Frankl had seized upon this vast body of literature and not honored the thin documentation handed down to him, he might have been persuaded finally to alter the plot of the story. The alleged "representatives" and their innumerable representees do not form a tight circle but make up a variegated republic of arts and letters in which, handily and even handsomely at times, against undeniable attacks and yet with support from classical quarters as well, the taste for Gothic survived. Among the ampler sections of the book, those devoted to more recent generations could themselves have acquired more blood and color.

Readers may also object, perhaps with reason, that Professor Frankl limits himself to the written word and excludes, as nonverbal tributes to the Gothic, the structures erected or restored through the post-medieval centuries in imitation of the Gothic style. Over against the familiar story of recurring vandalism and mutilations, the fortunes of neo-Gothic construction would be worth retelling, and would certainly be an additional index of attitudes and interpretations. Surely the movement called in England the Gothic Revival belongs in a history of taste. Yet Professor Frankl's position should not be too arduous to defend, even aside from the fact that his task was forbidding enough as he had delimited it. In a study of this kind, concerned with the reputation of a style, the question that it was indispensable to ask, in order to arrive at a sufficient answer, could not but concentrate on the reputation of those manifestly basic, original, outstanding creations which for all concerned embodied the style, historically and aesthetically. It is not because construction went on in neo-Gothic style that post-medieval generations reacted to the Gothic, but evidently the reverse is true, and if necessary we can gather these reactions to the Gothic of the Middle Ages, which are primary, without or before surveying imitations. One can find responses to the Pyramids, surely, in periods or lands where such structures never gave rise to new modes of building. Hard pressed to throw an immense field into focus, Professor Frankl understandably chose to dwell on what was decisive. The only problem is that, despite his decision, he does easily enough become involved in a discussion of questions besetting architects of the Italian Renaissance in charge of completing Gothic monuments at Milan and Bologna; these exceptions to his rule remind us all the more of the numerous temptations to which he did not yield. The rule undoubtedly remained too rigid. How, for example, may one simply bypass the Sainte-Croix Cathedral of Orléans, destroyed in the religious wars and completely rebuilt by the Bourbons?

It should be added that Professor Frankl does more justice to another variety of nonverbal appreciation of the Gothic. He appropriately calls attention to the pictorial artists, their development of architectural painting in seventeenth-century Holland, and their interest in depicting on canvas their impressions of the Gothic. He mentions engravers and notes the rise of illustrated books on the Gothic. Some of these pioneer publications remained serviceable and worthy of interest for a long time—one might have cited here, by way of significant illustration, the fact that a leading architect of the Victorian Gothic Revival, A. W. Pugin, possessed a library of seventeenth- and eighteenth-century books which were his principal resource not only for the history of the Middle Ages but for illustrations of Gothic building as well. However, at the top of pages that dwell on all this, the running head incongruously still stares at us: "Reaction against Gothic." *Quod scripsi, scripsi.*

In noting all that is lacking in this enormous book, it would be gross insensitivity not to prize all that Professor Frankl poured into it, and not to be enlightened and stirred by his own final pronouncement on the Gothic. To indicate that the historical part of his treatise remains incomplete, particularly as to the period he accepted as a depressed area, is to say, in the final analysis, that he undertook what at this juncture was unfeasible. A history of the taste for Gothic art through eight centuries and over most of Europe, to be definitive, would need to draw on a corpus of studies devoted intensively to each of the countries and major periods. Each society and age confronts us with such a ramified network of facts and problems that no one investigator alone, surely not even in twenty years, could range with sustained success over nearly a millennium. For his guidance, Professor Frankl at certain points had nothing better than flippant, biased, scandalous reports like the one of Jules Corblet. It is a commentary on the tenacity of prejudiced historicism that a Paul Frankl, himself so powerfully under the spell of the Gothic, could not more boldly yield to the evidence that was nevertheless available to him and recognize that, through all the vicissitudes of ideology, the Gothic as a thing of beauty did have its way of remaining a joy forever, if not for everyone everywhere.

Eugène Vinaver, ed. *Racine: Principes de la tragédie en marge de la Poétique d'Aristote.* Manchester: Editions de l'Université de Manchester, 1944.

THIS BROCHURE affords us a glimpse of Racine in a studious mood. We can see him, as it were, attentively examining his old copy of Pietro Vettori's *Commentarii in primum librum Aristotelis de arte poetarum* (2d edition, 1573). He has before him, in his treatise, the Greek text of the *Poetics*, a Latin translation by Vettori, and the latter's lengthy commentaries. Thus equipped, he ponders the terse, at times obscure Aristotelian critique of poetry. Here and there, in the margins, he pauses to paraphrase or translate a passage into French.

Originally published in *Romanic Review* 38 (1947): 270-71.

These marginalia, which are of signal interest, have been published be-fore—fourteen times in the past century—but not as a separate unit. Of rather slight bulk, they remained for many decades thoroughly submerged in voluminous collections of Racine's works. Professor Vinaver now makes them available in a special and more handy pamphlet edition. The new editor lavishes every care on the invaluable fragments, tidies the text more meticulously than his predecessors, and appends two sections of commentary, "Remarques" and "Notes," with a glossary of terms used in an unusual seventeenth-century sense. Whenever necessary, Racine's French can be checked, on the same page, with excerpts from Vettori's edition of the Greek; it can also be closely compared with Vettori's Latin translation, by which the poet often allowed himself to be guided. Simple typographical devices point out Racine's errors of interpretation, and, more important still, additions that he made to the original; these help to show to what extent he elaborated or even modified the Aristotelian doctrine; in particular, they illuminate his views on catharsis and the tragic hero.

As Professor Vinaver suggests, it all reads like a subtle, leisurely dialogue between the philosopher and the poet; that impression, one must add, is made the more vivid by the editor's skill in confronting the texts. But there are gaps in the dialogue. Two substantial passages (one on the necessity of "un commencement, un milieu et une fin" and another containing Aristotle's eulogy of Homer) have been lifted out of their place in the text and relegated to the notes (see pp. 5, 63, 68); and here, for some unspecified reason, they are transcribed, unlike the rest, from Paul Mesnard's older edition. The real lacunae, however, are due not to the editor but to Racine himself. Why did he translate certain passages and not others? Though many a possible explanation comes to mind, none appears conclusive. Professor Vinaver seems willing to take for granted that the poet deliberately chose those points in the *Poetics* most meaningful and interesting to him (p. 39). But there is no evidence. We do not know just when, or in the courses of how many readings, or above all for what purposes, Racine wrote his marginal notes. Can we explain, for instance, why he appears ready on two occasions to start a new paragraph and, each time, in the middle of the first sentence, stops short? The editor, here, offers no comment. He transfers one of the unfinished sentences to the notes. The other, to be found in Mesnard's edition, is wholly struck out; it should come at the end, in a chapter where Aristotle considers whether the epic is superior to tragedy; Racine writes out in French that part which summarizes the argument in favor of the epic and merely adds: "Je réponds à cela premièrement. . . . " Could we be very wrong in believing that although he did not go on translating the rest—a firm defense of tragedy—the tragedian surely was deeply interested in it?

What is undeniable, and stands here solidly demonstrated, is Racine's preoccupation with matters of doctrine. A consummate artist, he was also, as we are shown, a competent theorist of his art; he seriously probed the nature and principles of tragedy. Nine years ago, to be sure, this whole question was discussed most extensively by Sister Mary Philip Haley. In her *Racine and the "Art poétique" of Boileau* (1938) she dwelt on "an important trait of Racine's mind that is seldom fully recognized: the scholarly and critical bent of his temperament," and learnedly analyzed his views; one of the many texts that she examined was the very one edited in the present study. Professor Vinaver, apparently without any assistance from Sister Mary's work, reached conclusions remarkably close to hers. We learn from both—and the thesis can bear repetition—that pathos was to Racine the heart and essence of tragedy; to awaken and chasten emotions of pity and fear was his central purpose, in the light of which all problems, whether of plot, character, prosody, or any other phase of dramatic composition, were to be resolved. Both scholars compare the Aristotelian and Racinian concepts of *hamartía*, Professor Vinaver more briefly but with a livelier sense of differences. He neatly distinguishes the tragic flaw defined as error of judgment from that passion which drives and impels certain Racinian characters, like a furious, inward fate.

Needless to say, Professor Vinaver does not deduce all that exclusively from his one piece of evidence. He cannot but cast a glance now and then at the tragedies and their prefaces. All to the good, for his "Remarques" and "Notes" are not merely an explication of marginalia; they constitute, in sum, a valid critique of Racine's art.

Martin Turnell. *The Classical Moment.* London: Hamilton, 1947.

IT WOULD profit readers of French seventeenth-century literature to examine this work, although some of the material is stale, and some raw and undigestible. Not frequently, we are offered matter that is fresh and satisfies the desire for new understanding. Mr. Turnell has rare talents. He knows as few others do how to read a play, that is, how to visualize it as action and performance, sense the dramatic drive of the whole, and feel what the single word, line, or scene adds at every step to the momentum. He also knows how to read and bring vibrantly to life the old alexandrine, which to so many remains but a droning meter. He has a good ear, and a keen eye. It would seem that Mr. Turnell, however, does not know his strength or, knowing it, makes light of it. The perceptive critic must needs also play here, in dead earnest, the psychoanalyst, the sociologist, and the historian. In these roles, unhappily, he grows erratic and unconvincing, and cuts a rather awkward figure.

To find one's bearings here becomes a major task in itself. Just what did Mr. Turnell set out to do? The rather catchy title, *The Classical Moment*, points in directions which throughout, somehow, he forgets or disdains to follow. There is no study, no definition of the "classical" in general or of French classicism in particular, no inkling of the many discussions which in recent years have reopened this whole question. Mr. Turnell assumes apparently that this is a self-explanatory household term, or expects perhaps

Originally published in *Symposium* (1950) 4: 435–41.

that without much ado whatever he ascribes to Corneille, Molière, and Racine will readily be understood as classical. But here would lie part of the difficulty. One grows to feel that it is in the author's mind and not on paper alone that the idea of "classical" remains undefined; at times, one cannot but suspect, he lapses into the old-fashioned habit of picturing enormous areas of the seventeenth century bathed in classical sunshine (e.g., p. 6). Does Corneille, for one, speak a language intelligible to Molière or Racine? Any reasoned definition of French classicism, I believe, would prompt a literary historian to exclude the powerful but unclassical Cornelian drama. Just as he does not make clear why the three poets form a "classical" trio, Mr. Turnell does not explain why to him a stretch of some sixty years, from *Le Cid* to *Athalie*, constitutes a "moment." *Sub specie aeternitatis*, to be sure, six decades lose all shape and duration. But to literary historians those long years appear as a chain of perceptible length, marked off into successive links (or moments)—as this very work sometimes suggests (e.g., p. 44). According to Professor Henri Peyre and others, a brief phenomenon of equilibrium, in the second half of the century, following and preceding periods of unrest, produced masterpieces bearing a common stamp that we can agree to call classical; but that manifestly is not what is meant here; it is not evident that Mr. Turnell has absorbed or put to use the interesting essays on this point.

Thrown off by indefiniteness in terminology and thinking, the reader must also pick his way through errors and eccentricities. By now even nonspecialists would not go on blithely repeating that *Phèdre* "was a complete failure," or one "skilfully engineered by Racine's enemies" (p. 215); or that Henriette d'Angleterre "suggested to Corneille and Racine that they should write plays on the love of Titus and Bérénice" (p. 188). Phèdre, for a moment fantastically confused with Hippolyte's mother, becomes "the ageing Amazon"! (p. 209)—"ageing," she who in the play remains so wondrously ageless. When we hear to boot of her "simultaneous discovery that Thésée is living and Hippolyte is in love with Aricie" (p. 208), or of "the curse which Phèdre persuades Thésée to lay on Hippolyte" (p. 214), we wonder what unusual edition of the work Mr. Turnell might be discussing. And what strange version of Racine could make him appear "a reckless champion of the primacy of passion" (p. 15)? We are accustomed to extravagant musings on Racinian passion, but few so bizarre and unaccountable as this:

> the principal character suffers from a fatal passion which infects those who surround him or her, so that each of them develops the same passion for a third person. Oreste infects Hermione who becomes infatuated with Pyrrhus who in turn is infatuated with Andromaque. Roxane infects Bajazet who falls in love with Atalide ["Déjà plein d'un amour dès l'enfance formé," says Bajazet! "Je l'aimai dès l'enfance," says Atalide!] Phèdre infects the "insensible" Hippolyte who becomes desperately in love with Aricie (p. 213).

Infected or infecting, "when Hermione is finally thrown over by Pyrrhus" she is alleged to say (p. 177): "Ah! je l'ai trop aimé pour ne le point haïr," famous words which in fact she utters upon her first appearance, in Act II, scene 1. And in Molière's *Misanthrope*, it is of course Philinte and not the Cléante of *Tartuffe* who tries to moderate Alceste (p. 54). In *Tartuffe*, Elmire strives to help Damis and Mariane but, surely, these are not "her children" (p. 77).[1]

The most disconcerting fancies or errors are those that concern the meaning of words—important words like Tartuffe's "discipline" (p. 71), "innocence" in *Phèdre* (p. 209), and "gloire" in *Bérénice* (p. 190). The greatest jolt, perhaps, comes (p. 199) from the commentary on "Athènes me montra mon superbe ennemi," in Phèdre's confession to Œnone: " 'Superbe,' " writes Mr. Turnell, "with its suggestion of 'glamour' and 'romance' "! Phèdre is all set for Hollywood.

This work can be misleading, confusing, erroneous. More is the pity, since one of Mr. Turnell's objectives is "to encourage English readers to study 'the three poets' more carefully." He introduces learning of a different tone. Addressing a general public of English readers, traditionally cool to Racine, he explains the latter, along with Corneille and Molière, with the help of two highly respected techniques of analysis: the sociohistorical and the psychoanalytical methods. These, when handled by experts, are invaluable tools of criticism. Here, they throw more obstacles in our way.

One grows to suspect that if Mr. Turnell frequently scans the historical background, he may be doing so largely out of deep respect for the feeling we all have today that this is the thing to do. He sounds like one acknowledging and meeting standards, without expressing or communicating any thrill of discovery or true vision. Too frequently his sociohistorical observations are hackneyed, made to order, couched in language of this sort:

> The seventeenth century in France, as in England, was a period in which civilization was undergoing revolutionary changes. The old world was crumbling and a new world was emerging. There were curious cross-currents in France, where, more than in England, two orders faced one another (p. 143).

Here is an abridged lexicon of the clichés so current today. There is always someone to melodramatize and Hegelize any age, in any part of the world, in these very terms. If some author of the past never thought of himself as standing with one foot on a crumbling universe and the other on an emerging world, his modern biographer will surely put him in that uncomfortable acrobatic posture. Turmoil and consolidation—all that is certainly present, in the seventeeth century as along almost any stretch of time, but each of these "revolutionary changes" could be recounted with a realism appropriate to it, and without this haze of stereotypes. And without erroneous fancies. Where is this "unity of throne and nobility" (p. 2), in the seventeenth century? "The keynote of the century is authority [Descartes, for example?] and the word which occurs perhaps more frequently than any

---

[1] Cf. also untenable or disputable remarks on Boileau's "influence" and "propaganda" (p. 8), on Pascal and Bossuet as "admirers of Cartesian philosophy" (p. 21), on some sort of "conversion" at the end of *Tartuffe* (p. 120). On p. 111, "Rien ne m'appelle ailleurs toute la journée" (from *Le Misanthrope*, Act II, sc. 2) should read "*de* toute la journée."

other is 'les règles' " (p. 7)—it is just possible that "l'art de plaire" and the "je ne sais quoi" are invoked at least as often. One particularly unconvincing technique is to establish a relationship between a social and a literary phenomenon by merely assuming that the former, preceding or paralleling the latter, cannot but have influenced it: "The interest that [Corneille] shows in family feuds in the 'Cid,' in political intrigue in 'Cinna' and religious dissensions in 'Polyeucte,' is clearly a reflection of events that were going on around him" (p. 21). One can only ask, in rather elementary fashion, "how do you know?" and "when were there not feuds, intrigues, dissensions, and when did authors not write about such things?" "A direct preoccupation with morality," says Mr. Turnell, "and the constant recurrence of words denoting moral qualities like 'honneur,' 'gloire,' 'grand coeur' and 'mâle assurance' are usually a sign of literary decadence—a sign that society is becoming self-conscious about qualities it is in the process of losing" (p. 22). Only if terms lose all sense can we label as "literary" a decadence perceived and described as social. And is it decadence? That rests on the bald assumption that the frequent use of terms intimates the loss of those values they designate—a notion not foreign to modern psychology, but one that would require here more ample demonstration than a flat statement. Consider this cryptic assertion, among others: "The tendency to rhetoric, which is inherent in French verse, becomes more pronounced during the seventeenth century and is a sign that the poet is already conscious of the instability of the society in which he is living" (p. 3). Mr. Turnell no doubt intended the meaning to be transparent.

Age of Corneille: Man of Honor. Age of Molière: Natural Man. Age of Racine: Man of Passion. That is the nutshell formula. But how, chronologically, could two distinct Ages occupy the same space, as those of Molière and Racine would have to do? Mr. Turnell would be against setting rigid lines of demarcation. And yet, he takes his tripartite scheme much too seriously: in *Nicomède* (1651), Prusias, "an ironic figure," marks the discovery of a "new manner" and "points the way straight to the Age of Molière. Yet when Molière tried to do the same thing in 1658 the result [*Dom Garcie de Navarre*] was a failure." Why? "Molière was not sufficiently mature. . . . It was only in the 'Misanthrope' . . . that 'Nicomède' bore its full fruit" (p. 45-46). *Dom Garcie*, be it noted, was first performed in 1661, and probably composed in late 1659. But Pascal had not waited for the Age of the Mature Molière to write the *Provinciales*; if to him we add lesser ironists of the early century, including the "libertins érudits," what becomes of this distinction between the Ages of Corneille and Molière? One is not sure, besides, whether each of these representative poets is really one with his contemporaries. Now we hear that Molière, for example, "believed in his age," possessed a "sense of society as a coherent whole," and now, with reference to the *Misanthrope*, that Molière "lived in an age of intellectual scepticism" and that "at the close of the play society . . . leaves by one exit and Alceste abandons society by another, leaving an empty stage"; "complete disbelief" is the dominant note (pp. 119-20, 131-32).

To modernize an old play, we not only sociologize it, we often psychoanalyze it. Mr. Turnell cannot resist the manifold opportunities thrown wide open by this method, especially in the case of Racine. And it is indeed very difficult to withstand the temptation. Those in particular who have been fascinated by "le féroce" in Racine have made repeated analyses of the biographical data and the plays, at times with interesting results. Following Denis de Rougemont, Mr. Turnell finds something important to say about the Racinian expression of the death wish—although J. Segond's treatise remains a more systematic exposé of that subject. One difficulty, in the present work, is that the critic's purpose is not very clear. At times he seems to be psychoanalyzing the poet, and at times the very characters of the plays—a more hazardous enterprise; at other times, it does appear as though the poet himself is presented somewhat as a master pre-Freudian tying egos and ids into knots. For instance, "Aricie's declaration that she is not attracted by Hippolyte's physical beauty is perfectly sincere; she does not know that an unconscious fear of physical love is making her hide her real feelings" (p. 197). But does Racine know this? Can anyone be sure this was his conscious or unconscious meaning? Herein lies the chief objection to this whole procedure. Professional psychoanalysts would be the first to caution us against applying their methods to the dead, or to the fictitious, for reasons that should be all too evident. Yet "there can be little doubt," guarantees Mr. Turnell, "that Abner's return to the Temple symbolizes the return of the prodigal but repentant Racine to the bosom of Port-Royal" (p. 225); temples and palaces, the usual settings for the plays, were to Racine symbols not only of "refuge" but of "prison" as well (pp. 159-60). All that may be; but it is possible that, being princes, high priests, and monarchs, Racinian characters just naturally settled down in palaces and temples. Thus, very often, there is more than one plausible explanation, and Mr. Trunell appears rather willful in insisting on his own.

With rectifications, and with much of the sociologizing and of the psychologizing cut out, this work would shine, for powerful insights abound. In general, Mr. Turnell performs a rare service in calling attention to the deep, expressive ambiguity in the poetry of French classical drama, to which our routine commentators fail to respond sensitively. Others before have written effectively of the seventeenth-century "ambivalent attitude towards authority," "tension-and-repose," "poise," "concentration." But he very appropriately makes us focus on these again.

Mr. Turnell has a way of suggesting how to reformulate and invigorate our old impressions of the poets, and to reconsider some of their plays in a new light. He does not, however, retouch Corneille's portrait boldly enough. Even when insisting (pp. 29-34) that his real theme is not duty versus inclination "but the subordination of one set of values to another," or that "Corneille's characters are people 'qui se construisent' " (Sartre would agree), he does not go far enough in abandoning the dichotomy of sense-passion and will-reason; the duty, will, or reason of a Cornelian character can be a force as fierce and passionate as passion itself—witness Emilie, who opens the action in *Cinna* with outcries of impetuous, irrepressible, blind longing for revenge. For all this, to argue that "Corneille was not a master of pathos" (p. 35) seems basically sound, although our author could have supported his contention more vigorously had he absorbed the early comedies and the later plays into his general discussion.

His treatment of Racine in many ways is disappointing. He underscores too heavily the features of "ferocité," and generalizes too sweepingly: "In Racine's poetry love is always . . . a blind urge for possession which sees consummation not in union with, but in the pursuit and destruction of its 'prey' " (p. 171). Perhaps because this does not fit a Monime, a Bérénice, or an Iphigénie, the plays in which these appear are given rather scant attention; for *Bérénice* especially, the reader will discover, Mr. Turnell shows what may be called a blind spot. *Britannicus*, in which love-passion has but a very secondary role, is discussed most summarily; Agrippine, truly a central character, is barely mentioned. *Bajazet*, and more surprisingly *Andromaque*, are passed as rapidly in review. But powerful emphasis is placed on *Phèdre* and *Athalie*. In the former, symbols of light and darkness, intimations of the death wish, and the tragic "process of progressive and destructive self-knowledge" (p. 202) are unfolded with a skill that impels one to reexamine the whole play. A fresh, suggestive approach to *Athalie* brings out the ironic notes of the play, the full measure of the old queen's tragedy, and the ambiguity of the religious sentiment—for ambiguity is there, discernible especially through Abner's important role: this could be one of the most interesting commentaries on the religious feeling of Racine during his last decade.

Excessive selectivity also impoverishes the treatment of Molière: one paragraph for *Les Femmes savantes*! But this chapter, supported by theories of comedy already familiar to us, drives home many a capital point, and especially the comic nature and mechanism of that "esprit malade" which Molière laid bare in *L'Ecole des femmes* and later continued to probe. Mr. Turnell dwells on *Tartuffe, Dom Juan, Le Misanthrope*—the three most difficult to explain. Psychoanalysis at times offers dubious assistance: "Tartuffe is the scapegoat whose chastisement provides a release for the audience's primitive desires and emotions" (p. 91). Twentieth-century jargon at times obscures the seventeenth-century poet's strategy: " 'Tartuffe' is first and foremost a sociological study of the corrosive influence . . . of a decadent religiosity on the life of the community" (pp. 61-62). A paradox is propounded: "Tartuffe is in his way genuine—genuine in that his hypocrisy is an integral part of his character—and deceives himself as well as other people" (p. 63): we must then conclude that he is not a hypocrite at all! But the meaning of the plays breaks through. The most provocative essay is the one on *Dom Juan* as a comedy of "extreme incredulity" and "intellectual pride."

There are, scattered about in the sections on Molière and Racine especially, "explications" of a type that Mr. Turnell manages in a felicitous manner all his own. He moves swiftly to the core of a dramatic passage selected for analysis; with sure insight into the poet's use of language he fastens upon the focal terms and fashions the rest about them, like a configuration around the corner. He may torment a word or line now and then, and wring astonishing connotations out of it. Usually, however, the meaning of scenes and dialogues naturally opens out, as it were, and spreads to the whole play. That is surely the chief merit and attraction of the book.

But Mr. Turnell can best set an example of discrimination and sensitive critical imagination—and can show technical precision as well, as a skillful detector of sound effects in alexandrine verse—when he bends directly over the text at hand. When he would wander off into the sciences of man and society, it becomes difficult to follow him with assurance, with enthusiasm, or with patience.

Georges May. *Tragédie cornélienne, tragédie racinienne. Etude sur les sources de l'intérêt dramatique.* Urbana: University of Illinois Press, 1948.

SETTING CORNEILLE against Racine is an old ritual. Other tests-by-confrontation—pitting Racine, for example, against Sophocles, Euripides, or Shakespeare—could perchance have afforded equal sport and enlightenment, but have never attained a comparable vogue. "Le *parallèle* entre Corneille et Racine," Henri Bremond once remarked, "est un de nos grands jeux nationaux." These two alone are the standard, official opponents—are they the most felicitously matched? Do they belong at all in the same contest? This technicality has been rather overlooked; it would deserve to be argued before the strictest of referees. In the meantime, however, Dr. May offers here one of the most absorbing rounds in the history of the traditional bout.

There are, of course, certain rules of the game, which Dr. May very appropriately follows. Let our interpretation of the two poets lead where it will, we cannot but take into account Corneille's stated doctrine of "admiration" and Racine's declared adherence to the Aristotelian poetics of pity and terror; one fancies a relatively complicated form of dramatic composition, the other aims at simplicity; one defends "invraisemblance" in theory and courts it in practice, the other shuns it. So runs the conventional *parallèle.* It is all "matière de bréviaire," which Dr. May honors soberly, without laboring the point. The obvious is merely gathered into his own new scheme of things.

We are urged to fasten upon one simple fact: Corneille and Racine were playwrights. It would seem rather late for anyone to raise this point, but how many *parallélistes* thus far have borne it rigorously in mind? Before a welter of irresistible questions concerning duty and passion, heroism and realism, reason and inspiration, rhetoric and poetry, and other topics of great moment, we apparently need, in order to bend our attention toward problems of dramatic craftsmanship, something like Pascal's special "esprit de géométrie": "on a peine à tourner la tête de ce côté-là, manque d'habitude." But, "pour peu qu'on l'y tourne, on voit les principes à plein." A play, manifestly, is meant to be performed—to be seen and heard, in its entirety, on one occasion. Hence, communication must be direct and immediate; there is no poring over a text, no rereading, no pondering, no browsing back. We cannot but follow, without retracing our steps, a pace already set for us; and if this forward motion is to be compelling, the impetus must be continuous, unbroken, cumulative. Whatever else may be the purpose of the playwright, then, he must without fail capture our attention, and hold, in-

Originally published in *Romanic Review* 41 (1950): 135–41.

tensify, sustain our interest. Resolutely turning "de ce côté-là," Dr. May concentrates on the "sources de l'intérêt dramatique" in Corneille and Racine.

Shall the playwright begin by choosing a subject unfamiliar to the audience, or a well-known incident of history or legend? Corneille readily adopted the first and Racine the other technique, although perhaps not quite so consistently as Dr. May would have it appear. He ingeniously accounts for the intrusion of famous characters like Medea, Oedipus, Titus, and Bérénice upon a Cornelian world of obscure heroes, but in the face of other difficulties seems somewhat awkwardly to force the issue: the subject of *Horace*, for instance, was illustrious enough; granted, but it was the idea of putting it on the stage that was novel. This argument somehow does not apply to Racine's *Bajazet*, although the story had never been dramatized before; if indeed it was widely known at all, it was by no means so famous or classic as that of *Horace*, yet the latter is presumably a clear example of drama with original content, and we are asked to grant that in *Bajazet*, as in other Racinian plays, "une fois encore, les personnages sont familiers au public de la cour et l'intrigue est connue à l'avance." This shifting of ground puts a strain on the goodwill with which we receive Dr. May's thesis. We also wonder about plays like *Attila* and *Cinna*. In the former, the episode related by Corneille of course was not commonly known, but the central character—the scourge of God—surely was no obscure individual of the past; in the latter, there appeared the renowned Augustus. As for the *Cid*, is it demonstrable that "le sujet en était . . . inconnu des spectateurs de Corneille?" One of those cited as supporting authorities speaks in effect of a "tradition désormais établie" in France before the Cornelian masterpiece.[1] All this, however, is but the overstatement of a sound thesis. By and large, Corneille does show a tendency to go off on a "chasse à l'inconnu," and Racine noticeably leans in the opposite direction. That is a capital point.

Corneille by his very choice of subjects shows that he depends heavily on the technique of surprise. Just why? To *plaire*, to stir an audience, the poet strove to inspire a sentiment of "admiration," which is not to be construed, in a moral sense, as admiration-approval—witness his *héros scélérats*; it was closer to a feeling of wonder, to be inspired by characters who, in a spirit of "nietzschéisme avant la lettre," transcended the common, observable pattern of humanity; hence their "outrance," whether in virtue or in crime, and hence their "invraisemblance." The artist whose strategy thus tended toward the extraordinary could be expected to apply, in every phase of his art, tactics of surprise, and to be drawn to unusual subjects. Whether Dr. May himself would fully subscribe to this reading of his exposé is not clear. At one point,

---

[1]Gustave Reynier, "Le Cid en France avant 'Le Cid,' " *Mélanges offerts par ses amis et ses élèves à M. Gustave Lanson*, (Paris, 1922), p. 217. Through Mariana, among others, elements of the Cid theme could in fact have been known. The Spanish historian, it is true, appears in Dr. May's list of relatively unknown authorities whom Corneille was wont to consult (p. 55), but that list needs checking: if the fortunes of scholars like Mariana, Baronius, and du Verdier in the seventeenth century were better known, it might appear that Corneille, in turning to them, did nothing notably original.

he seems ready to argue that Corneille fancied surprise simply for its own sake, or for the privilege it conferred upon him of being the one to reveal the novel material (p. 58). Yet elsewhere he does relate it more intimately to the basic Cornelian drive; he shows that the master combined effects of surprise with feelings of "admiration" in his first, great dramas, only later allowing himself. in some weaker productions, to rely preponderantly on tricks of the trade (pp. 63, 233). Be that as it may, in weak or powerful works, throughout the execution of a play and not only in the choice of subject, Corneille's skill in holding an audience consisted—now more, now less—in stimulating curiosity and exhibiting the unexpected. A twofold suspense is built up: what will befall the individuals we see on the stage? how will the playwright disentangle his plot? A character goes off, between two acts, to face some peril or make a fateful choice, and if in his own mind he knows before disappearing what course he will follow, we are not taken into his confidence; at times his fate is determined by decisions reached, also between the acts, by other characters. Corneille will even mislead us, give us false or vague premonitions, send us off on "fausses pistes"; characters will whisper, or interrupt an exchange of remarks before the secret is out, or hint darkly at what will be more clearly unfolded later. Unexpected developments not uncommonly sustain the suspense. The *coups de théâtre* may come occasionally at the end of an act, to allow the consequences to materialize amply before the action goes on, but they generally open an act, especially the fifth, where they help to unravel the plot. The denouement is set to occur as close to the end of the play as possible; Dr. May convincingly argues that it is never predictable purely on the basis of the characters' psychology but is itself a final surprise, like the conversions at the end of *Polyeucte*. Our attention is prodded and kept awake to the last; particularly in the most complicated plays, it is perforce so taxed that all the intricacies of the action can be grasped only at a second performance; at that point, however, the initial element of surprise will have vanished, an impasse which clearly defines the limits of this technique in the manufacturing of dramatic interest.

Undeniably, Racine did the very opposite, but not doggedly, as if he had come into this world solely for the purpose of reversing Corneille's technique. Yielding very little ground on this score, Dr. May will concede that Mithridate undergoes an unprepared "revirement psychologique." Much more could be added. The Néron of *Britannicus*, for instance, keeps other characters in the dark. So does a Joad; he keeps his own counsel, answers Abner indirectly, and traps Athalie with a metaphor-lie. Above all, it is surprising that Dr. May, reacting so exactly to the timing of every exit and reappearance of a hero in Corneille's theater, does not feel the suspense created by Racine at the end and start of many an act. Is there no tense awaiting of developments, for example, as Acts I, II, III, and IV of *Phèdre* come to an end? That feature of Racinian stagecraft is ignored, and unaccountably so, since it could without difficulty be absorbed into what is here described as the characteristic technique. The latter consists not in surprising the spectator but rather in letting him know in advance what is to happen. Even before the play begins, he presumably is familiar with the story, if he knows his Latin and Greek classics or the current literature from which the playwright had drawn his material. Within the play itself, we are reminded before very long of the inevitable conclusion. Scenes of exposition, without being patterned after the prologues of Euripides, serve the same purpose. If an unfamiliar denouement is required, as in *Iphigénie*, it is carefully prepared; so are the occasional "coups de théâtre amortis," like Thésée's return in *Phèdre*. Shocks are avoided, or deadened. Racine does not wish to divert our attention to the incidents of the plot. He leaves us no opportunity to expect a turn of events other than the one we expect. And in its most drastic application, this method produces a *Bérénice* almost devoid of external action. Our attention is thus concentrated on complications of another kind, which are deeply within the characters themselves; the tragedian is free to probe this inner life, not having to labor the literal facts; and often, by his use of familiar lore, he can enrich his tragedies with the "parfum poétique" of evocative names of old. Corneille's spectator usually does not have foreknowledge of what is to come, while some of his characters do. Racine's spectator, no less than Sophocles', is like a seer or omniscient witness; it is the hero on the stage who gropes blindly or furiously forward to an end we foresee; the dramatic tension in us arises from our viewing this tragic fulfillment, this coming to painful awareness.

We discover a Racine and a Corneille in many ways already known to us, but the method is new. It has the precision and definiteness of a mathematical operation—a careful weighing of the pressures that unknowing and omniscient listeners, present before the poet's mental eye, bring to bear on processes of dramatic composition. Now and then, as noted above, Dr. May yields to the temptation of balancing those pressures too rigorously; like an athlete playing at Bremond's "grand jeu," he goes all out for a perfect equilibrium. But he bolsters his *parallèle* with strong arguments, and with solid evidence drawn from the two poets' plays and from their theoretic writings as well. No wall is raised tightly around Corneille and Racine; the former is compared, in passing at least, to the Spanish theater, and the latter, in some of the finest pages of the book, is viewed at some length against the background of Greek drama. The central thesis is systematically elaborated, acquiring momentum step by step. Comments on related topics open interesting areas of research still to be explored: thus, in one passage which deserves particular attention, Dr. May views with appropriate skepticism the notion that the Cornelian spirit can be understood in terms of a certain heroic atmosphere that blew about in Corneille's day (a superficial idea of the early Lanson, but still all too influential today). Throughout, Dr. May proceeds with manifest confidence—in himself, but not so much in the reader, however. Various points seem needlessly reiterated. With most uncommon frequency, the author interrupts the exposition, which is methodical and easy to follow, in order to point parenthetically to what has already been said or will later be taken up, as if he feared that the simplest relationships of ideas might not be self-evident. A plain, unpedantic terminology is set up, but one "ism" (always a source of confusion) is used rather carelessly in two unrelated senses: the rationalism of Racine (and Euripides) signifies a disposition to see human action as purely human, without supernatural intervention or motivation (p. 183); Corneille's "conception strictement rationaliste" of drama has to do with a "conception logique du spectacle" with inductive and deductive aspects (pp. 212–14). Difficulties of a different sort, here and there, may cause the reader to stop, and resist. May one in all seriousness speak of "un génie aussi divers et ondoyant que Corneille" (p. 18)? Do we know anything, concerning Racine's long silence, that would permit one to speak with assurance of a "conversion" to Jansenism (pp. 185, 230)? In his famous letter of reconciliation to Perrault, did Boileau accept without a smile Corneille's "nouveau genre de tragédie inconnu à Aristote"? Dr. May sees no malice, yet this piece is one of Boileau's most felicitous attempts at sustained irony; the passage quoted here (p. 23) is patently equivocal: consider "une certaine admiration, dont plusieurs personnes, et les plus jeunes surtout, s'accommodent souvent mieux que des passions tragiques."

The whole problem of tragedy, like a haze, hovers indistinctly over the *parallèle*. All along, as in the title, it is rather taken for granted that Corneille was a writer of tragedies. Is that so irresistibly self-evident? More than twenty years ago, Jean Schlumberger denied it, for reasons far from frivolous, and proposed that Corneille be understood essentially as a creator of "comédies héroïques."[2] That point of view, of course, is not the prevailing one. But to my knowledge there is no reasoned, searching study of Corneille considered specifically as a tragedian—none, that is, based on any rationalized, comprehensive theory of tragedy. A habit, time-honored but hard to justify in terms of explicit critical standards, prompts us to admit Corneille into the company of Sophocles, Shakespeare, and Racine; yet if *Oedipus, Hamlet,* and *Phèdre* are what we mean by tragedy, neither an *Attila* nor even a *Cid* can be absorbed into that concept, however broadly we define it. Powerful, but with a spirit and a ring utterly different from and contrary to the tragic vein, the Cornelian drama remains apart. To be sure, Dr. May was not bound to raise this particular issue; his task was not to analyze the nature of the genre but to describe a process of dramatic composition. Yet "tout se tient"; and inevitably Dr. May becomes a party to the discussion. He even compels us to ask the embarrassing questions. He underscores all the "trucs," as he calls them, and all the melodramatic features in Corneille, pointing out that our attention, drawn to the plot, "ne permet pas de jouir, à supposer qu'elles y soient, des qualités plus universelles de la tragédie" (p. 207): "Que l'enveloppe soit quelquefois vide, ou que son contenu soit souvent bien mince, nous n'en disconvenons pas" (p. 231—see also p. 211 and passim). The difference will out, and Dr. May will note in passing Racine's search for "les plus authentiques beautés tragiques," "une autre fin plus haute et plus authentiquement tragique" (pp. 224, 144). Are Corneille's productions less authentic tragedies, then? Are there, indeed, degrees of tragedy? It is not simply a matter of separating the empty shells from what might be called the "enveloppes combles" of the great plays, for an "enveloppe" with "un contenu bien mince"—*Oedipe*, for example, on Dr. May's own showing—is still a "tragédie" (p. 208): Corneille-tragedian-for-all-that. For a moment, the idea of drawing the latter closer to Aristotle grows tantalizing; curiosity and surprise, we are urged to consider, are like

---

[2]"Corneille," *La Nouvelle Revue Française* 33 (1929):337ff.

"les avatars modernes" of the pity and fear of tragedy described in the *Poetics* (p. 114). Some links do exist between the two sets of words; but essentially they stand for two distinct modes of reaction; pity and fear are twin emotions, or one ambivalent emotion betokening the complex identity between spectator and tragic hero, whereas curiosity and surprise are successive states of the mind seeking answers to riddles: what is the identity between a spectator and a riddle? Discovering, with Dr. May's unintended help, what separates Cornelian dramaturgy from tragedy, we also discern more clearly what relates it to comedy. "Des pièces comme *Othon*, *Agésilas*, *Attila*, *Tite et Bérénice*, *Pulchérie*, *Suréna* ressemblent étrangement à des comédies. . . . il n'y a pas jusqu'aux vers qui ne soient des vers de comédie" (pp. 92-93). But why "étrangement"? For "il ne paraît pas douteux que ç'ait été sur la scène comique," in his early creations, that he learned all the "ressorts de surprise et de curiosité" (p. 74).

The Corneille-Racine *parallèle* remains a "grand jeu" largely, perhaps, because it is confidently assumed that these two are comparable as tragedians. It will undoubtedly be always instructive to confront them, as it is to confront any great writer with another, even at random. The differences in technique between Racine and Corneille, skillfully analyzed by Dr. May, are most interesting, because all techniques are of great interest to us. But the authors of the *Cid* and of *Phèdre* did not work out their different methods for ends comparable with one another. It is possible that the final *parallèle*, to end all *parallèles*, will show that there is no *parallèle*.

Jean Pommier. *Aspects de Racine. Suivi de l'histoire littéraire d'un couple tragique*. Paris: Nizet, 1954.
John C. Lapp. *Aspects of Racinian Tragedy*. Toronto: University of Toronto Press, 1955.

MUCH OF the accumulated commentary on Racine has to do with "aspects." He is reckoned a difficult poet, whose classicism runs deep, but businesslike commentators prefer to seek after what is accessible, in research localized and at times immobilized on the periphery of Racine's works; they appear to consider themselves rewarded with aspects, or facets. But in the presence of an art so sustained and intensively unified, modest restraint of this sort is out of place. Nothing less than a feeling for the total sweep of Racinian tragedy, as in the dynamic critique of a Thierry Maulnier, can be very satisfying. Aspects should be used to round out a broad prospect.

In Professor Pommier's book of aspects, which brings together, with some revisions and accretions, articles and essays already published from 1943 to 1953, the most tantalizing part is perhaps the table of contents, where for certain sets of chapters there are improvised, resounding group titles like "De l'aube au midi," "Rayons et ombres au couchant," "Sur les deux rives du silence," and "Langage et poésie," which seem to promise great flights of the critical imagination. But from Dawn to Noon we review circumstantial evidence about the relationship of the boy and the man Racine to Antoine Le Maître and Jean Hamon, of Port-Royal; about the identity of "la déhanchée," who turns out to be the actress Du Parc; and about the reasons for Racine's silence, the "chapitre à faire" in all Racinian detective lore. The four-chapter sequence on Sunset Shafts and Shadows confronts us suddenly with side disquisitions on the life and trials of the Comtesse de Grammont, "la grande dame dont l'amitié sérieuse pour Racine donne, croyons-nous, le secret des dernières années du courtisan et du chrétien"; but Racine himself, for long stretches of time, simply vanishes from sight. On the farther Shore of Silence, where Racine reawakened to poetic creation, Professor Pommier commemorates this event by engaging another scholar in a dispute as to possible political allusions in *Esther* and *Athalie*.

Each of these questions has its importance, to be sure. Some have been discussed previously, and with authority: Henry C. Lancaster, for example, showed before the present writer that Racine's appointment as historiographer of the king helps to explain his withdrawal from the stage. Fresh or merely restated, every point is here established with veritable virtuosity in documentation and debate. Journalese mannerisms unfortunately mar this impression somewhat, as when we read: "Car . . . Mais laissons ici parler un témoin direct," or "[il promet] à elle-même . . . Mais laissons-le parler"— suspension without suspense. But what is basically disappointing and vexing is that the biography and background material, occupying nearly half of the thick volume, was thrown together in an amorphous pile. The bodies of facts have little relationship to one another, despite the catchy captions, and are not made to have any bearing on the literary values of the great plays.

There are other chapters more directly concerned with Racine at work as a creator. "Construction de *Phèdre*," on the hither Shore of Silence, is a study of construction in two senses of the term—the structure of the play and the constructing or putting together of elements borrowed from ancient and modern sources. It is perhaps Professor Pommier's strongest offering. Also of special quality, chapters on Racine's language persuasively point up the need for expanding and correcting the work already done by Marty-Laveaux and Jacques Gabriel Cahen; here we come closer to seeing the true nature of the taboos observed by Racine in his choice of words, and to opening our eyes to the color and the technical, or familiar, or material, or sensuous shades that his vocabulary can take on. There are suggestive discussions of "polyvalence" and the "franche jouissance" that Racine found "dans la chair, la pulpe des mots" (p. 282).

But there is still no center of interest, no reason why these chapters should be stacked up in their present order. There is no study of Racine's "Poésie," as announced, but only a slight chapter on versification. A long "Histoire littéraire d'un couple tragique" here again reviews the ancient and the French works concerned with Phaedra and Hippolytus, presenting a double series of portraits with captions often trivial and more snappy than accurate, such as "Une Patricienne emballée" and "Un Beau Cavalier." But Racine's own two characters, for whom all these forerunners might have been expected to serve as prologue, are left out of the procession; few buildups could be more anticlimactic. Finally, the most disappointing chapter of all is perhaps "Le 'Crime' de la reine," the only one in which the author faces directly the question of tragedy in Racine, or at least "aspects" of that central problem. He can paint a dark picture of Phèdre and yet declare himself unable to detect in it any but venial sins. Against every discernible intention of Racine, he clears her of responsibility as a "victime" of Venus, and as a wife deceived by Thésée; she may say of her marriage: "Mon repos, mon bonheur semblait être affermi," but what of that? "Bonheur assez pâle, puisqu'elle le met après son repos" (p. 211). Is it possible not to see that the very opposite effect, in ascending gradation, is produced? The argument never seems to achieve firmness. Now the preface of the play is cited as conclusive evidence, and now rejected as suspect. "*Phèdre* ou la tragédie de l'expiation," we read in a surprise conclusion—expiation, then, of venial sins, and by a victim not responsible for them! The point that struggles to emerge here is that Phèdre, not knowing that Hippolyte is already dead, at the end wishes to make known his innocence, though she has persecuted him, and to permit his reunion with Aricie; she dies to make a brighter day possible for them. But had she not resolved to destroy her life before ever becoming aware of his feeling for the captive maid? At the moment when she expires, and even before, when proclaiming Hippolyte's innocence, she does know of his death. For the alleged act of expiation, besides, the confession without suicide on her part would have sufficed. What happens while her life comes to an end and she gathers the meaning of her tragedy remains unexplained in these confused pages.

It would not be unfair to say that most of the articles and essays here collected did not urgently require to be published anew. Surely, readers of Racine had already sufficiently absorbed what knowledge and understanding these items had had to contribute. The latter had gained from remaining scattered, according to their nature, as so many random "aspects." Linked and forced together, they are disappointing as a body, like a very incomplete ten-year adventure in criticism.

The title of Professor Lapp's work, in the circumstances, is rather unfortunate, for this is no book of "aspects" like the other, although it is also in part the product of various articles previously brought out. Contrast is more in order than comparison. The title of the final chapter, "The Essence of Racinian Tragedy," makes a brave promise, such as one rarely sees in the most enterprising studies on Racine; much in the other chapters and the conclusion bears on the same subject, and so recurrently in fact that diffusion rather than concentration sets in. In chapter 1, devoted to the Themes, these often are not really themes but elements or modes of tragedy.

The question of time and space is lifted out of the realm of worn doctrine-by-rules, and the unities, quite properly, are interpreted as aesthetic strategy, which by various means condenses the past into the present moment and far lands and seas into the visible setting. Professor Lapp is at his best as he argues these points, showing especially how "time is dramatic in Racine; his characters are its prisoners, bearing the onus of the past and confronting a future that brings catastrophe" (p. 81).

The relationship between this sense of time and the sense of fatality, perhaps, could have been more explicitly brought out, as in Professor Georges Poulet's *Etudes sur le temps humain*. Fate, a crucial problem for any theorist of tragedy, is here strangely skirted as a topic of discussion; it is introduced only in passing, in phrases like "the pull of fate" or "playthings of destiny." The ultimate significance of expanding time and space lies elsewhere: that "the obsessive past . . . should, in all its glory and awesomeness, take such precedence over the frenzied and passionate present of the play itself, underlines the theme of the disintegration of the hero" (p. 45). This takes place, presumably, in an early play like *Andromaque*. Something analogous occurs within the framework of space but apparently—that is a first difficulty—not so early; from *Andromaque* to *Bajazet* Racine would seem in varying degrees to have limited the scene of action and from *Mithridate* on to have broadened the expanse. Conceivably, a poet could simultaneously contract space and expand time, as much as he pleased. But there is something askew in this picture of Racine, for with the initial contraction of space does come, as Professor Lapp recognizes, a "claustrophobic effect": do not lines such as "Nos vaisseaux sont tout prêts, et le vent nous appelle," then, break through even in *Andromaque* like an urge toward outlying spaces and, psychically as it were, extend the setting powerfully, before *Mithridate*? Why, moreover, is it contraction, spacewise, that causes claustrophobia, and on the contrary extension, in terms of duration, that makes of Racinian characters "prisoners" of time? If these characters are ensnared by the time that has passed, are they not also held back in the distant regions inhabited in that time past, like Andromaque in Troy or Antiochus in "l'Orient désert"? What especially takes the reader by surprise, leaving him lost behind the author, is the claim that Racine's "conscious restricting of the scene in the earlier plays gives prominence to human instrumentality; the reverse is true when the area beyond is widened" (p. 76). Human instrumentality and stature are linked. When the gods' role is found to grow prominent in *Iphigénie* and *Phèdre*, this "stress on divine instrumentality," like the expanding setting, is made to correspond with the tragic character's "diminishing in stature" (p. 35). But why does the hero disintegrate, against a widened background of time and space or in the face of divine intervention? These seem to be beliefs of great importance to Professor Lapp, but they are never explained or justified. One might more easily maintain the contrary thesis, that it is when pitted against gods, and the whole universe, and the maledictions of all elapsed time that the tragic hero, if truly tragic and not merely pathetic, rises to his highest possible stature. What is the exact relationship between human instrumentality and stature? There is only a human and no divine instrumentality in farce or comedy—who in *Le Bourgeois gentilhomme* or even *Le Misanthrope* has what may properly be called heroic stature? One source of Professor Lapp's, evidently, was Paul Bénichou's *Morales du grand siècle*, which he cites on the theme of Racine's "demolishing" the hero; but there what is successfully demonstrated, in the chapter on "La Démolition du héros," is Racine's destruction of the Cornelian hero, but not of the tragic hero. The difference is enormous.

Many elements of Racinian tragedy are probed with discrimination and uncommon felicity: solitude, incommunicability, "the agony and tension resulting from the mere placing of characters together," the "electric effect" of "presence" and "constraint," the confrontation of the watched and the watchers. Professor Lapp has many a penetrating page on these subjects, important but often neglected in routine discussions. Some elements, like "reason and passion," "control and abandon," or "the control beneath which we can yet sense smouldering fires," are better known, and somewhat worn by now; they are *matière de bréviaire* in the Racinian canon. Perhaps the abandon and the violence could have been described less toughly than is done in spots, in the Masson-Forestier tradition; it is excessive to see Phèdre's passion as "animality," or the whole dramatic poem as "the mocking of man's aspirations by malevolent and universal forces" (p. 26). It might be fruitful to explore the possibilities of a different interpretation, viewing *Phèdre* as a play in which all, from beginning to end, is contrived so that the heroine's dying word could not but be *pureté*.

In a new study of Racinian tragedy, one would have expected some reference to Professor Eugène Vinaver's recent, provocative *Racine et la poésie tragique*. Convincingly, it defines tragic catharsis, in Racine, as that which, in arousing pity and fear, tempers these states of our moral being: "ce n'est pas nous ôter toute terreur ou toute miséricorde, c'est les ramener à un état d'équilibre où, au lieu d'obscurcir notre vision du vrai, elles l'intensifient" (p. 45). This sets Racine among the poets for whom the sense of tragedy arises out of an experience of enlightenment, self-recognition, and inward rediscovery; it goes deeper than the formula of reason versus passion. On his own, or on the basis of some undisclosed source (this work, like Professor Pommier's, offers no bibliography of any kind) Professor Lapp has arrived at a very similar insight: the "agonizing lucidity" with which tragic characters face their nature, their impossible position, and their will to deceive themselves. But why is this true only of Roxane and Phèdre? What "compelling difference," in substance, between these and an Hermione? "Crois," she says desperately to Cléone,

> que je n'aime plus. Vante-moi ma victoire.
> Crois que dans son dépit mon coeur est endurci,
> Hélas! et s'il se peut, fais-le-moi croire aussi.

"Hélas!" echoes Bérénice, "pour me tromper je fais ce que je puis."

If painful self-knowledge is at the heart of Racinian tragedy, it would seem possible finally to question the conventional position, defended by Professor Lapp, that there is a significant kinship between Racine and Euripides. Their affinity, it is argued, is "tonal." Yet Sophocles and Racine, it is also argued, are close in the use they make of irony—a tonal resemblance if ever there was one. But this can be carried farther. Karl Reinhardt in his *Sophokles* has drawn attention to the "Enthüllungsszene" or scene of revelation, a resolution of the desire to conceal and the desire to reveal: it conveys the meaning of an Oedipus, but would as well unfold the meaning of a Phèdre. Chiefly on that basis, the important, essential comparison to make would be between Sophocles and Racine,[1] *mutandi mutandis.* It would entail a debate about another, related position of Professor Lapp according to which "the Racinian character is hardly tragic in the traditional sense that has developed out of neo-Aristotelian theory" (p. 180). Sister Marie Philip Haley, among others, has shown in her *Racine and the "Art poétique" of Boileau* that a contrary view may not be difficult to defend.

Many of these points may remain forever debatable. But there are few works in English, or in French, in which "The Essence of Racinian Tragedy" claims attention as centrally as here. Professor Lapp compels us to isolate, confront, fit together, and adjust many attributes of that elusive essence. For such "aspects," no reader will owe him a light debt.

[1] Dr. John A. Stone has presented a very challenging dissertation on this subject at Columbia University (1955), published as *Sophocles and Racine: A Comparative Study in Dramatic Technique* (Geneva, 1964).

René Bray. *La Préciosité et les précieux de Thibaut de Champagne à Jean Giraudoux.* Paris: Albin Michel, 1948.

M. BRAY reopens the question of *préciosité.* In a previous publication, his *Anthologie de la poésie précieuse de Thibaut de Champagne à Giraudoux* (1946), it was already apparent that he had gone beyond the routine accounts, which perpetually revolve around a group of silhouettes narrowly confined to seventeenth-century France; that little volume, however, was simply a display of widely scattered *précieux* specimens, with most cursory comments attached; it remained a vague exhibit. Here the author's new outlook clearly unfolds. He would add a dimension to *préciosité*: extension in time. He would immensely expand the perspective to encompass century upon century, from the Middle Ages to the present. A complete survey of *préciosité* against such a setting, of course, would be impossible at this stage. M. Bray appreciates that such a work would have to be an exhaustive study in comparative or general literature, and that numerous exploratory investigations must come before. He directs his attention to France, and in one brief chapter on Lyly, Marino, and Góngora, sketches in some of the other areas still to be searched. Even within the limits of his special province, he has had to forego the triumph of bringing every scrap of evidence to light. To make an issue of this and list all the additional writers he could have touched upon would be to misunderstand his purpose, which was to initiate a full-scale discussion, but hardly to settle it. A wide sampling was enough.

The evidence, spread out in a straight chronological line, graphically conveys an impression of the long duration of *préciosité.* But M. Bray, point-

Originally published in *Romanic Review* 42 (1951): 223-28.

lessly complicating this effect, introduces what I should call an awkward myth. He would have us develop the feeling that *préciosité* will make itself known only at the end of his investigation: "notre objet," he announces in a foreword, "est d'aboutir à une définition," and fairly close to the end (p. 343) he still imagines himself straining toward "la définition à laquelle il faut arriver"—as if *préciosité* could be a word in search of a meaning. We are invited to sustain an inductive sort of experience where, manifestly, we do not take a step without already knowing what we are looking for. How do we determine as we proceed that a Desportes, say, is the very thing? By making the final definition retroactively guarantee the examples on which that definition was based? M. Bray may simply have wished to create a feeling of suspense, or may have merely been expressing a basically laudable distrust of foregone conclusions. In practice, to be sure, he does not rest his case on that wait-till-we-know-how-we-know dilemma. He does the very opposite; from beginning to end, he accumulates not only examples but definitions and descriptions galore, leaving very little to add in the "conclusion." Thus, *préciosité*, in the service of courtly love, is a "jeu d'esprit" practiced in a closed, aristocratic circle according to conventions of word and gesture— a poetry of conceits, devices, and artifices—or a poetry of elegance and style—an intellectualized form of love, Platonistic and Petrarchian—a taste for refined analysis and subtle expression of feelings—a Baroque phenomenon—a display of the incongruous and the hyperbolical—a bid for distinction, a tendency toward affectation—an excess of wit—a sort of egotism akin to dandyism—a love of the useless and formally perfect . . . this is by no means a complete list of the reasons why, at every step, M. Bray is sure this or that poet was a *précieux*.

At times he is too sure. Fastening upon one frail criterion, he lays upon it a heavy burden of proof—again, before the long-awaited conclusion. Too much weight particularly is placed on such figures of speech as allegory and metaphor. Theoretically the latter, to be sure, is declared a symptom of *préciosité* only when the relationship it establishes between two things is farfetched, oversubtle, and based on a comparison of unessential features; but even then the testing device is too easy, or can grow too vague in the presence of certain concrete examples: "appeler l'amour un *feu*, c'est se servir d'une métaphore précieuse"! In Racine's poetry, then, is Phèdre's "feu fatal," alive in her "brûlantes veines," a conceit? In the case of allegory, defined as a prolonged metaphor, apparently no hesitation is possible: with its network of relationships, multiple, drawn out, and presumably artificial, "c'est un des stigmates de la poésie précieuse." This rule of thumb produces meager results, nowhere more disappointing than in the pages on *Le Roman de la Rose*. Such a poem, indeed, cannot but be included in a history of *préciosité*, but for a variety of reasons that would call for ample discussion. M. Bray, in a brief, hostile chapter that is largely a summary of the work, merely decrees: "L'allégorie seule donne au *Roman de la Rose* son caractère précieux"; he finds it difficult to follow the story on both the literal and the symbolic level, and "cet effort est le symptôme de la préciosité." One could argue that no exceptional effort is required, at least in reading Guillaume de Lorris' verse. But that would not be the point: allegory is not of itself a sufficient criterion; it is not what we mean by *préciosité*. Surely the *Divine Comedy* is not.

Sometimes, as in the case of Théophile Gautier, or of Théodore de Banville, the poet's use of personification, or of imaginary transpositions of reality, leads the critic to detect *préciosité* even in poems (cf. pp. 260–62, 272) where, I believe, the reader will not spot any. In a dozen poems of Baudelaire, again, the only test is "l'abstraction," equally inconclusive; we are told, moreover, that in the *Hymne à la Beauté* the linking of an abstract idea with a concrete, objectified symbol is not startling; the illusion seems perfect, and although elsewhere this stands as a sign that figures of speech are free from *préciosité*, here the point of view is reversed: "la préciosité est la même dans tous les cas." That is rather extreme; it is as if the author had grown to feel: an abstraction is an abstraction, *préciosité* is *préciosité*, and the two are the same! In addition, the equation fluctuates, admitting various criteria in the place of abstraction. Shifts of position give one a sensation of indeterminate gliding: what is *préciosité*? A "labeur," as for the trouvères? A "création jaillissante," as in Thibaut de Champagne? "La démesure de l'imagination," as with Voiture? Or, à la Giraudoux, an art never labored, but never careless? At such points, we have an uneasy feeling that *préciosité* too freely borders on or absorbs whatever for the moment lies about, and is the opposite in other circumstances. When in *Au sujet d'Adonis* Paul Valéry admires the beauty and power inherent in conventions, rules, and set forms of art, M. Bray too casually converts this feeling for classical discipline into a sort of *précieux* taste for conventions; the transfer is possible only if we confuse two meanings of "convention."

All this is not to argue that M. Bray's long list of *précieux* needs drastic revision. It would require adjustments. A Baudelaire could well be left out; say what one will about his dandyism, his "esthétique de l'inutile," his figures of speech and ambiguities, *Les Fleurs du mal* was not a landmark of *préciosité*. It is equally doubtful that a Victor Hugo or a Giraudoux (despite Claude-Edmonde Magny's *Précieux Giraudoux*) can play a part of any importance here. But by and large, the list will stand. Most of the objections previously raised have to do with confused or arbitrary justifications of certain choices, and not with the basic validity of those choices; some of these, moreover, weakly supported at one point, are more strongly backed up at another. Repeatedly, the critic's method grows more firm, incisive, and searching, and penetrates closer to the heart of the matter. His procession of *précieux* impressively gathers momentum. In the Middle Ages, the poets of courtly love, Thibaut de Champagne, Charles d'Orléans, and even a much belabored Guillaume de Lorris; Scève, Desportes, and many others in the sixteenth century; all the familiar *précieux* of the seventeenth century; a considerably smaller group of eighteenth-century figures, among whom Marivaux; and more recently, poets of varying importance and depth, ranging from Gautier and "les Jeune-France" to Mallarmé and later still the surrealists; all invite consideration, and as a group suggest an infinite variety of possibilities. M. Bray makes them particularly interesting when he draws out of their texts ample, diversified patterns of *préciosité*. Then, he no longer evaluates the literature before him in terms of allegory or any other single feature, but undertakes to see it whole, as a complex phenomenon of motive, disposition, and technique. Thus, in one definition (p. 396): "Le jeu inutile et sans cause d'un oisif à l'esprit agile et à l'imagination féconde, hanté par l'ange du bizarre, riche de culture, se plaisant dans une création de luxe qui traduit par des gestes arbitraires une exigence interne de distinction, voilà comment nous apparaît l'art précieux."

But a new difficulty arises. What are we to understand by that "jeu" around which the rest of the definition appears organized? Is it a clear and fundamental characteristic of *préciosité?* Voiture, to be sure, is forever playing, like a cultivated idler. But is Scève? or even Charles d'Orléans? M. Bray elaborately establishes that his poets took delight in plays of fantasy, imagination, irony, in interplays of fact and fancy, and so on; but these are something else again; they are modes of high poetic strategy, cultivated by artists of every school and not by the *précieux* alone; essentially, they are by no means a "jeu *inutile* et *sans cause,*" and one does not see why they would be just that when they happened to fit into *précieux* writings. Indeed, in the same definition, that very form of purposeless play turns out at the end to be a creative act giving expression to an "exigence interne de distinction."

The contradiction could be resolved, in some such fashion: let this urgent inner requirement be understood as the more fundamental impulse, preceding the other, and let the playful manner, whenever it is put on, be seen as an outward show or even a disguise of that need. M. Bray himself does much to help us reach this view. In general he is not averse to probing *préciosité* in depth, and not surprised to uncover now an underlying "métaphysique du hasard," now a tension between "la poésie rêvée et la poésie exprimée," and other mysteries of that nature; these may in fact show through in some of the *précieux* writings, and may be quite absorbing, but again they are not of the essence here; they are the stuff of literature at large. But in the case of Mallarmé, among others, we ultimately come to the vital point, after devious discussions, not uninteresting in themselves, of the poet's "expression de l'être" and his creation of a hermetic world all his own: "il est précieux, au sens exact, par sa volonté de se donner du prix." That of course is a rather traditional description of *préciosité* (to the abbé de Pure, the *précieuses* were ladies "qui ont su se tirer du prix commun des autres") but it remains one of the truest; it fits every example long familiar to us.

The relationship of *précieux* (*pretiosus*) to *prix* (*pretium:* price, value, worth) brings home important connotations of the term. That is precious which, literally and figuratively, has an uncommonly high price or worth; in both senses, this valuation reflects a condition of scarceness or a quality of uniqueness (in English, we even say "precious little" and a "precious fool"!); that is rated precious which, matchless and irreplaceable, must be sought after or vigilantly guarded—thus, precious stones. But in effect, what is set at a price out of the ordinary, and therefore prohibitive, is frequently out of our reach; what is precious can be unavailable. The monetary sense of *précieux,* far from lowering the expressiveness of the word, discloses its full range of meaning and, what is essential, its ambivalence: it stresses worth and attractiveness along with inaccessibility. M. Bray's felicitous phrase, "une exigence interne de distinction," could be similarly expanded. To achieve distinction is to receive special public recognition; in another, ety-mological sense, distinction, as a distinguishing mark, establishes a differ-ence and a separation. The elect are distinguished by and from others. Now, the strategy peculiar to the *précieux* is to strain for both effects at once, whereas normally one is simply an unpremeditated outcome of the other. They wish to be and to appear select, uncommon, unmatched, distinct from the crowd; their manner proclaims a rejection of the usual values, but it simultaneously bespeaks a need to make their rare quality conspicuous be-fore those whose standards they yet despise and from whose midst they would withdraw. They would be attractive in virtue of that very exclusive-ness by which they would be set apart.

They are egoists to their fingertips. Their gesture is never an outgoing motion, a reaching out for identity with other beings. The *précieux*, both in withdrawing and in attracting, is self-centered, self-engrossed—Narcissus-like, he is absorbed in a "danse devant le miroir," as M. Bray aptly suggests (pp. 293, 343, 348, 395). One could wish that this, rather than any other, had been made the central theme; around it could have crystallized what-ever else needed to be said. Call a *précieux* a fop, a sophisticate, a wit, a trifler, or an idler; say that he is eccentric, or imaginative, or ostentatious, or consummately refined; show that he toys with language and with sentiments, or ritualizes them, or complicates them; each of these impressions may be true in some specific case or another; but similar impressions are made by those we do not find *précieux*. What endows all features of *préciosité* with their essential character and unity is the irreducible presence of one who interposes his rare, artful self. It is not simply that a *précieux* is or proposes to be unique, but that he confidently and knowingly watches himself as he contrives to be so. He does not necessarily tend to be obscure. Desportes, for example, calls the tears he sheds on Diane's account an essence that he dis-tills from her flower-like, youthful, fragrant beauty; in that process, he ex-plains, his love is the fire, his heart the stove, his sighs the wind of the bel-lows, and his eye the still; violent heat sends the fluid up in vapors and causes an overflowing. The meaning, far from abstruse, is all too transparent, and that is why at the same time the metaphor is strained: not so much because it is incongruous, but rather because the poet exerts himself to hit it off with a show of rigorous consistency—with an "imagination logique," as M. Bray comments—multiplying with studied verve all the unexpected but conceivable comparisons between love and distillation. His own rare form is really what constitutes the limpid content of the sonnet.

The *prix* is the thing. All the ambiguities that this entails, in terms of egoism, self-display, withdrawal, and attraction, have already been per-ceptively analyzed, with reference to *précieux* love, in M. Paul Bénichou's *Morales du Grand Siècle* (1948). It remains to show elaborately that *pré-cieux* manners, language, wit, and art betray the same basic compulsion, and that essentially, therefore, they are not games without cause or purpose. Does not M. Bray himself consider the "danse devant le miroir" a rather desperate pose? So it is, very often. It expresses self-sufficiency, and yet requires a public. While holding us off, the *précieux* also needs to hold us; his dilemma is to combine both gestures in one. Sometimes he achieves a triumphant pose, as does the Cornelian hero in stirring, ambiguous victories that strike wonder into the hearts of the very ones he sacrifices for his "gloire." Equivocal, enterprising, or ruthless, *préciosité* is not aimless but fulfills an "exigence interne de distinction"; it is a form of mentality with a sincerity, a drive, a goal—and disappointments, no doubt—peculiar to itself.

Préciosité is certainly, as M. Bray intimates in the introduction, a "tendance naturelle à l'esprit humain." What the innermost source of its energy may be in human nature he does not indicate with precision or consistency; in attempting to reach it, one could derive invaluable help from his numerous insights into the egoism and ambiguities of *préciosité*, but one encounters interpretations that persistently obscure or cancel these gains. Yet, in another and most important way he has renewed our thinking on the subject by showing us how to project *préciosité* over an enormous span of time. If nothing else, the duration of *préciosité* alone demonstrates that it is an important and permanent mode of self-expression.

Index

Library of Congress Cataloging in Publication Data

Edelman, Nathan, 1911-71
    The eye of the beholder.

    Includes bibliographical references.
    1. French literature—To 1500—Addresses, essays, lectures. 2. French literature—17th century—Addresses, essays, lectures. I. Title.
PQ153.E4   840'.9   74-6813
ISBN 0-8018-1621-1